PARENTING THE FIRST TWELVE YEARS

VICTORIA COOPER
HEATHER MONTGOMERY
KIERON SHEEHY

Parenting the First Twelve Years

What the evidence tells us

A PELICAN BOOK

PELICAN
an imprint of
PENGUIN BOOKS

PELICAN BOOKS

UK | USA | Canada | Ireland | Australia
India | New Zealand | South Africa

Penguin Books is part of the Penguin Random House
group of companies whose addresses can be found at
global.penguinrandomhouse.com.

First published in 2018
001

Text copyright © Victoria Cooper, Heather Montgomery, Kieron Sheehy, 2018

The moral rights of the authors have been asserted

Book design by Matthew Young
Set in 10/14.664 pt FreightText Pro
Typeset by Jouve (UK), Milton Keynes
Printed in Great Britain by Clays Ltd, St Ives plc

A CIP catalogue record for this book is available from the British Library

ISBN: 978-0-241-27050-9

Contents

INTRODUCTION   1

CHAPTER 1

How Should Babies Be Looked After?   13

CHAPTER 2

What Are the Influences on Becoming a Parent?   47

CHAPTER 3

What is 'Family' and Are Some Families Better Than Others?   71

CHAPTER 4

How Should Children be Socialized?   97

CHAPTER 5

How Should Children Play?   121

CHAPTER 6

What Matters in Education?

159

CHAPTER 7

How Can Parents and Professionals Promote Resilience and Autonomy in Children?

187

CHAPTER 8

What Should Children Look Like?

215

CHAPTER 9

Was It Really Better in the Past?

239

CONCLUSION

269

NOTES

275

FURTHER READING

319

INDEX

329

INTRODUCTION

There has probably never been a time when parents simply raised their children without advice from families or outsiders, when they were spared criticism, judgements or the suggestion that others knew best or that things were better in the past. Parenting has always been a topic in which there are multiple conflicting opinions, viewpoints and ideologies and people have been always very willing to discuss, share and sometimes impose their own viewpoints on others. Advice manuals, written by experts, have been around for hundreds of years and debates about the nature of children and what sort of parenting they need to grow up as 'well-adjusted' adults have an even longer history. In his book, *Far From the Tree*,[1] on parenting 'different' children, Andrew Solomon wrote that 'parenting is no sport for perfectionists' while it is at the same time something that the vast majority of parents struggle and strive to do as well as they can. So often parents are told they are failing, that their children aren't right in some way – too fat, too thin, too self-confident, too lacking in self-esteem, too connected with the digital, as opposed to the real, world – that it can seem very much as if parenting *is* a competitive sport suitable only for perfectionists and that those who fall short in some way (or any way) must be held up to account and general opprobrium.

This book is neither a parenting manual nor does it set out the right way to bring up children or to spell out the dire consequences of not doing so 'properly'. It is not a polemic, nor does it promote any particular philosophy or way of child-rearing. Rather, it aims to provide a pathway through the proliferating amount of literature published in recent years on parenting, probing and questioning some of the taken for granted assumptions about how to raise children. It is a book written not only for parents but also for researchers, professionals and policy-makers engaged with childhood. While the phrase 'it takes a village to raise a child' has become a cliché, it remains true that many people have a stake in how children are parented and want to know what researchers and academics have discovered about the ways of doing so.

While parents have always had an (obvious) interest in their children's lives, since the late 1980s there has been an upsurge in interest in children's experiences and understandings from both policy-makers and academics. Childhood Studies has become an established and still expanding subject in universities throughout the world and, while there has been an interest in improving children's welfare for many centuries,[2] recent interventions in children's lives have been based on taking on board children's own views and on understanding their needs above and beyond physical survival. Yet this research is not always well disseminated and does not always reach parents or practitioners: sometimes it is full of either medical or sociological terms which make little sense to those outside the medical profession or academia, or else it is only available in academic journals which few people have access to outside universities. There can also seem so much of it as to be overwhelming. What we have tried to do in this book therefore is to identify, summarize and sometimes critique the academic work out there, explaining its significance and implications but also pointing out some limitations. It is not exhaustive: there has been so much academic work done in the last forty years on childhood and parenting that it couldn't possibly be, but it does try and be representative, using examples from research studies which illuminate particular aspects of children's lives and which present broad themes and concepts developed within studies of parenting and childhood.

The authors of this book come from a variety of disciplines: we have backgrounds in education, psychology and social anthropology, but have also written about and taught sociology, history and development studies. The book therefore has a largely sociocultural focus – and concentrates on the social landscape of parenting. While it touches on research in medicine, genetics and neuroscience, the majority of the evidence we examine is from the social sciences and is largely qualitative rather than quantitative. There are of course huge debates about the relative merits of each type of research, as indeed there are about how 'scientific' social science research really is, but one of the greatest strengths of qualitative research is its ability to look in depth at what sociologists call the 'lived experiences' of individual people and to place them in their social, cultural and political context. This is not to claim that genetics are unimportant or that we believe entirely in nurture rather than nature. Indeed, the reason we have discussed neuroscience or genetics in places is to show the interaction between nature and nurture (or, as the debate is now more usually framed, between genetics and environment). If there is at times a slight scepticism towards neuroscience, this occurs when it is used as an over-reaching and generalized explanation for everything without looking at the wider setting and background. To give an example: Robert Plomin and colleagues conducted a series of studies examining behavioural genetics in which they looked at children who had been adopted and whether those children went on to develop the same traits as their biological parents or their adopted parents.[3] They found that adopted children were significantly more likely to develop schizophrenia if their biological parents suffered from it, even when their adopted parents did not. Such a result strongly suggests that schizophrenia has a largely genetic basis. And yet this is not the full picture (as the researchers acknowledge). It is very hard to conduct studies on adopted children and isolate one factor: numerous other experiences such as their experiences before adoption, their general health or that of their parents or the number of other children in their adopted families, have all been shown to have an influence on a child's susceptibility to schizophrenia. Further studies have also revealed that children with a biological predisposition to schizophrenia are more likely to show symptoms of the disorder when brought up in certain environments rather than others, meaning that disentangling these various factors from each other is not always possible. More broadly, such findings emphasize the need for an understanding which places the child and her experiences at the centre of analysis rather than attempting to discover one biological or medical 'key' which unlocks the entire mystery of why a child develops as she does.

This book therefore focuses on two areas: the broad conceptual theories relevant to 'parenting' and the impact these have on both individuals and institutions; secondly, how individual children, mothers and fathers experience family, community and educational life. The word parenting is a recent one within sociology and is now used more generally to mean the processes, actions and behaviours of adults that shape the child's physical, emotional, social and cultural development.[4] The last forty years have seen important changes in ideas and understanding of what both parenthood and childhood mean – this book examines the notable move away from 'parenting' in the sense of the study of the mechanics of childcare onto a focus on adult behaviour, attitudes and identities: people no longer simply *are* parents but have to *become* parents, *doing* parenting by learning the skills, attitudes and practices that come with this new status. Parenting is a word which is supposed to apply equally to both mothers and fathers, although in the majority of the literature it is used synonymously with 'mothering' and it is only recently that a specific set of studies looking at fathers and fatherhood have come to be written.[5] In the UK, parenting has also become part of the political landscape and is closely associated with the New Labour government of the late twentieth and early twenty-first century which blamed poor parenting for rocketing rates of obesity, anti-social behaviour, cycles of poverty, low self-esteem, teenage pregnancies, early sexualization, stalled social mobility and lack of social cohesion.[6] This makes parenting an area of concern beyond individual families.

The second area of focus is how individuals experience

childhood and parenting, both as children and as parents. This is inevitably an emotive topic and it is extremely hard to separate personal experiences, as both a parent and child (or indeed as a researcher and a policy-maker), from more general research findings which may run counter to one's own experiences and beliefs. Our book will argue that parenting changes throughout time and also throughout individual lives. For many people parenting is more challenging at particular times of their lives, either because they find it harder to relate to teenagers, for example, than babies, or because their own circumstances and experiences have changed. This need not be anything dramatic or even negative, but the same person who has two children will be a very different parent to the first child than to the second. No two children are ever brought up the same way, even if they have the same parents and all their external circumstances are identical; adults change, adapt and develop alongside their children and it is these changes on a micro, even individual, level which are as fascinating as the larger social changes. This emphasis on individuals also allows for an analysis of the experiences of all children – both those who are viewed as 'ordinary' as well as those regarded as 'different'. It also acknowledges that the parent–child relationship is a reciprocal one, in which both parties shape and change the other.[7] Parenting is not a one-way process during which adults impose ideas on children, but a relationship between them; children play an active role in their own upbringing, turning adults into parents with particular styles and ways of parenting. Children make parents as much as parents make their children.

In this book we examine the many debates, complexities

and paradoxes around the subject of parenting. We draw upon a broad range of research studies that explore many aspects of parenting and set out to consider what the evidence can reveal and where it is contested and even contradictory, in that two research projects on the same subject can come up with radically different findings. An example here is the way that children interact with their disabled peers. Some research (discussed in Chapter 6) argues that children feel relatively positive about inclusive education and value having disabled children in their classrooms. In contrast, research presented in Chapter 8 states the exact opposite: children remain uncomfortable and even hostile to children who are different from them. Both these studies are valid but they need to be understood in a wider perspective. What was the background of the children? What was their school like more generally? How well integrated were the disabled children? Even though the research might seem, at first, contradictory, the twin emphases we have followed – context and individual experience – offer a reflection of the nuanced, and even messy, realities of people's lives: all kinds of experiences need to be acknowledged if relevant and effective interventions are to be put in place.

The book also aims to look at 'obvious' problems in a different way and to challenge some of the accepted wisdom around them. An example is the discussion in Chapter 8 on obesity. While acknowledging that overweight and obese children suffer from risks to their health because of their weight, we also examine how these risks to individuals have been constructed and promoted as a social problem which requires intervention not just from a child's parents but also from the state. Again, this is not to argue that obesity is not a health problem, rather that it has different aspects from the way it is often presented and that sometimes there is a conflation of the medical with the moral: overweight children not only *have* health problems, but they, or their parents, *are* social problems, letting society down with their self-indulgence and lack of self-control. Similarly, advice on pregnancy and childcare, while often claimed to be ideologically neutral and based on the best interests of mother and child, is highly influenced by politics, culture, social norms and environments. In both cases understanding the interface of the social and individual is central to the book and we argue that recognizing this is imperative if parents and policymakers are to receive advice which is useful and relevant.

We concentrate on ideas about parenting children from approximately 0–12 years. One of the features of childhood is that its stages and progressions are often defined rather arbitrarily by cut-off dates and birthdays rather than by measures of biological or psychological development. In both national and international law childhood is defined as being under the age of 18, although there are obvious differences between a newborn baby and a 17-year-old in terms of their needs and capabilities. There are also great debates on when childhood (and therefore parenting) begins. Does it begin at birth? Or conception? Or even earlier when potential parents are told they must start getting ready for parenthood by preparing themselves physically, emotionally and behaviourally before they even start trying for a baby? Furthermore, parenting is a lifelong process – it is not a series of events or skills to be learnt and ticked off and it does not have an end point at

3, 12, or 18 or even 40 years of age. Indeed, twenty-first- century phenomena such as the 'Boomerang Generation', those young adults who return home time and again in their twenties, having previously left for university or a job, or even the so-called 'Doomerang' children – those who return in their thirties and forties after a marriage break-up – suggest that parenting never ends. Any book is likely to be somewhat subjective in its cut-off dates, and given the vast scope of the literature we have decided to stick to the approximate limits of the age group 0–12 years – a large enough topic in its own right. There are other aspects of children's lives not covered here –their physical health is mentioned only in passing, or their lives outside the family or in school, for example in clubs such as Brownies or Boy Scouts where, it might be argued, other forms of parenting take place. Nevertheless by taking major aspects of children's lives in turn and discussing the evidence and what we can learn from it, the book aims for a holistic account of the ways in which children have been thought about, how their individual experiences have been studied and represented, and how these have enhanced and deepened our understandings of many aspects of their lives.

How Should Babies Be Looked After?

Pregnancy, giving birth and caring for infants are often seen as the most natural processes in the world, things that women have been doing instinctively for millennia. And yet, in reality, they are nothing of the sort. Many people find getting pregnant difficult (one in six couples struggle to conceive) and, once pregnant, women are offered endless, often conflicting, advice about what they should do, what they should eat and how they should behave. They are closely monitored by doctors, midwives, fellow parents-to-be and their employers so that pregnancy is anything but a private, natural business. Birth has become similarly ideological – with women being criticized as 'too posh to push' if they have an elective Caesarean or ridiculed as 'hippy earth mothers' if they want a home birth or a birthing pool. Once the baby is born, the debates over breastfeeding – whether or not to do it, how long for and whether it should ever be done in public – are also heated. Even before a child is born it seems that there are many people making judgements on how to be a good parent and predicting lifelong damage to a child if a parent (especially a mother) gets it wrong. Yet being a parent means much more than learning the correct techniques to ensure that a child enters the world in the 'right' way or eats or sleeps according to the 'right' schedule. Parenthood is a relationship which develops and changes over time, depending on a child's, and a parent's, individual needs, desires and circumstances. There is no one correct way of looking after a baby or child that works for everybody. There are many beliefs about what to do during pregnancy and childbirth, and about how to care for the very youngest; these are often contested and conflicting – and have always been.

What should women do when pregnant?

In almost all cultures parenting starts well before a child is born, with pregnant women advised to avoid doing or eating certain things and to behave in certain ways. While today much of this advice is based on medical science, the idea that a mother's actions while pregnant might affect the long-term outcomes of the child's development is widely held, even among people without access to Western medicine. While women in the West might be told to avoid uncooked eggs, liver, sushi, soft unpasteurized cheeses and, of course, alcohol, women elsewhere are placed under a variety of other dietary restrictions. In parts of Ghana for instance, women are told to avoid eating snails or okra, as these might cause a baby to drool, while consuming pineapple or ripe plantain can mean a painful labour, a premature birth or even bring on a miscarriage. Coconuts, too, may be forbidden because they are believed to cause blindness. Other communities forbid pregnant women to buy tomatoes, peppers, okra and aubergines from the market, which are believed to cause rashes and lead to disability. In some areas of Tanzania women do not eat fish while pregnant, while others avoid farm animals in case their baby takes on the characteristics of those animals. Anthropologists have found evidence from parts of Europe as well as from Israel, Egypt and Brazil of beliefs linking food cravings with particular birthmarks, so that a child born with a strawberry shaped or coloured birthmark is thought to have a mother who craved strawberries excessively during her pregnancy.[1]

In Europe, advice to pregnant woman has changed continually and is often bitterly fought over by experts. In the late nineteenth century women were encouraged to diet during pregnancy in order to reduce both their own weight and that of the baby in the belief that a smaller baby would make for an easier birth. Some doctors recommended corsets that would both hide the growing bump and keep the baby small and easy to birth – although others were equally happy to admonish women for damaging their babies by lacing their corsets too tightly. Older superstitions about birth defects lingered on as well, especially those concerning 'maternal impressions' or the idea that a woman's experiences and emotions during pregnancy could have a negative impact on her child. In 1858 Archduchess Sophie of Bavaria wrote to her son, the Emperor Franz Joseph of Austria, to warn him about his pregnant wife's love of animals: 'I do not think Sisi ought to spend so much time with her parrots, for if a woman is always looking at animals, especially during the earlier months, the child may grow to resemble them.' There is a long-standing English superstition, recorded until the middle of the nineteenth century, that a woman who sees a hare (an animal with a long association with witchcraft) when walking alone will give birth to a child with a cleft palate (a so-called harelip).

Into the twentieth century, women were advised to rest and be as calm as possible while pregnant, to avoid family quarrels, exciting books and even breathtaking views. They were told to avoid salty or sour food, including pickles or under ripe fruit, in case these resulted in a child with a sour disposition, but all pregnant women were exhorted to drink at least two pints of milk a day. Bicycling was forbidden and even travelling in a car was to be avoided in case it went over too many bumps. While all these restrictions might be laughed off now as outdated beliefs, the idea that a pregnant woman's environment and emotions can affect the character, appearance or health of her child has not gone away. Contemporary research suggests that stress during pregnancy can harm unborn children and affect their development, although what constitutes stress is contested. One way of measuring it, however, is to look at levels of cortisol – often known as the 'stress hormone' – in both pregnant women and their babies. American psychologist Elysia Davis has carried out several research projects on the impact of stress during pregnancy. While all pregnant women in the studies show a rise in their cortisol levels, those with levels consistently higher than normal are more likely to have children showing higher distress levels at birth and beyond, and these children are also more likely to be anxious as 2-year-olds.[2] Although research on this is still at an early stage, and advice to avoid or minimize stress during pregnancy may be easier said than done, such work emphasizes the need to focus not only on physical health but also mental health during pregnancy. It also links back to older ideas, with very long historical precedents, that a woman's emotions and state of mind have a direct effect on her unborn child.

One of the key messages today for pregnant women in the West is the need to give up alcohol for the entire nine months and ideally also during the period in which a woman wishes to conceive. Yet again this advice is not without controversy, and while it is presented as a straightforward medical concern of posing a risk to the foetus, it has also become bound up with moral issues around good parenthood.[3] For many years the issue of drinking during pregnancy was largely ignored by doctors and health professionals and seen as being of little risk to women or their babies. Indeed, many women were encouraged to drink Guinness regularly to keep their iron levels up. This began to change after 1973 when doctors in the USA observed that a small number of children born to alcoholic mothers had a collection of birth defects including low birth-weight growth, facial abnormalities and some intellectual and developmental delays – a condition they christened Foetal Alcohol Syndrome (FAS).[4] They presented their evidence in three influential articles in the British medical journal *The Lancet* and while they focused on only seven case studies, they concluded that maternal alcoholism was directly linked to foetal abnormalities and birth defects. Initially, however, the syndrome was considered very rare and subsequent research showed that it did not occur in all babies born to alcoholic mothers; indeed, one study based on data from 55,000 women from the Collaborative Perinatal Project of the National Institute of Neurological Disease and

Stroke found twenty-three cases of women with a history of chronic alcoholism and six cases of suspected FAS among these women (although this diagnosis was not confirmed by direct observation).[5] FAS also appeared to be linked to other factors such as general maternal health and nutritional status (the mothers in the original study had been alcoholics for over nine years and suffered from cirrhosis and nutritional anaemia), as well as socio-economic status.

After these initial reports appeared, concern grew very rapidly and by the 1980s a new and much broader diagnosis of Foetal Alcohol Spectrum Disorder (FASD) was produced which suggested that alcohol use in pregnancy was not only associated with these very specific birth defects, but also with a wider variety of symptoms such as low IQ and sleep and behavioural disorders, including hyperactivity. By 1981 the US Surgeon General was advocating abstinence for all women who were pregnant as well as those trying to get pregnant. In the UK, doctors argued that one or two glasses of wine or beer a week was safe in pregnancy, although the Department of Health issued guidelines in 2007 which mirrored those of the USA and recommended total abstinence. The idea behind this was that, as no one knew what the safe limits were, women should err on the side of caution and assume that any amount of alcohol carried a risk and therefore that they should avoid it entirely. Today, most pregnant women do give up alcohol once they know they are pregnant (and there is an increasing social stigma against women who continue to drink while pregnant), but as up to 20 per cent of pregnancies are unplanned in the UK many women will unwittingly drink for a while.

Sociologists such as Elizabeth Armstrong and Ellie Lee have done extensive research on social reactions to drinking in pregnancy and the ways in which the moral and medical have become entwined.[6] Their interest lies less in the medical effects of alcohol on foetuses and more on the ways that drinking during pregnancy has emerged as a social and moral problem. They argue that the message of complete abstinence during pregnancy is motivated not only by concerns over babies' health, but is also used as a way of policing pregnant women's bodies and making judgements about a woman's moral character and her suitability as a parent. Giving up drinking when pregnant not only shows that a woman is following medical advice but also signals to the outside world that she is a good person, sacrificing enjoyment for the good of her child. It is both a public and a private way of beginning to parent many months before giving birth.

Policy-makers have continually promoted the no-alcohol-at-all message since the early 1980s ('to avoid confusion') and yet many studies have failed to show evidence that low levels of alcohol cause FASD. One study based on 10,000 children in the UK compared mothers who had abstained completely from drinking in their first trimester against those that drank a glass of wine a week and found no difference in their children's mental health or standardized test scores at the age of 11.[7] A 2017 study from Bristol University seemed to confirm this and concluded that light drinking in pregnancy (less than four units a week) appeared to have little detrimental effect on babies, although it may be linked to lower birth weights in a small number of cases.[8] Another report coming out of Denmark in 2010, based on 63,000 pregnant women, suggested that children whose mothers drank small amounts actually did *better* in terms of some developmental outcomes than those who abstained.[9] The authors emphasized that this link was not causal – the mothers who drank tended to have a higher socio-economic and nutritional status – and that these other factors might be equally important. This study certainly did not prove that drinking carried no risk at all (it is impossible to prove a negative), nor did it suggest that drinking in pregnancy was beneficial and that women should use it as an excuse to get drunk regularly. What it did is suggest that women knew about the advice on drinking, thought about the risks and weighed them up against other factors in their life, such as their diet or rates of exercise, and were unconvinced by what the experts had told them.[10]

Perhaps not surprisingly, this study was met with outrage in certain quarters – campaigners against maternal drinking have called it 'child abuse through the umbilical cord' and are unlikely to change their minds on the basis of this one study. Also, for every study such as this, there are others which offer contrary findings; a study published in the British medical journal *Paediatrics* in 2007 found that women who drank a glass of wine a week were more likely to have children with mental health problems at the age of 4 than those who did not.[11] Such studies, and their vastly differing conclusions, do not tell us whether drinking in pregnancy is safe or not, or at what levels it becomes unsafe, only that research findings can be highly contested and that 'evidence' is a sometimes slippery concept.

If childbirth is so natural, why can it be so difficult?

There have been many changes in beliefs about childbirth over the years, not just in medical or technological terms but also in terms of social attitudes and understanding of what a 'good' birth might mean. Whereas once a mother and child who survived childbirth might be seen as the only thing that mattered, today survival is more likely to be taken for granted and the experience of childbirth has become as important as the outcome. Mothers are now encouraged to write a 'birth plan', to make choices about where the baby should be born, whether at home or in the hospital, whether or not the fathers should be there (although today this is much less of a choice than it was and almost 86 per cent of fathers attend their child's birth). In particular, there is an emphasis on 'natural' childbirth and this is often presented as the ideal to which all women should aspire. The phrase 'natural birth' means different things to different people, but mostly it is used to mean a minimum of pain relief (if any), no doctors, only a midwife or another birth attendant such as a doula, and the mother being as active in the process as possible. This has even been taken to extremes with the 'free birthing movement' (also known as unassisted childbirth or unhindered birth) when a mother gives birth alone without any assistance.

There is an argument that women have been giving birth for millennia and thus it is a natural, biological, universal and instinctive event that women's bodies are 'designed' to do.

Yet this idea is undermined by the fact that, while women have been giving birth for centuries, they and their children have also been dying for centuries and continue to do so in many parts of the world. It also ignores the fact that evolution is not a design process, it is an adaptive one, and one of the strongest arguments against the idea of childbirth being something that women 'ought' to be able to do without difficulty or medical intervention comes from evolutionary scientists. In the early 1960s they began to look at why childbirth is so difficult and perilous for humans and why it almost always needs the help of others. Other primates give birth without assistance, with less pain and difficulty and more quickly: the average human labour lasts for nine hours; in apes and monkeys it is only two. Childbirth for humans therefore seems a rather hazardous way for children to arrive in the world and doesn't seem to make much evolutionary sense. Surely, from an evolutionary perspective, it would be better for female human bodies to have developed in a way to allow easier, lower risk deliveries, or for women to have smaller babies?[12]

Human babies are born with comparatively large and well-developed heads and brains but under-developed bodies (in contrast to many other mammals who give birth to young who can walk at birth or shortly after, but who are born blind or deaf), and this adaptive feature comes into conflict, at childbirth, with another unique human characteristic – walking on two legs. This necessitates delivering a child at an earlier stage of physical development than other mammals, meaning that human babies are uniquely dependent and vulnerable for much longer. This has been called the *obstetrical dilemma* – the fact that humans need a narrow pelvis in order to walk and run efficiently, but a wider one to bear infants with comparatively large brains. The evolutionary compromise is for a woman to carry a child for just as long as its brain takes to develop and then to give birth before the baby's head is too large to fit through the birth canal. This suggests many things: that childbirth is an evolutionary compromise, not an ideal adaptation, and that simply because it is 'natural' does not mean it is easy, uncomplicated or that there aren't inherent difficulties. It also guides us away from thinking that women from 'primitive' cultures give birth with a minimum of fuss and are back on their feet again within hours. They do not – and rarely are – and this natural process can cost them their lives, just as it has done for Western women throughout history.

In the West, childbirth has always been acknowledged as dangerous for both mother and child. Mortality rates for both were high and did not start to fall significantly until after 1935 when antibiotic drugs (sulphonamides) first became commercially available and enabled doctors to treat post-partum infections which might have previously proved fatal.[13] However, the pain and dangers of childbirth were often seen as part of God's plan because He had ordained that women should 'sorrow' to bring forth children in atonement for Eve's sin. Pain relief was both unavailable and morally unacceptable because it flew in the face of this divine injunction. It was not until the mid nineteenth century that this idea was challenged, most famously by Queen Victoria's doctor. Victoria had endured many difficult labours and so for her seventh child and subsequent children her doctor gave her ether (chloroform) in labour. She referred to it as 'that blessed chloroform', describing its effects as 'soothing, quieting and delightful beyond measure'.[14] Once the Queen had used it, the idea that women's suffering in childbirth was both natural and religiously ordained was abandoned, although such relief was available only to the richest women who had access to a personal physician or who went into hospital to give birth. There was almost no pain relief for women labouring at home. This remained the case until the 1930s when midwives were able to take gas and air into women's homes for the first time.

In the early years of the twentieth century obstetrics began to be recognized as a separate medical speciality and childbirth was rapidly drawn into the medical sphere of largely male doctors. The idea that it was a normal, if dangerous, event in women's lives, rather than an illness, began to fade. In 1920 the first volume of *The American Journal of Obstetrics and Gynecology* described childbirth as a 'pathologic process' from which 'only a small minority of women escape damage during labor' and which was in serious need of modern, technologically advanced interventions by doctors in hospitals (during the 1920s 80 per cent of births still took place at home with women attended only by midwives).[15] The rise of obstetrics meant that childbirth became increasingly scientific and hospital deliveries seen as a triumph of medicine over superstition, science over unpredictability. The process of childbirth became standardized and labour was measured and monitored with the use of charts and graphs. In 1955 Emanuel Friedman published his 'Friedman's curve', a graph which depicted normal labour by plotting foetal descent against dilation. This allowed doctors to see childbirth as a series of stages and any deviation from these norms would mean immediate intervention. While done for the ostensible good of both mother and child (and obstetricians have undoubtedly saved millions of lives, these new practices meant that women were distanced and even disempowered from birth, expected to be passive and to allow the experts to take over, and there were much higher levels of medical intervention than there had been previously. In hospitals, women routinely had their pubic hair shaved, were given enemas, made to lie on their backs, and then drugged, both for pain relief and to keep them quiet. Women were regularly given an injection of morphine and scopolamine (a drug which causes amnesia) to sedate them into a 'twilight sleep' and sometimes woken up after the baby had been born. American doctor Barbara Behrmann has compared her experience of giving birth with that of her grandmother. She describes her grandmother's experience as follows:

> 'Mrs Weingarden, will you please stop screaming? You're bothering the other patients.'
>
> It was 1936 and my grandmother was in labor. A nurse periodically woke her out of a drugged stupor to admonish her for her inconsiderate behavior. This is all my grandmother remembers of giving birth to my mother.[16]

In English hospitals too this would have been standard: men were forbidden from being at the birth (or indeed seeing their wives outside visiting hours) and babies would have been taken off to the nursery immediately after birth.

Yet not all male doctors were convinced of the necessity

of this and the first person to coin the phrase 'natural child-birth' was obstetrician Grantly Dick-Read in his 1933 book *Natural Childbirth*, which was followed up in 1942 by the still-in-print *Childbirth without Fear*. He argued against the use of drugs, 'twilight sleep' and forceps deliveries, viewing child-birth as an emotional event as much as a physical one. He believed that the pain of childbirth was caused by fear and could be overcome by knowledge and understanding. Although his ideas were welcomed by some women and his books were bestsellers, he was considered a maverick by his medical peers, who warned that women might kill them-selves or their babies if they laboured on all fours as he sug-gested, and it took some years until his ideas were viewed differently by the mainstream medical profession. He has also since been criticized for his anti-feminism (some of his writings suggest that he saw no role or purpose for women other than as mothers) and his racism ('primitive' women felt no pain and didn't mind dying anyway, he claimed).[17] His legacy lives on however and natural childbirth is now a popu-lar and heavily promoted aspiration. Ante-natal classes, which Dick-Read championed, are commonplace and midwife-led care, whereby doctors are called only in the case of serious problems, is also seen as best practice. Home births too are increasing in popularity. Women are much more active in the birthing process, making choices as to the sort of birth they want and many aspects of this are undoubt-edly good: the days of women lying drugged and semi-conscious have long gone.

The assumptions that childbirth is all about choices, and that knowledge and education are always empowering, are both problematic though, as are attempts to equate natural with better. Childbirth can still be risky and dangerous and the idea that technology over-medicalizes a purely natural phenomenon is not completely accurate. Natural childbirth is only possible, as Dick-Read acknowledged, because of advances in anaesthetics, the invention of antiseptics and the development of antibiotics. Without these innovations, 'natural' childbirth would have very high levels of mortality. Furthermore, many women, even those attempting a natural birth, are happy to accept certain forms of technology such as ultra scans during pregnancy or foetal heart monitoring during labour, making the idea of a totally 'natural' birth a fiction. The promotion of natural childbirth can also stigmatize women who do want pain relief or other interventions, as it can those who have Caesareans for whatever reason, leaving them feeling as if they have failed in some way or as 'not really have given birth' – even though telling a woman she has 'failed' when she has given birth to a healthy child after a Caesarean or an epidural is nonsensical. No birth is completely 'natural', every birth relies on some form of intervention – and always has done from the earliest humans onwards. Indeed, perhaps intervention rather than the reverse has always been the more 'natural' option.[18]

Does attachment matter?

When a child is born, one of the first concerns of healthcare professionals, as well as parents themselves, is how the mother relates to her infant in his or her earliest hours and days and how well attached and bonded the mother and child have become.[19] Midwives encourage immediate skin-to-skin contact between mother and child after birth and emphasize the importance of placing a child directly on a mother's breasts; there is a very widespread belief that successful attachment is the key to future happiness and success in relationships. Women are told that they should feel a rush of love (or hormones) when they first look on their baby's face and commercial ultra scans claim to encourage bonding even before birth. Maternal love is seen as an overwhelming, natural instinct, although in reality many women report feeling a mixture of thoughts and emotions, including curiosity, protectiveness, distance or simple exhaustion when they initially meet their baby.[20] Even so, early attachment is promoted as one of the cornerstones of good parenting, especially good mothering, and one of the key objectives of the NHS's health visiting service in England is to 'promote secure attachment' between mother and child.[21] There have also been attempts to identify possible problems with attachment in the first six to eight weeks of the child's life in order to intervene and to flag up future problems.[22]

The importance of attachment between mother and child was most famously discussed by John Bowlby, an English paediatrician who wrote a report for the World Health Organization on the mental health of children. He wrote a bestseller based on this work in 1953 – *Child Care and the Growth of Love*. He followed this up in 1969 with *Attachment and Loss* and his ideas about attachment continue to have an important impact on policy to this day (even if Bowlby himself might not recognize the way attachment is now used). Attachment, he claimed, was a biologically adaptive, species-wide mechanism that had evolved to protect vulnerable young humans by ensuring that mother and infant remained in close proximity. He argued that all children needed a stable, permanent care-giver to be attached to in their earliest years (almost always a mother). If this bond was broken in any way, or if babies were separated from their mothers at this crucial stage, then the result could be pathological – insecure, unhappy adults who struggled to form relationships. He believed there was a critical period in children's development – between birth and the age of 2 – when attachment bonds were first formed which influenced all future life chances. He argued that if mothers were separated from their children at this age (and the risk was still there until the age of 5), then their children would be 'maternally deprived' and this would lead to lifelong harm. Bowlby's theory was, for its time, a radical child-centred argument for the importance of early close relationships, and thus for providing young children with consistent loving care. It was prompted by his concern as a psychiatrist about the longer-term effects of children's loss of caring relationships, for example if they were maltreated, hospitalized (at a time when parents were not typically allowed to visit their sick child), housed in large, impersonal institutions, or separated from their parents during war or other social upheavals.

Bowlby argued that ideally mothers (or a single key maternal carer) needed to care for their babies exclusively in the first few years of life and that the results would be catastrophic if they did not do so or got it wrong.[23] Using his theories, later researchers found evidence of the long-term impact on children with poor attachments. In their pioneering work in the 1950s and 1960s, Barbara Tizard and Judith Rees compared the psychological health and social behaviour of sixty-five young children who had been placed in residential nurseries in London in the 1960s soon after their births.[24] Between the ages of 2 and 4, twenty-four of these children were adopted, fifteen returned to their birth families and twenty-six remained institutionalized. The researchers were thus able to compare these three groups of children and assess their behaviours when they were older. They found that at the age of 4, eight of the institutionalized children appeared emotionally withdrawn and unresponsive; they displayed unusual social behaviours and had found it very hard to form attachments to their care-givers. Another ten showed signs of indiscriminate attachment, going off with or seeking attention from strangers – both visitors to the institution and those outside. The remaining eight children managed to develop a preferred attachment to a care-giver at the nursery and displayed less of this behaviour. Such studies demonstrated the risks faced by insecurely attached children, and emphasized the dangers posed to children when they lacked a close, loving relationship with an adult they could trust and who would respond to their needs. They were also used to show the importance of forming secure early bonds between parent and child.

Not everyone is convinced by the idea of attachment, however, and some authors, particularly the psychologist Diane E. Eyer in her 1992 book *Mother –Infant Bonding: A Scientific Fiction*, have argued that attachment and bonding are highly plastic and flexible phenomena among human beings rather than universal, natural instincts and that many women throughout history have been good, loving mothers without necessarily having bonded with their children.[25] Psychologist Wendy Hollway has also found that many women feel challenged and even dislike their role and identity as mothers even while they feel deep love, affection and care for their children (this will be further discussed in the following chapter).[26] These authors argue that the overwhelming emphasis now placed on attachment only adds to the distress and guilt that women feel when they cannot or do not bond with their children straightaway – those whose babies are premature and kept in incubators, those who suffer post-natal depression or other debilitating illnesses which have an impact on their ability to care for their child, or those who adopt children and might believe that without their presence in the child's earliest days they will grow up to be insufficiently attached.

Looking at Bowlby's work in a wider sociopolitical context reveals other problems.[27] First, he based his ideas on a study of a group of delinquent boys already in trouble with the law for stealing. He then traced back their life histories to investigate whether they had been separated from their mothers at a crucial age. When he found that a high percentage of these boys had indeed been separated from their mothers, he argued that maternal deprivation was the cause and delinquency was the effect. His critics claimed that all he had shown was that there was a correlation between the two; he did not look further than maternal deprivation, giving little consideration to many other forms of deprivation such as poverty, social exclusion or discrimination, all of which might contribute to later delinquency.

Although Bowlby did acknowledge that women other than a mother could care for a child, he stressed the importance of a single maternal carer; a mother-centred version of attachment theory resonated politically and historically in parts of Europe and North America for much of the twentieth century. Feminist scholars have argued that his work was used by governments to push women back into the home and out of the jobs and financial independence they had become accustomed to during the Second World War.[28] When men came back from the fighting and were in need of employment, working women became a problem that needed to be solved. One way of doing this was by promoting the scientific discovery that children needed their mothers at home in the early years and that mothers should always be the primary caretakers of young children – a topic no one was especially concerned about during the war when it was necessary for women to work. Women could then effectively be removed from the workforce and pushed back into the home for the good of the children and the future society. The state was thus absolved from all responsibility to help women with childcare and the traditional nuclear family and the division of labour between the sexes were reinforced. As a counterbalance to this argument, however, it should also be noted that the British state had achieved a post-war removal of women from the world of work after the First World War, without recourse to attachment theory, with the 1919 Restoration of Pre-War Practices Act.

It is also unfortunate that fathers should have been largely excluded from the work on attachment and bonding. For Bowlby, fathers were largely irrelevant and had little role in a child's early development, though other research has shown that they can be highly significant.[29] In some societies men do as much infant and child care as women and it is central to their role as fathers. Anthropologists have found high levels of father involvement in childcare in other communities, especially among the Aka pygmies of central Africa who have become the poster tribe for involved paternal parenting; they even encourage infants to suck from their father's nipples. Aka fathers hold their children almost 50 per cent of the time and male and female roles are almost interchangeable: when women hunt (and they are very good at doing so), men look after the children, cook or plan where to set up the next camp.[30] Such insights have led anthropologists and some psychologists to suggest that it does not matter who does early parenting as long as someone does it.

Infant and child care is also something that increasing numbers of men in the West want to be more involved in and 53 per cent of fathers in their twenties and thirties in the UK claim that they would seek a less stressful job and 48 per cent would take a pay cut in order to get a better work–life balance, including doing more childcare.[31] Yet fathers can be overlooked in discussions not only of attachment but in all forms of parenting in the earliest days. Some report feeling excluded from family life with the arrival of a new baby – a position possibly encouraged by the intense focus on mother/child attachment and on services aimed almost exclusively at mothers and children. Despite the introduction in law of paternity leave and shared parental leave in the UK, take up has been limited (less than 10 per cent of new fathers apply for extended leave), which suggests that there is still ambivalence about paternal roles in childcare in modern Britain (see Chapter 2).

Should babies be breastfed and for how long?

The message that 'breast is best' is now a well-established mantra from health professionals and policy-makers, and women are regularly told that breastfeeding their children will boost their intelligence, protect them from obesity and promote their immune systems. Today the World Health Organization and the United Nations Children's Fund (UNICEF) recommend a 1–6–24 approach to breastfeeding: breastfeeding within one hour of birth; exclusive breastfeeding for the first six months of life; and continued breastfeeding, combined with safe and nutritionally adequate solid food up to 2 years of age and beyond. As ever, behind this approach are enormous differences in local practice and individual and social circumstances, and these, as well as wider cultural beliefs, will work against implementation of this prescription. Take for instance, colostrum, the milk produced in the later stages of pregnancy and immediately post-birth. It is densely packed with nutrients and also has a mild laxative effect to flush out the baby's first stool. It can help prevent jaundice and other infections and it is seen in Western medicine as vitally important that a child is fed on this as soon as possible. Yet there is a great deal of anthropological evidence that many cultures consider this sort of milk bad and dangerous for babies. Research amongst different societies in Uganda found that only one or two looked positively on colostrums, while the majority referred to it as 'bad', 'thick', 'watery', 'unclean' or 'diseased' and preferred to wait until their real milk came in. Some believed that colostrum could scald a baby's mouth or cause diarrhoea.[32] In the UK, until the late 1930s, it was not uncommon for women to be told only to give water to babies for the first three days of their lives to allow the early 'bad milk' to dissipate.[33]

The medical advice seems unequivocal and yet the 1–6–24 approach is far from universal, especially in the West. In the USA, for example, 79 per cent of newborns are breastfed at birth, but this percentage drops to 49 per cent at 6 months and 27 per cent at 12 months. The UK has some of the lowest rates of breastfeeding in Europe and, in 2012, while 81 per cent of babies were breastfed at birth, by 6 weeks old these figures dropped to around 24 per cent. Indeed, the UK has been described as the worst country in the world for breast-feeding because at 12 months only 0.5 per cent of children are still being breastfed in any degree whatsoever. This com-pares with 23 per cent in Germany, 56 per cent in Brazil and 99 per cent in Senegal. The reasons for this are undoubtedly a complex mixture of personal choice, social attitudes towards breastfeeding and also the emphasis on a child having a rou-tine. Research by Amy Brown of Swansea University suggests that mothers are encouraged to get their babies into a routine which includes them sleeping through the night as soon as possible. However this is often incompatible with breastfeed-ing where a child needs food more frequently and is more likely to wake up in the night. Brown also claims that social ambivalence and even hostility towards mothers who breastfeed – and the many stories in particular sections of the media about mothers being embarrassed into 'covering up'– also leads to women, even those who would prefer to breastfeed, giving up early, as does the need or desire to return to work or to reclaim some independence. Of the 300 women that Brown interviewed who had stopped breastfeeding in the first 6 months, 80 per cent cited pain and difficulty as one reason, but 40 per cent also spoke of negative public attitudes, 60 per cent mentioned lack of support and 20 per cent blamed embarrassment.[34] Alongside the lack of support and negative social attitudes cited by many mothers is the existence of infant formulas designed to allow women greater choice about how to feed their children and to provide nutrition for children who cannot be adequately breastfed (although there is debate about how many mothers physically cannot breastfeed and how many lack confidence in being able to do so).[35] It is hardly uprising that a country such as Senegal has much higher rates of breastfeeding because formula there is expensive and many women simply do not have a choice about how to feed babies.

Before the nineteenth century, women in Europe and the USA who could not, or did not want, to breastfeed had to employ another lactating woman who could feed their baby, known as a wet nurse. Often this meant sending the child into the wet nurse's home and leaving the baby to be raised there until it was weaned. This practice decreased in popularity as cows' (or other animals') milk became accepted as a suitable substitute. The trend was accelerated after 1867 when the first manufactured infant formula, Liebig's Soluble Food for Babies, was developed, a product quickly followed by others such as Ridge's Food for Infants and Nestlé's

Milk.[36] By 1883 there were twenty-seven patented brands of infant food in the USA alone, which usually came in powdered form and consisted of a mixture of carbohydrates, sugar and starches. They tended to lack vitamins, minerals and protein, although as the importance of these became known they were often added individually. Infant formulas were promoted as a healthy alternative to mother's milk and many were developed in order to combat malnutrition in cases where mothers had no milk or an inadequate supply. Coming at a time when improved sanitation and water quality meant they could be more safely mixed with water, they undoubtedly saved many children's lives during that era. They were not, however, a panacea and their use did sometimes lead to fatalities, especially during summertime when mixed formula could not be properly stored and the milk became rancid. It was only when knowledge of germs became more widespread (around the turn of the twentieth century), and the importance of cleanliness more generally known, that these deaths began to abate. The invention of rubber teats which could be easily cleaned and disinfected and the increasing number of households with access to an ice box to store milk safely meant that infant formula eventually became a wholly safe substitute for breast milk.

Gradually, infant formula began to be seen not only as a replacement for breast milk in particular circumstances but as an improvement on it which allowed for a more modern, scientific way of feeding, meaning mothers could take greater control of ensuring that their infant's nutritional needs were met. Mothers could more accurately judge exactly how much formula the child had drunk and it was believed that this would help establish feeding and sleeping routines. Formula was therefore promoted as a way of ensuring a compliant baby, fed to the highest nutritional standards, which could be measured and monitored so that doctors and parents always knew they were getting the 'right' amount of milk. Crucially, too, companies which manufactured milk began to play on this forward-looking, scientific image and solicited support directly from doctors which could be used in their advertising. In 1929 the American Medical Association formed a Committee on Foods to oversee and approve formula and insisted on manufacturers seeking their 'Seal of Acceptance'. While this brought greater compliance and adherence to safety standards by the companies which produced infant formula, it also meant that doctors were seen as explicitly endorsing the products.

Formula feeding was not, it is important to note, universally welcomed. In 1913 New Zealand doctor Truby King published a book, *Feeding and Care of Baby*, which dominated infant care advice to mothers across the West for the next forty years. He advocated strict routines for babies, regular sleeping and bowel movements, the importance of being in the fresh air and compulsory breastfeeding. Infants were to be breastfed every four hours and mothers were never to use formula. If they were asleep, children were to be woken up and fed, and if they cried in between feeds on no account were they to be fed or even comforted.[37] Yet despite voices such as King's, rates of breastfeeding continued to decline and by the 1950s parents and doctors regarded infant formula as a safe, effective and scientific method of infant feeding. US doctor Helen Flanders Dunbar, for example, in her 1949 book *Your Child's Mind and Body*, wrote:

> You do not have to nurse your child. Scientific evidence today indicates that children who have never been nursed are just as healthy, sometimes more healthy, both physically and emotionally, as children who are nursed. If you want to nurse your child, by all means do so, but allow your doctor to suggest, from the very beginning, additions to his breast diet such as orange juice, extra formula, or cereal. If you are reluctant to nurse your child, if it makes you tense and uncomfortable, or if you are too busy and doing it because you have an idea that it is your duty, do not attempt it.[38]

As with childbirth, however, there began to be a backlash against the over-medicalization of women's bodies and the belief that 'doctor knows best'. The idea that formula was the better option for children increasingly began to be questioned and organizations such as the Natural Childbirth Trust or the La Leche League began to promote breastfeeding as the best and most natural way of feeding children. Infant formulas started to be criticized as a marketing gimmick that caused women to lose confidence in their own abilities to feed their babies and, even though critics acknowledged that they could be useful and necessary for a small number of children, they still argued that they should never be normalized as a substitute for mother's milk. Furthermore, in parts of the developing world where standards of nutrition, sanitation and health care were lower, the switch from breastfeeding to formula feeding has been disastrous – with women in poor health believing that they are too ill or malnourished to feed their children themselves and turning to expensive, and heavily marketed, formula.[39] Without access to the clean water necessary to make up their children's food or to sterilize bottles, these formulas pose a substantial risk to children. One study suggested that 823,000 infant deaths a year (and 20,000 maternal ones) could be saved worldwide if breastfeeding was universal.[40]

In the contemporary West, however, there is no evidence that using infant formula puts children's lives at risk and the health benefits of breast over bottle are still vigorously debated, not least because while large-scale studies may show overall rates of better health, less obesity or greater intelligence among children who are breastfed,[41] individual children and their mothers will respond in different ways. Individual circumstances are key to any mother's decision as to how to feed her baby and the impact this decision will have on her child's life. It is simply not possible to point to one factor in isolation – such as breastfeeding – and attribute all these consequences to it. While some women take very easily to breastfeeding, others struggle, or find the pain and discomfort intolerable. Some feel their babies simply aren't thriving or getting enough milk and switch to mixed feeding, while for others the rigid formula of 1–6 –24 denies the realities of their lives where they have to work, commute, cannot always produce enough milk, or leave hospital within hours of giving birth before they have had the time and support to establish breastfeeding. Breastfeeding is not possible for everybody, for whatever reason, and stigmatizing women who struggle with breastfeeding can become yet another form of mother-blaming which causes unnecessary anxiety and distress at a time when women can already feel over-whelmed by the daily needs of a newborn.

For some women, extended breastfeeding is a conscious choice about the type of parent they wish to be. This is shown most clearly among those who are part of the Attachment Parenting movement. This philosophy promotes an intense bond between mother and child which is formed and bol-stered by the child being carried next to the mother as much as possible (baby-wearing), where the child's needs are responded to immediately, where co-sleeping (when a child sleeps with his or her parents) is promoted, and where breastfeeding is extended until the baby or child decides not to feed anymore. In 2012 a striking image of a young mother proudly feeding her 4-year-old son on the front cover of *Time* magazine brought Attachment Parenting to the wider public and caused a considerable reaction. Was this a natural, normal experience that Western women had given up because of the demands of the marketplace, or was it a form of attention-seeking and, frankly, a bit creepy?[42] Opinion was divided, as it remains on all forms of public breastfeeding, no matter how young the child, but this image raised particular questions about how long is too long to breastfeed, who should make the decision about when to wean a child and the ways in which breastfeeding is socially and publically policed.

Attachment Parenting is intimately bound up with ideas of what is natural and how women in other cultures, espe-cially those considered more 'primitive', care for their new-borns. The movement was inspired, in part, by anthropologist

Jean Liedloff's 1975 book, *The Continuum Concept: In Search of Happiness Lost*, which portrayed how the Yequana people of the Venezuelan rainforest cared for their very young. This included immediate contact between mother and child at birth, co-sleeping, carrying children everywhere for their first few months, breastfeeding on demand and responding to infants' demands for attention immediately and whenever required. Liedloff suggested that when children's and infants' needs are not met in this way, as they frequently are not in the contemporary West, the consequence will inevitably be later psychological difficulties.

The Continuum Concept was extremely influential, selling hundreds of thousands of copies and was translated into over thirty languages. Although not designed as a childcare manual, the idea that there was a natural way of parenting which our ancestors had practised successfully for centuries and which those in the West had forgotten, or given up on, was very appealing and led to books such as *The Attachment Parenting Book* by American authors William and Martha Sears, published in 2001. This 'bible' of Attachment Parenting claimed that such parenting produces happy, confident children whose parents put their needs first. Others, inevitably, have deemed Attachment Parenting unrealistic and faddish (and even narcissistic by some who see it as fulfilling the mother's needs rather than those of the child).[43] Certainly, being an attachment parent in the UK or USA today relies on a certain level of affluence, where a mother does not have to work (or who can rely on carers who will continue co-wearing),[44] where she can be in close contact with her children and is able to breastfeed her children for extended periods. There is also very little research on whether the children of parents who practise Attachment Parenting do in fact grow up happy, secure and more content than children who are raised in other ways.

It is of course very tempting to believe that there is one way of looking after newborns to guarantee that they will grow up happy, healthy and securely attached, but unfortunately there is not. While non-Western cultures give an insight into how other peoples look after their children, they do not present a blueprint for perfect infant care or lifelong happiness and it is impossible to simply cherry-pick aspects of another culture and apply them to a totally different situation and expect them to have exactly the same effect. There is no research which interrogates whether the Yequana people Liedloff knew were happy and contented *because* of the way they were carried or cared for in their earliest years (or, indeed, if Yequana ideas about happiness were the same as Western ones). In contrast, it is possible to demonstrate that their children had much less chance of survival than their Western counterparts, lower life expectancies and very limited access to medical care.

There is no perfect, universal way to give birth or look after a newborn that works for everyone, wherever they are. It is also impossible to look at long-term outcomes and to disentangle any one factor, be it breastfeeding for six or twelve months, co-sleeping or controlled crying, from a myriad of other factors including individual personality and temperament, class, lifestyle, nutritional and general health status. The daily interactions between parent and infant are, and always have been, heavily influenced by cultural beliefs, social and economic pressures and medical and technological advances. Babies are born into a particular social and cultural world and how they – and their needs and desires – are understood influences how they are treated from the earliest days of their lives. Becoming a parent involves so much more than simply giving birth and while infant care varies very widely across the world, the vast majority of parents want to give their children the best possible start in their lives from their earliest days onwards and will do whatever they can to protect them and ensure their survival.

What Are the Influences on Becoming a Parent?

Understanding what it means to become a parent may seem fairly obvious. After all everyone has experienced some form of being parented, albeit by potentially different caretakers, including mothers, fathers, grandparents, step-parents, co-parents, adoptive and foster parents. Irrespective of these different experiences there can be no doubt that becoming a parent comes with certain expectations, both those of individuals and others around them. Many of these expectations reflect the values and norms associated with gender roles and the idea that mothers and fathers should behave in ways deemed acceptable to particular communities, societies and cultures. The idea that people learn to parent from their own family experiences and are apt to turn into a version of their own parents is also an area that has been widely researched. The extent to which becoming a parent is largely determined by family, social and cultural influences, however, runs counter to a wealth of research which argues that many aspects of parenting, particularly in forming parent–child attachments, are shaped by biological and neurological and neuro-hormonal influences. In this chapter we draw upon research spanning biology, psychology, neuroscience and anthropology to address some of these themes.

How much control do I have?

The process of becoming a parent is often viewed as quite simply a force of nature. Many of the changes a woman and man might experience are routinely explained as a mere extension of biology which can be understood through exploring physiology and brain chemistry. Indeed, the many physical and neurological changes taking place during pregnancy have increasingly become a focus of research. Studies within the field of neurobiology and neuroscience argue that many of the hormonal changes during pregnancy and following birth are important for the early stages of parenthood and particularly for maternal and paternal bonding.

Physiologically, pregnancy and birth bring about both permanent and temporary changes to women's bodies. These include morning sickness (and persistent sickness throughout the day and even for the duration of pregnancy for some women) as well as reactions to strong smells and certain foods, along with food cravings; extreme tiredness and fluctuations in libido; difficulties in managing body temperature, sweating, feeling faint as well as experiencing heightened emotional responses; frequent crying, and sometimes anger and depression.[1] As much as 90 per cent of women in the UK report nausea and sickness during the early stages of pregnancy, although intriguingly these symptoms appear culturally specific. Pregnant women in New Guinea and Jamaica tend not to talk about sickness, but instead share their experiences of sleep disturbance, vivid fertility dreams, infections, rashes and ulcers, suggesting that purely biological explanations are not wholly adequate.

An expectant mother's metabolism increases during the first few weeks of pregnancy with blood sugars and blood pressure tending to be much lower during the first trimester as a huge amount of energy is required to put in place the basics of survival for her baby. Many mothers in the West report 'brain fog' during pregnancy and in the early caretaking stages following birth.[2] Often termed *baby brain* –this refers to a pregnant and new mother's reduced mental capacities to remember and react quickly and is often assumed to reflect disorganized and unpredictable behaviours. There is some research which indicates that during pregnancy a mother's brain alters – with some parts of the brain increasing in size, such as the ventricular (which is part of the brain where cerebrospinal fluid is produced), whilst the overall size of the brain decreases, being at its smallest by the time the baby reaches full term.[3] Brain changes, however, are temporary and a mother's brain will increase in size again in the weeks and months after her baby is born. By the time the baby has reached 6 months of age, a mother's brain typically will have returned to its pre-pregnancy size.[4] Studies carried out in the Netherlands and Spain by Elseline Hoekzema and colleagues using MRI scans of fathers' and first-time mothers' brains before pregnancy and following birth suggest that while the brains of fathers remain unchanged, the mothers' brains demonstrate a number of changes: specifically, extensive volume reductions in grey matter affecting the anterior and posterior cortical midline and specific sections of the bilateral lateral prefrontal and temporal cortex. Changes in grey matter can reflect various neurological processes, such as a reduction in the number of synapses, glial cells (non-neuronal cells that maintain homeostasis and form myelin that surrounds and protects neurons in the central and peripheral nervous systems) and neurons and changes to dendritic structure. Often described as synaptic pruning, this development is regarded by many neuroscientists as an essential process of fine-tuning thought to represent a refinement and specialization of brain circuitry during pregnancy, which is critical for healthy cognitive, emotional and social development.[5] Hoekzema and colleagues argue that loss of grey matter does not therefore mean loss of brain function – in fact these changes appear to represent more of a refining process through which the brain can function more efficiently during this period. Further neurological research indicates that such changes to grey matter during pregnancy, which might affect the experience of so-called 'brain fog' for many women, may actually support maternal attachment following birth, suggestive of an adaptive process serving the transition into motherhood (although, as suggested in the previous chapter, ideas about attachment remain strongly contested). Developments in neurobiological research have revealed that regions of the brain that control social interaction, empathy and anxiety (prefrontal cortex, midbrain and parietal lobes) are stimulated by hormonal changes during pregnancy and following birth.

Researchers Andreas Bartels and Semir Zeki from University College London claim that maternal expressions of overwhelming love, fierce protectiveness and persistent worry reflect the way a women's brain adapts during pregnancy and following birth to promote attachment formation – which is often seen as fundamental to parenting.[6] Their research shows that maternal love involves a unique and overlapping set of areas within the brain which are responsive to hormonal stimulation during pregnancy and following birth. During their studies they measured the brain activity in twenty volunteer mothers who viewed pictures of their own infants, and compared this to brain activity evoked by viewing pictures of other infants with whom they were acquainted for the same period. Their research found that when viewing pictures of their own infants in comparisons to other infants, maternal attachment appeared to suppress activity in regions of the brain associated with negative emotions, as well as regions associated with social judgement. They argue that strong emotional ties to another person inhibit not only negative emotions but also influence the neurological network involved in making social judgements about that person.

Scientists have only recently begun to unravel the possible links between how a pregnant woman/new mother behaves and her hormonal changes, neurological activity and brain chemistry.[7] Examining the maternal brain may also help better understanding of post-partum depression and anxiety amongst new mothers.[8] One in six women report post-partum depression and many others express anxious and compulsive thoughts particularly in relation to monitoring their baby's breathing, sleeping and eating. The hormone oxytocin (which is also used to induce labour) has been identified as an important driver for all mammalian mother–infant bonding; it increases significantly during pregnancy and levels remain high post- birth. Pilyoung Kim from the Family and Child Neuroscience Lab at the University of Denver[9] describes how oxytocin levels increase when a mother looks at her baby, as well as when she hears her baby cry, and is also claimed to influence a father's reaction to his baby.[10] Such changes are vital for parent and baby bonding and Kim compares the parental experience to that of falling in love.

James Swain from the Yale Child Study Centre proposes a model of how an infant crying, for instance, can activate parent brain circuits that regulate motivation, reward and learning about their infants, and stimulate parenting emotions and behavioural responses.[11] These signals can include crying, visuals as well as touch and smell. Having studied brain images of human parents and considered earlier studies of animals, Swain proposes a 'parental brain' model to depict how mothers' brains and their subsequent emotional reactions and behaviours respond directly to their own babies' signals. Swain describes how a mother's brain circuits are activated as reflexive caring impulses and these impulses are configured into emotional and behaviour responses as an expression of parental love and attachment formation. Swain argues that a greater appreciation of the neurological influences on parenting has profound implications for understanding long-term parent and infant attachment as well as mental health risks and the development of resilience in children.

Brain changes are not confined to women. Studies carried out by Eyal Abraham and colleagues[12] note how men's brains also change when they are involved in caring for their babies.

Similar hormonal changes are evident in fathers and include increased oxytocin induced by contact with the mother and baby. Oxytocin levels in fathers are positively linked to displays of affection towards their baby. Many of these physiological changes are defined as adaption processes which enable parents to form an attachment with their baby. Many researchers, however, question how far neurological studies explain processes of adaptation and learning during parenthood.[13] Whilst it is difficult to ignore many of the physiological and hormonal changes which take place during pregnancy and following birth, neurological research does not fully explain away the vast differences in the ways women and men throughout the world approach their parenting roles. Many of these differences have been explored by drawing on anthropological, psychological and sociological research, which not only examines diverse parenting practices globally, but also how community, social and cultural influences can shape parenting.

Anthropologist Robert LeVine has studied cross-cultural parenting practices extensively and his work has illuminated parenting differences and demonstrated how these are learnt processes which help new parents adapt to the circumstances of their own cultures and communities.[14] So, whilst there can be no denying the physiological and psychological changes that many women and men go through during pregnancy and the early years of caring for their infant, different societies encourage alternative approaches about what is acceptable or typical for new parents in any given community. In places with high infant mortality, mothers sometimes do not become emotionally involved with babies that they expect to die. Anthropologist Nancy Scheper-Hughes has written much about infant death in the shanty towns of north-eastern Brazil. She has described great ambivalence about infants among the poor mothers that live there, suggesting that they do not 'trust' these children to survive and invest little emotional energy in them. They do not recognize or acknowledge individual personhood, reusing the same name several times over for successive siblings, and rarely mourn openly for infants. There is little personalization of the very young and it is only when children show signs of being active, of having the will to survive, and when they become older and therefore worth investing in emotionally, that mothers acknowledge them as more fully human. Mothers tend to neglect young children who seem passive or sickly. They feel that some children are not meant to survive and they do not fight to keep them alive, do not give them medicine (and usually cannot afford to) and treat their deaths with resignation and even indifference.[15] These findings are supported by a well-established body of anthropological research which highlights how family, community, social and cultural influences shape different parenting practices throughout the world.[16]

Will I become a version of my own parents?

As the sociologist Frank Furedi suggests in *Paranoid Parenting*,[17] becoming a parent is not solely about how mothers and fathers adapt to their new roles with their child, but also how they make statements about who they are. It is difficult to disentangle the hopes and aspirations a new parent might have, however, with the pressures exerted within society. All societies have and continue to present some sort of opinion, expectations or set of ideas about what it means to become a new parent and how one should behave.

It may be fairly obvious that people learn to be parents in some respects from their own parents and carers; and this may indeed explain why so many patterns of parenting are reproduced through generations of families, in what Professor Wendy Hollway from the Open University describes as *intergenerational echoes*.[18] Jay Belsky, professor of psychology at Birkbeck, University of London, and colleagues put forward a theoretical model in 2009 which attempted to try and explain how parenting behaviours are shaped by the ways in which the parents themselves were parented. Many earlier studies on this topic emerged during the 1950s with particular attention to *intergenerational transmission*[19] and the idea that certain behaviours such as abuse and aggression run through generations of families.

Intergenerational research takes a detailed look at how parenting identities develop through experiences within families where early beliefs are shaped. Studies of this type commonly use personal reflections and retrospective accounts of family life by questioning parents and grandparents about how they parented their children as well as how they experienced being parented. In addition, children are frequently questioned about how they experience being parented as well as the type of parent they think they might be or hope to become. During an infant's early years, for instance, the infant is exposed to a whole range of behaviours that will to a greater or lesser extent influence their thinking, beliefs and perhaps their own later behaviour. Research carried out in 2013 at the University of Louvain in Belgium by Isabelle Roskam[20] over three generations of families found clear patterns in parenting behaviours reported by grandparents, parents and their children, including positive behaviours such as warmth and sensitivity as well as more negative behaviours such as the use of harsh discipline. However, not all types of parenting behaviours appear to be handed down through the generations. The research found that children reporting experiences of supportive and warm parenting were more likely to imagine using these types of approaches themselves as parents rather than more controlling parenting styles and particularly the use of harsh discipline.

As is often the case with research which draws upon self-reporting approaches, these results are highly dependent upon memory and interpretation, which can be problematic. And of course the idea that projecting yourself forward – from a child to a would-be parent – and imagining the type of parent you wish to become isn't necessarily a good indication of how you actually turn out. Yet not all parents assimilate the behaviours and approaches of their own parents. Some reject and take issue with how they were parented and are at pains to ensure they do not turn out the same way. As Andrew Solomon has written:

> Insofar as our children resemble us, they are our most precious admirers, and insofar as they differ, they can be our most vehement detractors. From the beginning, we tempt them into imitation of us and long for what may

be life's profound compliment: their choosing to live according to our own system of values. Though many of us take pride in how different we are from our parents, we are endlessly sad at how different our children are from us.[21]

The psychologist and author Oliver James warns of the potential for parents to *F*** You Up*[22] and provides detailed evidence and support for parents and would-be parents about *How Not to F*** Them Up*.[23] James draws upon inter-disciplinary research to describe the complex processes through which children's behaviour is fashioned through the actions of their parents whose behaviour has similarly been shaped by their own parents – and so the process goes on. Such research is clearly useful in recognizing the importance of learning within families, yet does not fully clarify why some children identify and perpetuate certain parenting identities and others don't. This view also has the tendency to imply that children are fairly passive and that parenting is something 'done to them'. Child psychiatrist Sir Michael Rutter suggests that to underestimate the impact that children have in shaping how they are parented and how their parents interact with them fails to take into consideration what countless parents have observed for generations when they have a second child and experience not only how different their children can be, but how different they are in relation to them.[24]

Canadian psychologist Steven Pinker describes how easy it is 'to think of children as lumps of putty to be shaped'[25] and so to overlook how important children are in influencing how their parents behave. It is important to foreground this here as a steer for much contemporary thinking around parenting which pays far more attention to parenting as a relationship or series of relationships in which children play as important a role as their parents. Parent–child relationships have in more recent years become a focus for study, in particular the notion of *bidirectionality*, which recognizes how parents and children continuously and mutually influence each other. A number of studies have looked at children's personalities and behaviour traits[26] as well as those of their parents as a way of understanding how parent–child relationships influence how parents develop their identity as much as how children develop, acquire beliefs and learn within families. Research of this kind is quite complex as it attempts to unravel how and why children and parents interact and behave as they do. Yet there is much about parenting that is quite difficult to understand. Often parents behave in ways that cannot easily be explained or even rationalized.

In *The Psychopathology of Everyday Life* Sigmund Freud[27] suggested that adults are rarely masters of their own behaviours and frequently (maybe even always) react to deep-seated thoughts and feelings. Whilst Freud's work highlighted the importance for parents of trying to connect (through psychoanalysis) to inner thoughts as a way of trying to understand behaviour, more contemporary research now blends neurobiology and psychology to explain parenting identities. In *Why Love Matters: how affection shapes a baby's brain*,[28] psychoanalytic psychotherapist and author Sue Gerhardt describes the importance of understanding both the neurology and psychology of parenting. Her work focuses on how early experiences not only socialize and teach children but also shape neural pathways, particularly during the first few months following birth. Much of her work builds upon extensive research in *brain plasticity*.[29] Rather than view behaviour as predominately fixed, research in brain plasticity argues that neurological pathways within the brain that support and reinforce particular behaviours are plastic and quite flexible and able to adapt and change. Similarly, research conducted by Ruth Feldman[30] from the Gonda Multidisciplinary Brain Research Center, Bar-Ilan University argues that early emotional experiences lay down neurological pathways which can shape ways of thinking and behaving; so much so that this may explain why parents often fall back upon styles of parenting that they experienced during early childhood. Yet Feldman and colleagues argue that the plasticity of the brain and its ability to change means that the neural pathways established during early childhood can be adapted – an idea central to critiques of attachment, as discussed in Chapter 1. Brain activity is highly influenced by hormones – though not solely – and research suggests that brain changes are also influenced by parent–child interactions, wider environmental and social factors as well as learning. This may further explain why many new parents take steps to avoid the parenting approaches that they experienced themselves. Brain plasticity also connects to what countless parents have described – often following their experiences in parenting more than one child – that not only does your parenting identity change as you move through life, but that how you parent and interact with your children also changes to meet the very different needs and personalities of your children.

Of course parents have different ideas about how they wish to raise their children. Many of these ideas might well be influenced by how they were raised by their parents as well as the mass of literature and media coverage which conveys distinct messages about different types of parenting. Partnerships can break down and family situations change, yet being a parent is characteristically a lifelong role. An underlying and very potent belief, however, is that the type of parent people become has consequences, not only in how they raise their children but how their children turn out. So, not only are parents bestowed with the responsibility to raise healthy, happy and well-adjusted children, but if things go wrong – parents can easily be blamed.

For a significant number of men and women, becoming a parent can feel like a crisis which brings forth a set of new demands – physiologically, emotionally, psychologically and economically – including increasing financial responsibilities[31] and perhaps a degree of uncertainty as to the impact this new role might have upon existing intimate relationships, leisure time and home and work–life balance. Despite very different circumstances, women and men commonly describe the inner struggle that becoming a parent can arouse – often a strong sense of losing a sense of one's self, set against a background of competing individual, social and cultural influences.

Can I have it all?

How parents interact and raise their children is assumed to have far-reaching consequences and possibly even lay down the foundations for their children's future. Various newspaper headlines reflect and – some might say – ignite many concerns that parents have about how they raise their children. Whether sending their baby to nursery or a childcare setting is a good or bad thing, the consequences of raising a child alone, or whether working whilst their baby is still very young will impact upon their development are all much debated. What, then, are the implications of trying to balance so many responsibilities? Is it possible to maintain satisfying and enduring intimate family relationships, secure financial independence, and nurture a satisfying career and raise healthy, happy children? How can parents balance so many demands? There are many concerns and questions that new parents might have. Chapter 3 will examine what research can reveal about the impact of different family circumstances on children's social and emotional development. Here, we look at the impact of mothers working whilst raising their children.

Looking carefully at research evidence can be useful in recognizing that sweeping statements and assumptions that lump all working women into one category and all stay-at-home mothers in another does not acknowledge that all women, or indeed all children, and the circumstances of their lives, are not the same. It is important that parents have the opportunity to make decisions which reflect their own individual and family circumstances. In the UK the proportion of women who are stay-at-home mothers has declined by more than a third in the past two decades.[32] Many women are also opting to work throughout pregnancy and return to work shortly after giving birth. Since 1951 the number of UK mothers in employment has more than tripled and the latest figures show that 68 per cent of women with children are now working.[33] This changing parenting demographic has been reported with media headlines highlighting the potential dangers – suggesting that children of working mothers are more likely to under-achieve, be socially awkward and engage in risky behaviours, such as drug-taking and underage sex.[34] Indeed, research carried out in the UK, Australia and America, where incidences of maternal employment are increasing, found some potentially adverse effects on children's academic performance at school and their social development. Research commissioned by the Joseph Rowntree Foundation, conducted by John Ermisch and Marco Francesconi of the Institute for Social and Economic Research, University of Essex, in 2002,[35] measured the impact of parental employment. Using features of the British Household Panel Study (BHPS), their findings revealed that although mothers in full-time employment increased family income, working also limited the time available for them to interact with their families and tended also to reduce children's later educational attainments.[36] The study indicated that longer periods of full-time employment by mothers when their children were aged between 1 and 5 years reduced children's chances of obtaining academic qualifications, increased the child's risk of unemployment and other economic inactivity in early adulthood and enhanced the child's risk of experiencing psychological distress as a young adult. Part-time employment by mothers appeared to have few adverse effects on children as young adults. The effects of fathers' employment on the outcomes studied were considered less significant than those of mothers' paid work. Longer periods of work by fathers when their children were pre-schoolers was linked to a reduction in the child's risk of unemployment and other economic inactivity in early adulthood and less chance of experiencing psychological distress as a young adult. Generally this research suggested that parental working whilst raising young children may have a negative impact upon their development. Closer scrutiny of the research approach, however, reveals that much of the data used very general categories such as 'parental paid work' and 'parental time' spent in part-time and full-time employment without fully exploring the complex set of circumstances that surround family life. The socio-economic status of parents, for example, as well as parental choice whether to work or not, are categories that are also important to consider.

In 1991, the National Institute of Child Health and Development carried out a longitudinal study across the United States to examine the relationship between maternal employment and various outcomes in children. The study, conducted by psychologists Jeanne Brooks-Gunn, Wen-Jui Han, and Jane Waldfogel from Columbia University, found that full-time maternal employment which started before the child was 3 months of age was associated with significantly more behavioural problems, including aggression and social anxiety at the age of 4½ years. Children whose mothers worked part-time before their child was 1 year old had fewer disruptive behavioural problems than the children of mothers who worked full-time before their child's first birthday. With regard to cognitive differences, children of mothers who worked full-time during the child's first year scored lower on cognitive tests, whilst lower cognitive scores were not found in children of mothers who worked part-time during the first year of their child's life.[37]

Despite many negative associations between children's behaviour, outcomes and maternal employment, Brooks-Gunn and her colleagues nevertheless argued that maternal employment does not necessarily have a negative impact upon children's intellectual and social development. By looking at maternal employment in conjunction with other influences, including parent–child interactions, family income and childcare, they developed a more nuanced understanding of how maternal employment might affect children. They found that while early maternal employment may have some downsides, the links between working mothers and negative impacts on young children are complex. It is not a simple case of working mothers being bad for infant development, but more about weighing up the pros and cons in line with individual circumstances. For a high percentage of working mothers, increased financial security allows for high-quality childcare as well as enhanced opportunities to buy experiences that may enrich a young child's quality of life and that of other children within the family.

A large-scale study carried out at the University of New South Wales for the Social Policy Research Centre in 2005 found that the quality of time and care working parents spent with their new babies – that is often assumed to be sacrificed when mothers go out to work – actually remains high.[38] Looking at mothers and fathers of children under 5 years of age, Professor Lyn Craig, Director of the Australian Research Council (ARC), found that working mothers, rather than reducing the amount of time they spent caring for their infant, tended to sacrifice their own domestic, leisure and rest time in order to carve out quality time with their baby when not at work. In order to preserve time with their child or children, working mothers spent less time engaged in housework, personal care and child-free leisure time than non-working mothers. The research also reveals how working mothers 'time shift' and reorganize their home activities to set aside more time with their child, such as beginning their days earlier, spending more time with their child prior to work, and scheduling later bedtimes. Of course, many women do not have the choice whether to work or not – but have to do so for a number of reasons. Lyn Craig[39] acknowledges that it is the women who feel they have limited choices that have the most negative outcomes. Having to work and leaving an infant with other child carers can be emotionally difficult. In addition, a significant number of mothers cannot afford quality childcare, and for those who are parenting alone the issues are even more difficult to resolve. For a high proportion of women, becoming a parent not only presents challenges in terms of trying to balance a number of responsibilities, but also forces them to resolve psychological and social dilemmas and differing views about what is and isn't good for their baby.

For a number of working mothers, employment and having a career can impact positively upon their own well-being, security and life satisfaction; conversely, for many other women work may not reflect a choice or personal ambition but rather a necessity. In such cases, as Lyn Craig suggests, women may find working and balancing child-rearing as more stressful than those working mothers who choose to work for a host of very personal reasons. A number of studies indicate that parental well-being is one of the strongest indicators for a child's developmental outcomes and that children's social-emotional development is linked to levels of parental well-being, depression and also stress.[40] A body of psychological research demonstrates that parental depression and stress can place young children at risk of social and emotional problems.[41] In *Kids Pick Up On Everything: How Parental Stress Is Toxic To Kids*, pastoral counsellor David Code draws upon a broad range of psychological research and argues that parents' levels of stress can impact upon a child's social, emotional and cognitive development. Research carried out by Nicole Talge and colleagues in 2007[42] found that if a mother is stressed during pregnancy, then her child is substantially more likely to have emotional or cognitive problems, including an increased risk of anxiety and late development of language skills during childhood (a point also made in other research cited in Chapter 1). Maternal levels of the stress hormone cortisol are thought to be an influential factor here. [43] Taken on balance, it appears that perhaps parental stress rather than employment alone is a factor which may impact on a child's development. Although we do not look at the determinants of parental stress in this chapter, it is important to note that parents may experience stress in relation to a number of influences, including financial instability, housing insecurity and balancing work and family life. It is important therefore to consider the variety of influences that shape parental experiences.

Whilst there can be no denying the physiological impact

that underpins becoming a parent – from basic biological adaptation to accommodating birth, through to neurological changes that facilitate bonding between a parent and child – the capacity for parenting to be shaped and influenced by wider learning cannot be underestimated. Parents can and do make choices and rather than see parenting as a role mapped out and predetermined through biology and culture, research reveals that parents have the capacity to adapt and change their behaviour and carve out a role that fits their unique set of circumstances.

What is 'Family' and Are Some Families Better Than Others?

The word 'family' is one of the most loaded and controversial in the language; it is deployed and discussed endlessly by the media, politicians and academics. The family can be sentimentalized, demonized and seen as responsible for all the ills in the world, as well as much of the joy. It is viewed as both private, 'a haven in a heartless world', and as deeply politicized – a space into which the state has both a right and a duty to interfere. It is difficult to think about, or discuss, the family entirely rationally or dispassionately: everyone has, or has had, a family (of sorts) at some point and while experiences differ widely, the effects of these experiences may colour the rest of a person's life and, as discussed in the previous chapter, almost certainly have an impact on the ways that person parents their own children.

The ideal of the nuclear family – defined as a married, heterosexual couple who live with their biological children in one household and operate as a single economic unit – looms large in these discussions. The nuclear family has a long history in the West, particularly in Northern Europe, and is often considered as both the cultural and historical norm and the most effective, and best, way to raise children to adulthood. Yet this model is not universal and anthropologists have argued that while the family exists in all societies, the forms it takes are very different. Looking cross-culturally, there are many other ways that families are created and many other family models: children may live in three- or even four-generational households where they grow up with grandparents, aunts, uncles and cousins living in the same house. In small-scale African societies in the past children may have grown up in polygamous families where a man had several wives and children by different women who all lived together in one compound. Anthropologists have also found evidence of polyandrous communities where one woman marries several brothers and the children are raised by them all.[1] The nuclear family, while it retains an enduring cultural appeal in the West, is not the norm universally. This chapter will look at the different ways in which ideals of 'family' are presented and what the research can reveal about the impact of family dynamics upon children.

Who are family and what should they do?

In answer to the question, who is your family, many in the West would instinctively say their 'blood' (or possibly genetic) relations – their closest family being the people with whom they have a blood connection such as parents, grandparents, children or siblings. In English, phrases such as 'blood is thicker than water', or questions to those who have been adopted, such as 'do you know your real (i.e. biological) parents?', suggest that biological relationships are fundamental to ideas about family. Although other people may be acknowledged as relations by marriage, the idea of a biological connection remains significant. Yet this has little meaning to most young children in the West, especially before the age of 5, as psychologist Jean Piaget discovered in 1928.[2] He looked at the definitions of the family given by children at different ages and found that before the age of 5 children tended to see family simply as the people they lived with and did not talk about relatedness. More recent sociological work has suggested that this is still the case and that ideas of biological relatedness only start to become important to children after the age of 8, although certain minority groups may lay a different emphasis on the importance of biological relationships.[3] One UK study which looked at how children defined who was family and who was not found that Jewish children were particularly aware of biological connections, this being a reflection both of a specific understanding of religious identity (a child claims Jewish heritage through his or her mother) and the fact that many lived in small, tightly knit communities in which many people were distant relatives and where explanations for how children were related to other people were more likely to be given on a regular basis.[4]

More generally, sociologist Carol Smart has argued that children are much less concerned with blood or formal family ties than they are about being raised within families where adults provide love and security, and that it is the quality of family relationships and the provision of emotional and material security that is of much greater significance to children than the structure of the household or the gender or number of adults it contains.[5] Smart and her colleagues identified three aspects of family relationships which children value and which take on a different significance at different ages: residence (who lives where and with whom), which is especially important for children up to 7 or 8; family roles (what members of the family do for each other), a discussion which preoccupies children between around 7 and 12; and the quality of these relationships (the love, care and respect that children feel within the home) being most important to those over 11. They found that in many ways children are more flexible than adults about what constitutes family and they include a large number of people in their descriptions of their families, including relatives both living and dead, members of other households, and even pets.

The importance to children of having parents who love and care for them, but are not necessarily biologically related, has been explored by researchers from the Centre for Family Research at Cambridge University in relation to children born after sperm, egg or embryo donation. This body of work has looked at the long-term outcomes for these children and their own views on their origins. The numbers of children born as a result of assisted conception in the last twenty years has continued to grow and there are approximately 2,000 births each year in the UK which occur after either egg or sperm donation.[6] Such children may be born into a variety of family structures after their birth – to a single mother, a same-sex couple or a heterosexual one, and there has been research on all of these family types.[7] These studies have found that young children show little understanding of donor conception, but by the age of 7 can understand the basic outline. By the age of 10, however, they do understand that there is not necessarily a biological link to both their parents and their reactions range from indifference to curiosity. Researcher Lucy Blake asked a group of 10-year-olds born from donated sperm or eggs how they felt about this. One replied: 'I don't feel any differently, I'm just carrying on with my life. I don't really think about it much, because there's much more like, special on my mind, like cooler things. So I don't really care about it much.' Another said: 'Well, I do feel a bit as if he's not, he's like half-dad but I just forget about it a lot of the time.'[8]

Other work from the same research group has looked at children being raised by two mothers in a same-sex relationship and suggested that children are aware by the age of 5 that they do not have a father, but are not particularly concerned about this and do not see it as a great issue. Indeed, Blake and her colleagues have reported that 'Contrary to expectations, the quality of parent–child relationships in gamete [egg or sperm] donation families has been found to be similar, or superior, to natural conception families . . . Parents who conceive via assisted reproductive technologies have made an enormous effort to have a child, so it is perhaps unsurprising that these families are characterized by high levels of parental warmth and involvement.'[9] Children's responses seem to confirm this and they have reported that they felt close to their parents regardless of biological links and that they regarded their relationships as good, warm and supportive.

The importance that children place on different aspects of family life was explored in the mid-1990s by sociologist Virginia Morrow who interviewed 183 children between the ages of 8 and 14. She asked them directly how they understood their families and what they valued in their parents.[10] She found that the idea that family were who you lived with largely held true for younger children, as Piaget suggested, but after the age of 8 what families do became more important than who lives where. The view that family members provide mutual love and care took on greater significance at this point. Thus 9-year-old Nadia said: 'My mum is important to me because she feeds me and clothes me and loves me very much. My dad is important to me because he pays for the food I eat and the clothes I wear. He cares for me and loves me very much.'[11]

As children became older still (between 11 and 14) they tended to be more evaluative about their families. Whereas younger children tended to talk only about their own experiences and their own families, by the time they were 11 they were able to describe and analyse more abstract notions such as mutual respect or connectedness. Danielle (aged 13) said: 'A family is somewhere you are loved, wanted and spend time with, care for you and brought you into the world, important. Families are for love, homes, helping you, understanding problems.'[12] It must be remembered, however, that children may well be talking about a cultural ideal rather than their own actual experiences. There are many children who grow up without this help, or indeed care or love, and families can be a great source of unhappiness as well as mutual support. In a recent study on secondary school children in the UK, and their perceptions of whom and what makes them happy, Cordelia Sutton explored these ambivalences about family life. She asked forty young teenagers to draw a happiness map with themselves at the centre and then to draw a series of concentric circles in which they wrote down activities, people and things that made them happy. While family scored very highly as something that made them happy, several young people modified this, writing that only a happy or a calm family made them happy. When explored further, young people qualified this so that Paige wrote, 'I love my friends and family but sometimes they cause me sadness', while Sharina said: 'My family, but only when we're not arguing or no one's angry'. Other children in the study spoke of 'a negative aura around your family sometimes' (Holly) and even a pressure on them to act happy even if they did not feel like it, as it was what their parents demanded of them.[13]

Other aspects of family life also reveal some ambivalence amongst children in their closest relationships, especially those between siblings. Surprisingly there is little sociological literature on sibling relationships. Psychological studies have tended to concentrate on the potential for antagonism and rivalry.[14] Yet siblings, along with parents, are the people with whom children are likely to spend the most time in their childhood and indeed the sibling relationship may well be the longest continuous relationship that many people experience. In many parts of the world children spend much of their lives in the company, and under the charge of, their older siblings, who play a central role in their lives.[15] In the very recent past in the West also, many children, especially girls, were expected to look after, or at least keep an eye on, much younger siblings while their mothers did the housework or went out to work, and while this is less common today, the role of siblings remains highly significant.

While the types and variety of sibling relationships are

numerous, in general they are characterized by their strength and depth of emotion, be that positive, negative or ambivalent. Older siblings are often fundamental in socializing younger ones (and being socialized by them) and through each other they learn how to cooperate, empathize and play.[16] Such proximity also means, of course, that siblings learn from an early age exactly which buttons to press and how to rile each other, and this contrast of love and antagonism is one of the defining features of much of the literature. In the previously mentioned study of family life carried out by Virginia Morrow, 11-year-old Callum summed this up succinctly: 'My little sister is important to me because I can sometimes trust her. She does get very annoying, though.'[17] Despite reservations, children value the shared time and experiences of childhood and the fact that with their siblings they can 'be themselves' and don't have to put up any sort of pretence or be on their best behaviour. Samantha Punch has called this children's 'backstage behaviour' – the things they get up to when no one is watching and when they don't feel judged. Children generally feel accepted 'warts and all' by their siblings and in return accept their brothers' and sisters' foibles and failings: 'If you try to take your anger out on your friends then they'd think you're, like "Oh no he hates me or something", but they [siblings] know I hate them sometimes but I don't really hate them, you just say you do but you don't' (Craig, aged 11, a middle child).[18]

The evidence suggests that this is true for children regardless of age, gender and ethnicity. However, studies of siblings among ethnic minorities have shown particular patterns and noticeably more positive descriptions of siblings.

Virginia Morrow's study compared how children of Pakistani heritage in the UK talked about their families with how rural white children spoke about theirs. She found that relationships with siblings were discussed especially positively in the former group. There was less talk about how annoying they were and more about what the siblings did for each other. Shazia, 10, said 'My little sister is important to me because without her I would have nothing to do. My little brother is important to me because without him I would have no one to play with. My littlest sister is important to me because she always makes something for me to do.'[19] There appeared to be less expectation of going round to friends' houses to play and siblings took on a greater significance for these children, partly in line with community norms which emphasize the importance of close ties and emotional satisfaction within the family rather than through friends.[20] There could also be a fear of racial harassment which means that some children of Pakistani heritage may choose to remain closer to their homes and within their own communities and do not play in public spaces as much as their white peers, making sibling ties even more significant in their lives.

Despite the fact that children do talk about their siblings positively, there is also an underlying conflict for many that can be extremely hard for parents to handle, especially when the conflicts become frequent and aggressive.[21] Parents may be torn between wanting to step in and stop the argument escalating and wanting children to sort it out on their own so that they learn about conflict resolution and compromise. In the end most parents intervene by adjudicating and assigning blame to one or other of the children, but more recent psychological studies have suggested that this is not always the best way and that parents should try and mediate between their children, allowing them to come up with their own solutions within a structured negotiation process.[22] This may sound fine in theory, but it is unlikely to come naturally to many parents – indeed, it is suggested that parents need to be 'trained' in such strategies – and in the heat of the moment, it can be extremely hard to set up a negotiation between recalcitrant toddlers. Yet such suggestions highlight the difficulties of maintaining fairness within family life and dealing with the often conflicting needs of children with different personalities and at different developmental stages. Some children, like some adults, are simply happier alone or mixing with adults.

Grandparents can also have important impacts on children's lives but it is only recently that their role and their relationships to their grandchildren have been looked at in greater detail. In many older sociological accounts of the family, grandparents were often seen as somewhat peripheral to the main family, but in the new millennium there has been a greater understanding of their role and a recognition that it has, in many ways, expanded over the last thirty years, rather than contracted.[23] However in contrast to the research presented on how parental identity changes when a child is born (discussed in Chapter 2), there is almost nothing on how personal identity changes when a grandchild arrives. Grandparents now provide a significant amount of financial and practical support to their grandchildren, especially in the form of unpaid childcare. Studies which have focused on what children themselves feel about their grandparents have

also shown that in many cases children place great importance on such relationships. Grandparents are valued as
people who listen to them in a way that parents sometimes
do not, and are often used as mediators between parents and
children. Children greatly value grandparents' nurturing,
both physically and emotionally (children in one study talked
of the cooking and baking they did with their grandmothers),
while others spoke appreciatively of how their grandparents
listened to them without judging or interfering.[24] Although
the relationship changed as children became older, this sense
of closeness continued. Research from the USA suggests that
young children with close, loving and continuing relationships with their grandparents cope better after a parental
divorce than those without.[25] However, such research must
be balanced by the fact that many children do lose contact
with grandparents after a divorce (especially paternal grandparents) and that some grandparents may then have a difficult, distant or even antagonistic relationship with their
former daughter or son-in-law, meaning that continued,
enforced contact with them may be another source of tension and stress in children's lives.

Children's views on family life are complex and they talk
of the need for loving, supportive families and, not surprisingly, this is what most of them (and indeed the overwhelming majority of adults) hanker after. Most people want to see
the family as something they will be part of forever and to
which they can always return, but experience of family life
can also be destructive or suffocating and the family an institution into which they feel they don't belong or don't fit
and are not understood, loved or supported. Particular

relationships within the family, such as those with siblings, are often undercut by tension and antagonism. Harmony, therefore, is not always intrinsic to family life or to intimate relationships. Nevertheless, children consistently emphasize how important these intimate relationships are to them and how strongly they wish to believe in the family as a place where their best interests are looked after and where they are loved unconditionally. Not all children will experience this but the ideal remains strong.

Is the family in decline?

Although families in the West today are more diverse than ever,[26] the nuclear family retains (especially for policy-makers and politicians) a strong symbolic and ideological significance as the 'gold standard' of family and the best backdrop for parenting practices. Those who grow up in this sort of family structure – it is claimed – do better academically, have lower levels of psychological distress, are less likely to misuse alcohol or drugs and are more likely to delay sexual activity until later in their teenage years. They are also thought to have less conflictual relationships with their parents, who will probably be more involved in their lives and provide more emotional support, cognitive stimulation and supervision.[27] Yet this is clearly not the case for every child and while research can suggest that, on average, children do better in particular types of families, there are many children who do well in families that don't fit the 'norm', making generalizations contentious.

Since divorce rates rose across the West after 1945 there

has been a large amount of research on the impact of divorce on children. For many years it was assumed that divorce would have a significant and traumatic impact on a child and some longitudinal studies have shown the longer term consequences of parental separation on children's well-being. The most significant of these studies was carried out by Judith Wallerstein, a psychologist who set up the California Children of Divorce Study.[28] This research was begun in 1971 and followed 131 children (aged between 2 and 18) from sixty families whose parents had divorced. She followed these children for twenty-five years, undertaking extensive interviews with them every five years. She found that divorce was often extremely difficult and disruptive to children and that the effects were long-lasting. She claimed that half the children in her original study had become 'worried, underachieving, self-deprecating and sometimes angry young men and women'.[29] One of her findings, much debated ever since, was that 40 per cent of children of divorced parents never went on to marry themselves.

Wallerstein was called by *Time* magazine 'the godmother of the backlash against divorce' and her findings were extremely influential on both public opinion and social policy in the USA and beyond. She found that the younger the child the greater the initial impact on them: some regressed into babyhood and almost all were profoundly upset and feared that their parents would abandon them. After eighteen months they still seemed troubled, and boys in particular were more disruptive at home and at school. Five years after their parents' marriage ended the children were still depressed and anxious, although after ten years these children seemed happier and many said they had no memories of the divorce or of their parents ever having lived together. None of them remembered feeling frightened or abandoned, although they had spoken about it at the time, nor did they blame themselves for their parents' divorce – and some were glad it had happened when they were younger rather than later. In contrast, Wallerstein found that children who were older at the time of their parents' divorce may initially have seemed less affected, but appeared to retain their fears and upset for much longer and that these feelings sometimes carried on into later life.

Wallerstein's research was subsequently criticized for a number of reasons, both methodological and ideological. The children in her study were all white, middle-class children and her sample was small and narrow. Her comment in the *New York Times* in 1976 that 'I don't want to say don't divorce, but I think the children might even prefer having an unhappy family' led to accusations she was 'guilt tripping' women into staying in unhappy marriages for the sake of the children.[30] She denied this, claiming only that she wanted to give women advice on how to support their children after divorce and to make them aware of potential problems. She also changed her position somewhat over the years, so that by 1989 she was writing: 'a divorce undertaken thoughtfully and realistically can teach children how to confront serious life problems with compassion, wisdom and appropriate action'.[31]

Just as Wallerstein herself seemed to shift her position, so other sociologists and psychologists have moved away from assuming that children affected by divorce will be irrevocably and irreversibly harmed and have started to look at a more complex picture which takes into account a family's individual social, economic and psychological circumstances as well as more general social change. They have argued that a child experiencing divorce in 2018 will have a very different experience from one forty years previously: divorce is more common, more socially accepted and a child is very unlikely to be the only child in the class or peer group with divorced parents – something that might not have been the case in Wallenstein's cohort.[32] There is also recognition that, as some relationships break down, others are built and that living in a single-parent household is not necessarily a permanent situation, given that the average length of time an adult spends as single parent is five years. This means that the type of family a child lives in over the course of their childhood may change and that a child may be part of a nuclear family, a single-parent family and a step-family during his or her childhood. Some may repeat the transition a number of times.

Other research on the longer term impact of divorce on children has suggested that Wallenstein's findings need much greater nuance and possibly no longer hold true. Economist Richard Layard and psychologist Judy Dunn have looked at over ninety studies on the effects of divorce on children and found that these have shown that 50 per cent of children are negatively affected by divorce – in terms of academic outcomes, behavioural difficulties, popularity with other children, anxiety and depression. However, they also point out that these effects, especially behavioural difficulties, dissipate within two years, suggesting that, while divorce may be initially difficult for children to handle, they do adapt.[33] Talking to children and discussing their feelings with them has revealed that (not surprisingly) many do find their parents' divorce upsetting and disruptive, both emotionally and practically. The same is also true for adults of course and even the most amiable divorce is unlikely to be emotion-free. However, there is an increasing recognition that children find it easier to cope with divorce if they feel they are kept fully informed and that they still matter to their parents.[34] The idea of 'mattering' in a divorce is therefore central to how children adapt to it: children have told researchers in many studies that they want reassurances from both parents that they still care about them. Children want clear information about what is happening and some say in where they live (although there is often ambivalence about this, with children not wanting to make decisions that might upset either parent).[35]

For many children it is not the divorce itself that is the most upsetting part, but the conflict, confusion and uncertainty around it and the feeling that they are being kept in the dark about what is going on. The children's mental health charity Place2Be published a book in 2016 on the impact of divorce on children and included a number of case studies. Annaliese, a 9-year-old, described her parents' divorce: 'They didn't really say they were splitting up, but I could just see it coming because they were always fighting . . . Then, one day, when I got home from school, my dad and all his stuff was gone. I felt like they left me all by myself.'[36] It is clear that a badly handled divorce causes problems for children and if divorce represents the continuation of the conflict in the marriage rather than its resolution many children will find the process deeply distressing.[37] Equally important though is other research which suggests that when there is continued conflict in a marriage, or parents who are anti-social or violent, then this too is likely to damage children, making conflict and uncertainty within a marriage as harmful as separation.[38] It is important therefore not to see divorce as the only risk factor: family disharmony, poverty and poor parental mental health may pose equally significant, or even greater, risks to children than parental separation.

If divorce is upsetting, but not necessarily traumatic for children, we have to ask why children raised in single-parent families appear to have poorer longer-term outcomes with higher rates of underachievement and school drop-out and, later on, delinquency and anti-social behaviour. One reason which has been given is the fact that many studies of single-parent families fail to take into account the question of poverty and that it is a lack of resources rather than living in a single-parent family which is likely to cause the most adverse outcomes. One study concluded that up to 50 per cent of the instances of the link between family structure and outcomes, such as teenage pregnancy or school drop-out, could be attributed to poverty rather than single parenting – single-parent households being significantly poorer than those with two parents.[39] Furthermore, on a simple, practical level, having two people living in the same place and taking on a share of the day-to-day aspects of child-rearing, be that school drop-offs and pick-ups, getting lunches ready, reading bedtime stories or bath-times, meant that the daily routines were shared and that there was less of a worry about back-up and plans going wrong. Parenting can be much harder work, physically, financially and emotionally, when done alone.

Parenting need not depend on co-residency, however, and the majority of parents do continue to parent successfully after a divorce or separation. Indeed, there are few children who think of themselves as having only a 'single' parent and this term may well be an inaccurate way to describe a divorced family where the parent who lives apart from the child remains heavily involved. Many fathers remain intimately connected to their children and this involvement can take place in many contexts. Studies from the US have found that children had fewer behavioural problems when they remained emotionally close to their fathers and when these fathers paid child support, although they found little or no correlation between a child's emotional well-being and how much time they spent with their father, suggesting that the quality of the relationship was more important than the amount of interaction.[40] Again, this is not universal and there are many single parents who do parent with little outside help and who effectively raise children on their own. Around 13 per cent of fathers in the UK lose touch with their children after a divorce,[41] although behind these statistics lie a myriad of personal situations: fathers who want to remain in contact but are blocked by former partners; fathers who start again with new families and don't have the time or inclination to see their older children; fathers who are imprisoned; and fathers who believe their children would be better off without them. There is little research on how children feel about this, although there are some suggestions that older children will cease to claim their fathers as part of their families if they don't have a good relationship with them and if they feel they have been abandoned.[42] The majority of research suggests that children who have a good ongoing relationship with their fathers do better than those who do not – with one important caveat, that children whose fathers are anti-social or abusive do better with no contact.[43]

While divorce is still a messy and painful process for many adults and many children, new ways of coping with it are emerging which put children's well-being at the centre. There have been calls for the UK to emulate the system in Sweden in which parents automatically share custody and parental responsibility of the children after divorce, although there is still flexibility about the child's main residence. In Belgium, not only is there an assumption of shared custody, but also a system of alternating residence and care, so that, unless there are very strong objective grounds to oppose it, children spend equal amounts of time with each parent.[44] Other parents have begun to experiment with what has come to be known as 'bird-nesting' where the children stay put in the family home while the parents move in and out when it is their turn to have custody.[45] This has been claimed to be a uniquely child-centred arrangement as it keeps the interruptions to children's lives and routines to a minimum – they don't need two sets of everything to keep at different parents' houses, they do not have the disruption of setting off to school or nursery from different places, and are constantly surrounded by their own familiar stuff. It is, of course, easy to raise practical objections to these forms of post-divorce parenting – they rely on a good cooperative, ongoing relationship between parents, which is not always easy after divorce. Shared custody, while arguably fairer to parents, can be difficult for children, especially if the parents do not live close by and, if parents find new partners and start new families, such arrangements can become impossibly complex. Furthermore, both shared custody and bird's nest parenting depend on a level of affluence: bird's nest parenting means each of the parents having their own small house or flat as well as the larger family house. At a time when many people struggle to buy or rent one home, let alone two or three, a lack of resources can undermine the very best of intentions. Nevertheless the fact that such ideas are being discussed and taken seriously does suggest that parents are aware of the impact that divorce can have on children and are thinking of creative and constructive ways to overcome the difficulties.

Perhaps the best conclusion to come out of the often conflicting research literature on children post-divorce is that, in the words of University of Pennsylvania psychologist Sara Jaffee and her colleagues, 'a growing consensus reveals that living in a single-parent family is, on average, a robust risk factor for children's development, although it is also true that most children ever raised in single-parent families do not suffer long-term adversity'.[46] Despite this, single-parent families still provoke much anxiety, especially when they are found in Black or Minority Ethnic (BME) communities. Some have claimed that these families are disorganized and pathological, producing a generation of violent, anti-social young men who are ruining not only their own lives but are also socially destructive. In 2007 the then UK Home Secretary Jack Straw led a campaign designed to highlight and deal with the problem of absent fathers, predominantly in black communities. He was quoted as saying: 'As we know – lads need dads. Of course they need their mums as well, but there is a particular point in teenagers' development, of young men, where fathers are very important and they are more likely to be absent in the case of the Afro-Caribbean.'[47] When riots broke out in London in 2011, the absence of Afro-Caribbean fathers was offered up as one of the primary causes of this supposed social collapse. This view has a long history and was an echo of one offered almost fifty years earlier by US politician Daniel Patrick Moynihan in his 1965 book *The Negro Family*, which specifically linked ethnicity, fatherlessness and social chaos.

> From the wild Irish slums of the nineteenth century Eastern seaboard to the riot-torn suburbs of Los Angeles, there is one unmistakable lesson in American history: a community that allows a large number of young men to grow up in broken families, dominated by women, never acquiring any stable relationship to male authority, never acquiring any set of rational expectations about the future – that community asks for and gets chaos, crime, violence, unrest, unrestrained lashing out at the whole social structure that is not only to be expected; it is very near to inevitable.[48]

This view from politicians and the media has been countered by sociologists who have presented a different picture and suggested that being raised by single mothers, even ones living in poverty, is not automatically a high road to underachievement and anti-social behaviour and that comments like this are both racist and simplistic. Furthermore, very rarely are these women single mothers raising their children in isolation; they are well supported by their female relations and wider community. In her classic study from 1974, Carol Stack examined social relations in a poor, African American, urban neighbourhood in Chicago which she called the Flats.[49] Here she found groups of women raising their children in a variety of family patterns, swapping and sharing children as their social and financial resources permitted. Children lived in a variety of households at different times, including those of their mothers, their friends and their female relatives when circumstances required it. Despite this often being a necessity, and contemporary views that such parenting behaviour was proof that black families headed by women were chaotic and damaging, Stack showed that such arrangements could also be viewed as comprising a positive care system which reinforced social ties, rather than being a symptom of family breakdown. Even today, to talk about single parents in Afro-Caribbean or Afro-American families may be a misnomer as many women raise children with help from their mothers or siblings, making such networks closer to extended families than to single-parent families. There has been little research on whether it is poverty and social exclusion or lack of a father that causes problems and, while the two are closely linked, this connection needs to be carefully analysed if these families are not to be unfairly stigmatized.

In the first line of his novel *Anna Karenina*, Leo Tolstoy famously claimed that 'All happy families are alike; each unhappy family is unhappy in its own way'. While this might be a pithy aphorism it can hardly be said to reflect reality. There are many happy families headed by single parents, gay parents, older parents, adopted parents or foster parents, just as there are many unhappy children in nuclear families. Research on the family suggests very strongly that the shape and structure of the family may be negotiable, but children's need for love and security within it is not. Children need people around them to whom they matter, whom they love and who support them. Timothy Biblarz and Judith Stacey have concluded, based on many decades of research into same-sex parenting, that 'The bottom line is that committed, responsible parenting involves spending time with children, caring about what they're involved in, and providing structure, limits, guidance and affection. Good parenting is good parenting, whatever package it comes in.'[50]

How Should Children Be Socialized?

Socialization describes the processes by which children develop and learn to behave in ways deemed acceptable within particular families, communities, cultures and societies. Parents and carers play a key role in these processes through the ways in which they stimulate, interact with, discipline and support children to develop and mature into healthy, happy and successful adults. Yet how parents and carers do this varies considerably and a number of psychological theories continue to debate the 'best' and most effective parenting approaches. In this chapter we look at what research can reveal about different parenting approaches.

Supporting children to become successful adults is a primary goal for many parents throughout the world and yet what counts as success remains a topic of wide debate. The 'first three years' movement represents a body of interdisciplinary research spanning psychology and neuroscience and suggests that early stimulation is vital for infant brain development and can even shape ongoing development throughout childhood and into adult life. Failure to make the most of this critical period may limit a child's capacity to reach his or her full potential. Should new parents therefore be primarily concerned with the first three years of their infant's life and so provide rich and stimulating environments for them to play, learn and thereby reach their full potential, or are parents at risk of becoming over-anxious, controlling and perhaps even exhausted in their attempts to do what so-called experts deem best? Is there a right or wrong way? This chapter will look at what research can tell us about the relationships parents develop with their children, how they discipline and interact with – as well as how they stimulate – their children and will ask what 'good parenting' really means.

Stimulating children and when should parents start?

Childhood success and achievement – as a driving objective for many parents, particularly within the Western world – has been the subject of much discussion and yet remains a fairly contentious topic. This is especially marked in research exploring the importance of stimulation during infancy. The 'first three years' movement was a term coined by Davi Johnson Thornton, Assistant Professor of Communication Studies at Southwestern University in Georgetown, Texas, in 2011.[1] Jan Macvarish, Ellie Lee and Pam Lowe from the Centre for Parenting Culture Studies at the University of Kent describe in their paper '"The first three years" and the infant brain'[2] how this movement began in the US in the early 1990s and has expanded to become increasingly influential in Canada, New Zealand, Australia and the UK. The movement encompasses a body of interdisciplinary neurobiological and neuropsychological research which suggests that stimulation is vital for infant brain development and can influence development into adulthood. Many studies also argue that stimulation should start prior to birth – and that the first three years are crucial. From early communication using simple sounds and words to singing and storytelling, to encouraging learning through play and carefully selecting toys that stimulate infant development, including interactive cot mobiles and baby gyms – there are many things parents can do and purchase to stimulate their infant.

The 0–3 years movement has, however, aroused a great deal of debate, with many psychologists, neurobiologists and social scientists casting doubt on certain claims. The claim that if parents don't stimulate their infant enough during early childhood this may inadvertently compromise their child's development remains controversial. Here we look at some of the research and consider if there is indeed evidence for a critical period for children's development from 0–3 years and, if so, what the implications are for the ways parents raise their children.

Neurobiological research, such as the work carried out at the Center for Neuroscience & Society (CNS) at the University of Pennsylvania[3] during the last twenty years, using brain imagery techniques and MRI scanning methods to scan infant brains, identified how, during gestation and the first three years of life, the infant brain undergoes significant changes resulting in enhanced synapses and dendrite density (synapses control motor, cognitive and sensory functions and so regulate much of our behaviour).[4] In humans, synapse formation is a gradual process beginning at around two months before birth and continuing through the first few years of life (a synapse is a small gap at the end of a neuron that allows an electrical or chemical signal to pass from one neuron to the next. It is widely accepted that the synapse plays a central function in the formation of memory). Neurobiologist Patricia Goldman-Rakic explains that how synapses are organized within the brain largely defines a human's intellectual capacity.[5] The thrust of this neurobiological research is that, although some of the neurons in a baby's brain are genetically hardwired at birth to manage basic bodily functions such as breathing and digesting, others lie dormant, awaiting stimulation. The experiences and stimulation a baby and young child encounter during these formative years are therefore thought to programme the brain in such a way to determine how intelligent, confident and articulate a child becomes.[6] The assumption being that without early stimulation the potential for enhanced cognitive development will be lost. Many of these claims have become key topics in media debates, such as the 2012 *Guardian* article, 'Childhood stimulation key to brain development',[7] which presented the idea that enriched early environments potentially produce 'better' infant brains that will in turn create more emotionally attuned, cleverer and socially well-adjusted children and adults. Similarly, Martha Farah, director of the CNS at the University of Pennsylvania[8] led a longitudinal study (carried out over ten years) which combined surveys of children's home life experiences at ages 4 and then again at 8 years of age, coupled with brain-scan recordings during adolescence. The study recorded a series of details about the children's lives in an attempt to measure the amount and type of stimulation that these children experienced, such as the number of children's books they had, the type and number of learning and educational toys and games that the children played with, as well as other types of education such as learning a musical instrument. The researchers also looked at how parents interacted with their children and scored the interactions on 'parental nurturance' – which the researchers took as a measure of how much warmth, support and care the child received from a parent. The results suggest that stimulation at the age of 4 was a key factor in predicting the development of several parts of the brain cortex. The region in the brain most affected was identified as the lateral left temporal cortex – which is associated with memory, processing word meanings and general knowledge. 'Parental nurturance' and stimulation at age 8 had apparently no effect on brain development.[9]

Yet contrasting research from the fields of cultural, psychological and philosophical studies presents quite different results. Jan Macvarish and colleagues argue that despite apparent 'explosive synaptic connectivity' during gestation and the formative years, much of this research – although very powerful – rests upon rather inflated claims.[10] Macvarish and colleagues draw upon the work of John Bruer, a leading American philosopher working in neuroscience, and the psychologist Jerome Kagan to challenge some of the evidence put forward by neuroscientists.

John Bruer questions the idea that more dendrite density and enhanced synaptic development infers more brain power and claims instead that dendrite density can actually increase at any age. Although some human skills such as acquiring language and visual development are highly responsive to stimulation and environmental influence during the first few years of life, many other skills and behaviours such as the development of perception and social intelligence are learnt and developed throughout childhood and into adulthood. Bruer argues that a baby's brain develops appropriately and sufficiently in quite ordinary environments and the idea that parents should begin a focused programme of stimulation is therefore misguided. Whilst Bruer and other academic researchers such as Jerome Kagan do not suggest that playing with and stimulating children is not important – as clearly it is in a number of different ways for promoting warm, caring and loving relationships – they argue that neuroscience cannot claim that such activities always produce certain types of childhood behaviour and so infer better outcomes (ideas about how children should play is taken up again in the following chapter). Bruer contends that whilst a foetal and infant brain develops considerably during the early years it is misleading to suggest that this is the most significant, if not critical, period. Children develop and learn throughout childhood and adolescence and indeed many other academics would suggest that learning is a lifelong process. This view also aligns with research within the field of brain plasticity and the idea that pathways and connections within the brain can change and adapt throughout life. As Macvarish and colleagues argue, 'Brain development is therefore better described as plastic and resilient rather than determined and fixed'.[11] This supports the extensive research carried out by the leading psychologist Michael Rutter on children raised in conditions of extreme deprivation in Romanian orphanages which illustrates that the impact of limited stimulation and deprivation can be overcome in some cases.[12]

Bruer, along with many developmental psychologists,

critiques many of the research methods used in early neuro-science which relied on animal experimentation rather than the analysis of human infant brain development (which raises a number of ethical issues) and questions how much is really known about the impact of early stimulation and particularly parenting/caring on infant brain development. Macvarish and colleagues argue that many of the messages that neuroscience promotes may encourage parents to feel personally responsible for exhaustively stimulating, playing with and educating their children from a very young age. The strength of neuroscience in presenting an appealing and – as psychologists David McCabe and Alan Castel[13] would suggest – a rather beguiling message has become a topic of wide debate. They argue that brain images are more persua-sive and influential because they provide a physical basis for rather abstract processes.[14] In *The Seductive Allure of Neuroscience Explanations*, academics Deena Weisberg and colleagues report on their research which set out to examine people's ability to critically consider the logic of explanations by giving students on a neuroscience course, and neuro-science experts, brief descriptions of psychological phenom-ena, followed by one of four types of explanation. The study shows that people tend accept explanations that allude to neuroscience, even when they are not accurate.[15]

Mark Stokes, from Oxford University's Centre for Human Brain Activity, presents perhaps a more balanced perspective and suggests that many of the claims in neuroscience are somewhat premature and so it is of little surprise they have provoked debate.[16] Stokes describes how neuroscience is still a relatively new field of research in which developments in research approaches are still being refined. The extent to which stimulation beyond what might be considered 'normal' impacts on a child's later development remains open to debate, however there can be no doubt that parents throughout the Western world are encouraged to engage, play with and to stimulate their infant as much as possible.

Despite the lack of firm evidence to support the idea that the first three years of life are critical for a child's intellectual development, a number of initiatives throughout the UK and North America, as well as parts of Europe and Australia, have been set up which focus on the importance of early childhood stimulation, play and learning. These include 'Thrive to Five'[17] (which goes beyond three years, yet still emphasizes the importance of early development),[18] as well as information portals such as the Urban Child Institute[19] which encourage parents to exercise their baby's brain during what is considered to be the most important stage for learning, and provide support and guidance for parents, academics and practitioners. Whilst the 0–3 movement has raised awareness of the value of stimulating and educating infants, the claims that this can produce 'better brains' and lay the foundations for enhanced intellectual outcomes for children and adults remains open to debate.

Is there a right or wrong way to socialize children?

There are many approaches that parents can and do use to socialize their children and get them to behave as they see fit – from reasoning with them, punishing them for unacceptable behaviour, including through smacking, taking time out and the removal of privileges to use of the 'naughty step' (some of the debates around forms of discipline and punishment are picked up in the final chapter of this book). Discussions on parenting often convey the idea that socializing young children is actually quite difficult. Similarly, in a variety of TV shows, such as *Supernanny* or *Three Day Nanny*, parents are offered a series of techniques to help them manage their children's behaviour, establish more effective relationships between adults and children and get their children to behave in ways deemed acceptable.[20] In *Supernanny*, Jo Frost's Naughty Step, for example, is a technique whereby unruly toddlers are encouraged to reflect on their 'naughty behaviour' and recognize that behaviour has consequences – one of a number of techniques illustrated as effective 'toddler taming' methods.[21] But what does the evidence suggest about the most effective ways to socialize children?

In her leading research during the 1960s, psychologist Diana Baumrind[22] studied more than a hundred middle-class American pre-school children and their parents. Through extensive observations of parent–child interaction and parent interviews Baumrind identified three parenting styles termed *authoritative*, *authoritarian* and *permissive* – which are still influential and widely used today.

Authoritarian parents characteristically expect their children to obey certain rules within the family and are generally regarded as quite strict. Their child-rearing tends to make use of punishments, such as smacking and shouting, to teach children to behave according to their rules. In contrast, permissive parenting reflects a far more laissez-faire style in which parents place low demands on their children and do not impose boundaries on behaviour. While permissive parents tend to be warm and loving, they provide few guidelines and rules. Somewhere in between authoritarian and permissive parenting, authoritative parents set boundaries, yet encourage children to develop self-reliant behaviour and individual autonomy. Authoritative child-rearing typically reflects a child-centred approach in which parents attempt to understand how their children are feeling and support them to regulate their own emotions. They encourage children to be self-reliant but still apply boundaries and family rules.

Following the publication of Baumrind's classification of parenting, these different parenting styles and their impact upon children were studied extensively. A large body of research suggests that authoritative parents are apt to raise children who are more independent, autonomous and generally happier than children raised by permissive and authoritarian parents.[23] Similarly, the UK's Medical Research Council (MRC) National Survey of Health and Development tracked more than 5,000 children since their birth in 1946 through to adulthood in the 1990s to examine the links between parenting approaches and children's, young people's and adults' reports of their own well-being.[24] The researchers found that children who claimed that their parents had been controlling (examples of this include invasions of children's privacy and a reluctance to let children make their own decisions) during childhood were more likely to have low scores in surveys of happiness and general well-being carried out in their teenage years and then again during their thirties, forties and even their sixties. In contrast, the children who reported that their parents were more caring, warm and responsive to their needs tended to be more content well into adulthood.

These research findings are also supported by a large-scale study which was carried out at the University of Toronto by Maxine Wintre and Shawn Gates in 2006 which gathered data from 301 middle-aged couples. Using retrospective accounts of how they were parented and subjective accounts of their early experiences, the authors found a link between parenting style and psychological distress in middle age.[25] Further studies argue that children raised with warm, loving parents are more likely to display emotional security in later life.[26] In 1983, psychologists Eleanor Maccoby and John Martin built upon Baumrind's classification of parenting styles and identified a fourth parenting style, called neglectful or uninvolved parenting.[27] Typically this approach reflects parents who are somewhat detached and disengaged from their children and, although they fulfil their children's basic needs, are otherwise emotionally distant. The impact of this style of parenting has been linked to higher incidences of anti-social and aggressive behaviour in children.[28] Studies of this type have been criticized for using retrospective accounts of childhood experiences – which rely on memory, and self-reporting techniques – and are highly subjective. Despite these critiques, a number of studies exploring recalled parenting style through sibling and twin research support these findings.[29]

Whilst these types of studies are exceptionally useful in examining the potential impact of different parenting styles, when taking into account the critiques mentioned above it is important also to appreciate that individual child-rearing styles are rarely as neat as the classifications. As Baumrind's extensive research illustrates, parents can adjust their style at different periods of time throughout their lives and according to unique circumstances;[30] parenting approaches are both fluid and changeable. The child's contribution to the family dynamic, as well as their temperament and relationship with their parent are also important considerations which have become a feature of more contemporary research.

Swedish psychologists Geertjan Overbeek and Håkan Stattin[31] carried out a longitudinal study in 2007 examining the impact of children's relationships with their parents on their emotional adjustment in adulthood. The study followed 212 Swedish children and their parents from birth into adulthood. The research provided a detailed examination of social and emotional development across different developmental stages – infancy, childhood, adolescence and adulthood – with a key focus on child–parent communication and conflict to see how this impacted on the children's later relationships in adulthood as well as any experiences of depression, anxiety and dissatisfaction with life in middle age. The results suggest that early adversity in parent–child relationships, such as difficult parent–child relationships, conflict and discord, may signal the beginning of a developmental sequence in which communications with parents in adolescence predict low-quality partner relations in young adulthood, which in turn may be linked to dissatisfaction with life and poor quality of partner relationships at mid-life. In addition to the possible connections between parenting style and a childhood behaviour trajectory into adulthood, however, the researchers raise a number of important considerations. They suggest that it is necessary to look at how parents from different socioeconomic groups adopt particular parenting approaches; whether approaches are also different in relation to parental gender; and whether parents employ distinct care-taking approaches in relation to their child's personality or temperament. Overbeek and Stattin suggest that it might be that a child's difficult temperament or low sociability lead to difficult relationships across all domains, affecting relationships with parents but also later relationships with partners. In other words, the present study helps to provide insight into the explanatory role of difficult parent– child interactions in the development of social-emotional behaviour, but it does not determine the causes that underlie these detrimental parent– child interactions themselves. Few studies look at the multiple influences on family relationships and Overbeek and Stattin acknowledge that different measurements may indeed yield different results.

So whilst there is a body of research that suggests that parents do employ different approaches and some of these approaches can be considered better than others in terms of the long-term social and emotional development for children, the assumption that parents play a leading role – if not the leading role – in shaping their children's behaviour does not fully consider the intricacy of family relationships. Indeed, in the previous chapter the influence of siblings and grandparents was discussed and some scholars have argued that parents are not nearly as important as they think they are. Psychologist Judith Rich Harris, for example, has claimed that peer groups are often a more important factor in socializing children than parents. She writes: 'Socialization is not something that grown-ups do to kids – it is something kids do to themselves . . . Modern children do learn things from their parents; they bring to the group what they learned at home . . . This makes it look as though the parents are the conveyors of the culture, but they are not: the peer groups is. If the peer group's culture differs from the parents', the peer groups always win.'[32]

What is 'good parenting'?

Despite the many apparent differences in how parents raise their children, anthropologist Robert LeVine (introduced in Chapter 2) has identified three core goals which parents across the world typically strive for. He argues that first, all parents are concerned with physical survival and the health of their infant. Although now largely taken for granted in the West, in other parts of the world where this isn't the case this is clearly the first priority. Secondly, all parents are to a greater or lesser extent concerned with support for their child's developing capacity to look after themselves. Whilst cross-cultural differences are evident, socializing, educating and providing opportunities for children to work and lead an independent life are core priorities for parents throughout the world. Thirdly, helping children to do well and make the most of their lives – through greater wealth, religious piety, intellectual achievement, personal satisfaction and self-realization – are goals evident amongst parents. Of course, different communities and cultures have very different ideas about what 'doing well' and 'making the most' of one's life means. Much of LeVine's work is based on comparisons of middle-class mothers in the USA with those of mothers in rural communities in Kenya. He identifies two approaches – *paediatric* and *pedagogic* – which may help explain why parents prioritize different goals in different circumstances. The *paediatric* approach, which is customary across Africa, focuses on protection and survival in the early years, and the *pedagogic* approach, typically practised in the USA, is more concerned with teaching infants behavioural competencies. Middle-class mothers in America generally take the survival of their children for granted and so are more likely to devote time and energy to shaping how their children behave and get on socially and academically. They engage in 'proto-conversations'[33] with their babies (even when they can neither understand nor respond) and encourage them to walk and talk early.[34]

In contrast, LeVine argues, in African societies where infant mortality is high, and the early years of life most dangerous, mothers keep their children in very close physical contact, carry them everywhere and breastfeed them for up to two years. Mothers feed babies on demand but generally do not treat them as emotionally responsive individuals with whom they should make eye contact or talk. This is not because they are uninterested in their long-term development but because they are less concerned with moulding their infants' behaviour. Indeed, throughout the world different cultures have very distinct ideas about what is best and most appropriate for children and looking at these childcare approaches reveals some of the difficulties researchers encounter when trying to describe what makes a good parent. Cross-culturally, parents have strongly contrasting ideas about what infants are capable of at particular stages within their development, which further shapes their own approach to what is right and 'best' for their infant and therefore what constitutes 'good parenting'. Through his anthropological research David Lancy[35] has found a number of differences in how parents raise their children – much of which goes against a Westernized emphasis on the overwhelming importance of the first three years and the need for constant mental and physical stimulation. Among the Yucatec Maya people of Mexico for example, early parental care is primarily geared to raising a quiet, content and calm infant and over-stimulation is something to be avoided. Parenting aids such as swaddling, cradle boards and carrying slings[36] have been observed by anthropologists, particularly amongst Native Americans, as ways of keeping a baby in what Lancy describes as an almost 'benign coma' in which infants are afforded few opportunities to engage directly with their environment. Child–parent interaction may appear somewhat limited when compared to many of the more hands-on approaches common in the UK, America and Europe. In other cultures, such as the Kaluli of Papua New Guinea, parents do not direct speech towards their infants because they believe that they have no understanding or ability to communicate. Not all mothers play with their very young children, as the following chapter will document, and children are not stimulated because they are not seen as interactive or as able to respond.

Further studies exploring parental attitudes to child-rearing and child-rearing practices indicate, as the anthropologist Meredith Small[37] notes, how North American parents typically strive to foster independence and self-reliance in their children in contrast to other cultures which place a higher value on group collaboration and cooperation. Small describes how many American parents believe that a child is born with a temperament and a number of personality traits that can to some extent be shaped and moulded through careful parenting practices. For a number of parents this equates with providing opportunities for achievement and success and limiting experiences which might prevent this. Valuing the confidence and self-esteem of children rests on the idea that as individuals they have a growing sense of self. Yet Small notes that for many other cultures there is not a similar recognition of self. Indeed, for many cultures throughout the world the idea of 'I' and the individualistic notion of self-esteem is somewhat overlooked, with more emphasis on the collective 'we'. Collectivist cultures such as in the Far East, Africa and Latin America downplay independence and instead aim to promote mutual respect and activity as part of a group, thereby advocating reciprocity and cooperation. But how do individualistic and collectivist values play out in the ways parents approach childcare and what are the potential outcomes – if any?

Sara Harkness, psychologist for the Department of Human Development and Family Studies at the University of Connecticut found that nearly 25 per cent of all the descriptors used by American parents to describe their children tended to draw on terms such as *advanced*, *smart* and *gifted*. She notes a tendency among contemporary parents in the

UK and the USA to focus on children's future success rather than on the everyday enjoyment of childhood. In *How to Raise an Adult: Break Free of the Overparenting Trap and Prepare Your Kid for Success*, former University of Stanford Dean, Julie Lythcott-Haims defines over-parenting as a potential trap.[38] She goes as far as to suggest that many parents operate a 'checklist' approach to their child-rearing which has increasingly become overburdened with activities, clubs, attainment and success goals which are potentially damaging to children, particularly since such approaches tend to overlook the importance of children being valued for who they are rather than what they achieve. Not only does this type of child-rearing encourage parents to focus predominantly on outcomes and achievements in the future but, she argues, it also restricts opportunities for children to learn from their own mistakes and learn to value their own accomplishments – instead of a version of their parents' goals and objectives. Wendy Mogel, a clinical psychologist and author of *The Blessing of a B Minus: Using Jewish Teachings to Raise Resilient Teenagers*,[39] suggests that as parents are supposed to be raising children who will leave home and become independent, it is important for children to develop self-reliance, resourcefulness and resilience. This is, of course, challenging, because it means that children must be allowed 'enough freedom to make mistakes'.[40] We will return to issues of how to build resilience while also protecting children from their mistakes in Chapter 8.

A parental focus on achievement and success is not confined to parents from the UK and the USA however and has been recently claimed as central to Chinese ideas of good motherhood. In her book entitled the *Battle Hymn of the Tiger Mother*, Amy Chua[41] describes a type of Chinese mother who is a strict disciplinarian, yet is primarily focused on success and achievement. This is often played out through excessive parental stimulation, activity-focused play as well as the organization of endless classes to teach young children how to learn a musical instrument for instance, as well as literacy and maths. Chua suggests that many Chinese mothers actually believe that academic achievement reflects successful parenting, and that if children do not move through distinct developmental milestones, achieve particular intellectual success and do well at home and at school, then the parents are largely to blame. The growing tendency for parents to intervene and attempt to manage and control many aspects of children's lives from a young age is recognized by sociologist Frank Furedi in *Paranoid Parenting*.[42] It is also a belief further explored in a UNICEF report published in 2001 which, although acknowledging the importance of child protection and safety, suggests that a climate of parental surveillance can be potentially damaging for children 'whose lives and childhoods are being newly circumscribed by unprecedented levels of parental concern' (an issue which will be discussed further in the final chapter).[43]

The observation that child-rearing, particularly in the USA and the UK, is increasingly marked by over-parenting shares much with Foster Cline and Jim Fay's idea of the *helicopter parent*. This term was coined during the 1990s to describe over-protective, pushy, interfering and achievement-orientated parenting approaches prevalent in the Western world. Whilst the concept was first used by child psychologist

Haim Ginott in her book *Between Parent and Teenager*,[44] the term is now more widely used to encompass parenting from the early years onwards. In very general terms, helicopter parents attempt to make sure that their child is on the correct path for success, first by identifying which path to follow and secondly by ensuring they stay on that path. In *Parent and Child Traits Associated with Overparenting*, researchers Chris Segrin, Alesia Woszidlo, Michelle Givertz and Neil Montgomery examine the effects of helicopter parenting and argue that over-parenting can potentially nurture narcissistic young adults with poor coping skills, which in the long term can be linked to anxiety and depression.[45] In summary, the research evidence appears to suggest that while parental stimulation and engagement is important for children's development, over-parenting is associated with potentially more negative childhood behaviour.

Parents and carers throughout the world will employ different approaches in how they care for and raise their children. Research indicates that some parenting approaches are associated with better outcomes for children than others and that children raised by warm and loving parents/carers who set boundaries are more likely to develop into content and secure adults. Yet this is culturally specific and by no means universal. It is also – despite some of the claims that it has 'hard science' behind it – subjective and fraught with disagreement. Today it is hard to talk about parenting without coming across yet another new term – Tiger Mums – to describe a different type of child-rearing technique. From over-protective, helicopter and drone parents to Tiger Mums, there are many ways to describe and disapprove of parents trying to do what they think is best for their children. Evidence from neuroscience, anthropology or psychology gives no definitive answers about how to parent, what makes a good parent or the best way to socialize children. What these various fields can identify, though, is the distinct approaches and wide-ranging ideas about what counts as 'good' parenting and the many pathways that parents take to achieve it.

How Should Children Play?

Play is an activity that is important enough to be claimed as a human right for every child. It is a universal phenomenon, though the nature of play may vary widely.[1] Its importance in children's lives is of interest to parents and policy-makers because of the unique contribution that play can make to children's physical, social, emotional and cognitive development. Play is sometimes seen as the defining feature of childhood, so much so that its importance in children's lives is taken for an established fact. But is this the case or does the idea of play need more interrogation? Is it, in fact, universal? Is it a fundamental part of a healthy and happy childhood and what impact does it have when children cannot or do not play, or play in the 'wrong' way? To answer these questions it is necessary to examine what counts as play for young children today and to look at the cultural differences in how children play and the impact of play activities on various aspects of their development. It is also important to discuss the now ubiquitous new play technologies and the extent to which they have transformed children's play.

What is 'play' and is it universal?

Although there has been an enormous amount of research into children's play, the actual purpose of it and the definition of the term 'play' remain widely debated. This is partly because researchers are seeking to understand a phenomenon which changes across time and between cultures. Certainly, comparative international research suggests that play means different things to different communities and that there is no one universal notion of play.[2] Such work identifies a range of ways in which different cultures regard children's play, including situations where children play and work alongside adults, their play mirroring the adults' work; where children work if their families need the income, but also have separate play activities; or where children's play and adults' work is seen as completely separate entities. Furthermore, the way in which parents and care-givers play with their children is culturally mediated, so that, for example, American parents engage in different types of pretend play with their children from Chinese parents.[3] Anthropological research has also suggested that mother–child play is not universal and while the notion of mother–child play is seen as an essential part of a child's development in the West, international studies have shown that it is relative uncommon elsewhere. The existence of these diverse practices concerning children's play illustrates that the 'privileged' position that play is given in European-heritage cultures is not necessarily the norm in all cultures.[4]

Beliefs about play and its value vary by cultural group,

socio-economic status and ethnicity. For example, in China the one-child policy led to a situation where it was common for a single child to be the centre of a family with six adults (parents and two sets of grandparents). Although many Chinese parents believe in the importance of play in their children's lives, the broader cultural view of the importance of education, combined with family expectations for future success, causes a disconnect between parental beliefs and their actions.[5] In China, toys are typically seen as things which young children should play with freely, simply for enjoyment. However, after children reach about 7 years of age, parents begin to favour toys that are seen as serving an educational purpose, and this educational aspect is explicitly promoted to parents in the media.[6] Parents might have a desire to give their children a childhood that includes more free playtime; however, they also experience a cultural 'moral duty' to train their children for success, which runs against the notion of children being encouraged to play for the sake of play. Consequently, academic tasks take precedence and play opportunities are reduced for children, and this gives rise to activities such as computer coding classes for pre-schoolers.[7] Where economic pressures are greater, parents are more likely to see play as incidental to the development of necessary economic skills. For example, the belief in the precedence of 'education' over play for young children is more likely to exist in parents who have emigrated from China into situations that are economically more challenging, than those who have not.[8]

Similar findings have emerged from other countries. In diverse communities in India, nearly all parents valued their children's play, but placed a greater value on early educational activities.[9] Surveyed parents from low-income groups in the USA also saw play as an opportunity for children to learn useful things, and were disinclined to endorse statements where play might be purely for fun.[10] Cross-cultural psychologist Jaipaul Roopnarine has noted: 'It seems that parents from culturally marginalized groups . . . may fully understand the "social value" of play but want to "prime" their children for school readiness and school success through early academic training – not through the "frivolity" of play.'[11] Conversely, parents in more economically privileged societies and families have the luxury to 'invest' in their children's play, often believing this will enhance their child's development and achieve longer term social and economic advantages (an issue which will be explored further in the next chapter). This may suggest there is a risk that play, albeit highly structured and supervised, may well become the preserve of the better off and a privilege of the rich.

Most academic studies view play as an activity which is controlled by the child, is voluntary, spontaneous and enjoyable. It covers a very broad spectrum of activities: it can be inferred in the very early actions of children, for example where they might repeatedly drop or bang objects together to make noise in the first year of their life, or it may be seen in the form of organized games with defined rules as children get older. As children develop, the nature of their play changes; early in the last century Mildred Parten gave names to different types of play which can still be useful today (see below).[12]

In *unoccupied play*, children have only a fleeting interest in objects and other children. This type of activity is primarily about exploring the properties of objects. In *solitary play* the child plays alone in a focused manner, away from other children. This type of independent play is common up to 2 years of age and is followed, developmentally, by *onlooker play* where children appear obviously interested in watching the actions of other children. They want to be near the other children and may make some form of social contact with them, but do not 'join in'. *Parallel play* can be seen as a development from onlooker play. Here children are actively playing in the presence of, and close to, other children. Their play activity might mimic the actions of the other children, but they are still not playing with them. Their playing isn't cooperative and doesn't require others for it to happen. This type of play, seen in many 2-year-olds and some 3-year-olds, is a transition between the solitary play of younger children and the socially engaged and cooperative play of older children.

Following this, there is the beginning of active interaction of *associative play*. Children now play with friends by sharing and cooperating, albeit not for sustained periods. These activities may not be socially well coordinated and often involve lots of practising skills such as 'disjointed' running about by groups of children. It is often later, after 3 years of age and into middle childhood when *cooperative play* becomes most noticeable. Children are then interested in other children and also in a shared coordinated activity. They may take on explicit roles within their games, and invent, follow or break shared game rules. Their play interactions are dependent on, and complementary to, one another. Although the amount of cooperative play increases as children get older, they still play by themselves quite often. Young children enjoy playing socially and their ability to do so becomes more sophisticated with age. The early origins of children's playful social interactions can be identified in the responsive interactions of babies during early mutual exchanges with their parents or through visual exchanges with peers as early as 8–12 months.[13] Play is the way in which children develop their early peer relationships, and so the benefits that derive from these social interactions are mediated through the development of their play.

Such categorizations are very useful for understanding children's different types of play, but they should not be seen as an unvarying developmental hierarchy of stages or as developmental milestones. Viewing them in this way can underestimate young children's social abilities, the influence of the family and the cultural context as well as children's own personalities – all children are different and mature and develop at different rates. It may well be that an only child is more interested in solitary play for longer, and other children may not get to grips with cooperative play until later than 3 years, whereas 4-year-olds who take part in organized joint activities are likely to show increased rates of spontaneous cooperative play.[14]

What do children think play is?

Relatively little research has investigated what play means to the children themselves, or begins from the basis of what children value in their play. This is important because children are the experts on their own experiences, play is a central part of their lives, and decisions made about an issue of such importance to them should prioritize their voices. When they are listened to, it becomes apparent that adult notions of play do not necessarily match those of children, and children expect adults to have ideas about play activities that are at odds with their own feelings.[15] For example, when asked about play, 9-year-old Canadian children had a much broader view of what counted as play than their parents. Unlike adults, the children saw play as possible with almost anyone, i.e. friends, parents and neighbours, solitary activities and time spent with pets.

> I like to play with cats and dogs. I like to play on my Wii. I play soccer out in my backyard . . .
>
> I like horses. I like to ride my bike and I like to build snowmen.[16]

Play activities for these children depended not only on who they played with, but were also concerned with movement, creativity, imagination, entertainment, sport or social activities – or combinations of all of these. For children older than toddlers, play is often linked to a story or idea that can give their play a personal meaning. Without this, activities which adults may think children enjoy can be felt to be boring by children.

For most children, underpinning all play activities is the idea that they must be *fun*. This applies even to games and sports with strict rules, which adult researchers have not always classified as play. Children see play not so much about an activity or object itself, but in the *experience* of fun (expressed as pleasure, entertainment, amusement or satisfaction in studies with older children) – a view which may well conflict with their parents' views and priorities. Furniture chain IKEA commissioned an international study on play in which researchers interviewed 30, 000 parents and children across twelve countries and found that over a quarter of children felt that their parents organized too many things for them to do outside of school. A UK-based review concluded that free playtime may be seen 'as an "unaffordable luxury" in modern society, and instead children [are given] more organized activities which are thought to be more educational'.[17] Children often claim that they would like more playtime with their parents[18] and many parents feel guilty about how a lack of play will affect their children's lives and their relationship with them. This was a finding in both time-rich countries such as the Netherlands, and time-poor countries such as India, where 60 per cent of parents agreed with the statement, 'I don't feel I have enough time to play with my children.'[19] What this experience is like from a child's point of view is further discussed in the above-mentioned Canadian study of 7–9-year- olds' play. A consistent theme in the children's accounts of their play was of a conflict when parents needed space or an adult-only time.

'She [her mum] wants me to play a game that doesn't distract her making supper.'

'They just want to do stuff without us.'

'My parents say go play, they mean stop bugging us, or get out of my way, just stop bugging us.'

'They said go upstairs, shut up and don't talk to me so I can do the taxes.'[20]

Thus play can sometimes be experienced as something children are told to do as a way of shutting them out of the adult world.

Why is play important?

A large body of psychological research indicates that play, however it is defined, not only reflects a fundamental feature of childhood but also provides opportunities for children to engage with their environments, to learn, establish friendships, forge attachments with adults and develop self-confidence and resilience.[21] Through their early hands-on play experiences, children are able to learn about space, colours and patterns, concepts that underpin and – with adult support – can later be developed into a scientific understanding of the world. Perhaps the benefits of 'larger' physically active play are the most obvious. Children who are playing rough and tumble, running and jumping, throwing and catching are enhancing skills such as hand–eye coordination and developing physical strength and stamina, as well as gaining confidence in their own abilities. Yet the desire of children and their families to play physically differs between countries. A multi-country study showed that, on average, 44 per cent of parents would like to play sport as a family.[22] This wish is greatest in South Korea, where respondents had the largest gap between the amount of physical play they engaged in as a family and the amount they would like. Children also consistently reported a desire to go outdoors as a family, albeit for many (38 per cent) this was a second preference to watching television.

An important aspect of children's play, particularly in supporting their cooperative play, is the development of their ability to pretend or make-believe: the drive to 'pretend' is seen in children across international contexts and in children living in both impoverished and better-off circumstances.[23] *Pretend play* involves taking on roles, being able to imitate others and imagine oneself in another person's place. The ability to do this develops slowly, usually beginning in ' re-creations' of common everyday activities and as children pass 2 years of age, and their language skills develop, they may begin acting out real-life events using dolls or other objects. As children get older they need less support, and by the time they reach about 4 years of age they can usually initiate their own play stories. They are often able to use their imaginations to create relatively complex stories that go beyond play objects that directly resemble their real world counterparts. The ability to think beyond 'everyday constraints' has profound developmental implications (and will be discussed later in the chapter). As Lev Vygotsky, one of the most influential child psychologists of the twentieth century, has written:

> In play a child is always above his average age, above his daily behaviour; in play it is as though he were a head taller than himself. As in the focus of a magnifying glass, play contains all developmental tendencies in a condensed form; in play it is as though the child were trying to jump above the level of his normal behaviour.[24]

Pretend play therefore allows children to begin exploring the world from different perspectives, and their use of imaginative play correlates with their social development. Children who engage with this type of play more frequently are likely to be better at taking on roles outside of play situations, and are rated, by adults, as more socially competent. It also seems to help children regulate their emotions during stressful periods. The positive effects associated with imaginative play have led to it being advocated by many pioneers in early childhood education as essential for supporting children's healthy development.[25]

The imaginative games which children play are shaped by their cultural and family contexts. This is seen, for example, in the types of games played by boys and girls. A frequently reported gender difference in play relates to boys being more aggressive in their *rough and tumble* play. This type of play can involve play-fighting, wrestling, chasing or piggyback fights, and is often what first comes to mind when adults are asked to describe children's play. Studies of American 4 to 5-year-olds suggest that boys enjoy playing more roughly than the girls, although they do not seek to hurt their playmates.[26] However, it is not something that all boys enjoy. For example, about 40 per cent of 11-year-old boys (in a survey of American children) said they didn't like it.[27] Adults are frequently concerned by this type of play, perceiving it as fighting or something that will escalate into fighting or anti-social behaviour, and so may seek to discourage it. As psychologist Eileen Kennedy-Moore points out:

> If you watch a group of boys playing outside, chances are, at some point, one boy is going to leap on top of another boy. There will be a lot of yelling and ferocious roars, but

> also lots of grins. Other boys will try to pull the first boy
> off or grab on, too, and they'll all end up in a pile on the
> ground.
>
> If there's an adult around, especially a woman, the odds
> are good that the adult will tell the boys, 'Stop that right
> now before someone gets hurt!' [28]

In this quote the phrase 'especially a woman' might seem unusual or even sexist, but it may contain a grain of truth. Whilst over 85 per cent of 11-year-old children could distinguish correctly between examples of real and play fighting in a research study, adults performed less well. Men and women raised with brothers were correct about 70 per cent of the time, whereas women who did not have brothers were likely to see *all* the videos as fighting.[29]

Rough and tumble play can be distinguished from aggression as there is no dispute to be settled, and it involves features of cooperative play such as rule-following and turn-taking, and afterwards there are no ongoing hostile feelings.[30] However, problems arise when children lack sufficient skills to join in successfully. Those who lack the social skills necessary to play in this way, or children who are seen by their peers as unpopular, are much more likely to find themselves in situations that escalate into aggressive or hostile interactions.[31] This issue aside, it has been argued that rough and tumble play, which is common across cultures, has benefits for children's development because of the negotiation of rules and the social competence it engenders. Whilst both girls and boys engage in rough and tumble play, boys are likely to do so more frequently,[32] and the nature of their play can differ, with boys likely to be noisier and physically rougher in their play.[33] This has been seen as a consequence of girls being more able to moderate their behaviour in relation to the social context, but it also reflects their differing cultural norms and opportunities.[34]

The psychological benefits of pretend and cooperative play are thus well documented. Children are able to learn about and then practise their social skills in situations that involve negotiating cooperation and conflict, taking on different roles, and learning how to adapt to social groups of different types. Pretend play provides social situations in which children need to, and learn how to, practise socially responsible behaviour and self-regulation.[35] This involves managing their own emotions, overcoming their immediate impulses and solving social problems (such as resolving differences) in order to support their social play. Research has found that children who are involved in lots of social play are rated by their teachers as the most socially competent and popular in class;[36] pretend play was also associated with enhanced creativity.[37] Although the explanations as to why these associations occur may differ, it seems reasonable to suggest that giving children the freedom to explore and be creative in their play is supportive of their later intellectual and social development.[38] Play is therefore not only something that is fun for children, it is reasonable to suggest that it is essential for their social, emotional, physical and cognitive well-being.

Yet despite the evidence that some form of play is both beneficial and necessary for children's development, some have argued that the 'centrality of play in children's lives is misunderstood and ignored', and that children's *right* to play has never been properly implemented.[39] Children's rights activist and founder of the Children's Rights Alliance for England Gerison Lansdown has argued that young children's right to play has been infringed by highly structured curricula in their early years, whose targets are reached through formal direct teaching, or homework, intruding on young children's free time, giving an implicit message that play is wasting valuable learning time. Early years' specialist Liz Brooker and psychologist Martin Woodhead concur, highlighting the fact that worldwide, as primary school opportunities increase, the use of formal rote-learning approaches in many settings and at younger and younger ages relegates children's play opportunities to the edges of their day.[40]

Globally, the role of work in children's lives and the effects of poverty are also significant barriers to the realization of their right to play. Access to play may also be impeded by living environments that are hazardous in terms of traffic, pollution and crime, or lack safe play areas. Even though 7–12-year-olds in many countries, including the Netherlands, China and Germany, have told researchers they would like to be able to play more outdoors, they are not able to do so.[41] Across Europe children claim to enjoy the excitement and exhilaration of outdoor activities such as climbing, exploring, bike riding or playing hide and seek.[42] These activities challenge children's skills and push their limits as they learn to overcome anxieties, 'test' themselves and maintain their physical health, including their eyesight. Indeed, there has been a concern that the worldwide increase in children's short-sightedness (myopia) is related to the time spent indoors, often looking at screens.[43] The proposed remedy is simply to increase the amount of time that children spend outdoors, but achieving this change is not straightforward. If children's right to play is to be realized then, as Gerison Lansdown has argued, 'the adult world around them must remove the physical, social economic and cultural barriers' that prevent it.[44]

The implementation of this right also includes changing parents' attitudes about the risks involved for their children in unstructured outdoor play (an idea further explored in Chapter 9). Helen Little and colleagues at Macquarie University in Australia have identified a trend in which contemporary parents are increasingly restrictive with regard to their children's mobility in their own neighbourhoods.[45] For example, mothers of 4–5-year-old Australian children were keenly aware of the positive impact that 'risky outdoor play' could have on their children's development.

> I think for physical coordination and strength as well as mental; I think it embraces both in terms of their play and their development . . .
>
> Being able to have the amount of space to run around in and to experience the earth and being out in the earth is really important.
>
> They need the fresh air and it's good to learn their skills for climbing and maybe trying to play with other children too.[46]

Similar beliefs have been noted in other studies, in which parents see their children's development as enhanced by experiencing, and managing, the risks that outdoor play might bring.[47] These mothers felt that through this type of play their children would learn how to assess and deal with risk and that this experience could be 'a foundation for life and understanding themselves and their capabilities'. Learning to manage risk was felt to be a key part of life.

> I think nearly every aspect of learning involves risk. Not necessarily physical risk but social risk or emotional risk. Like learning to speak, learning new words, making new friends, all of that, there's potential for you to get hurt in some way.[48]

These Australian mothers' accounts of their *own* childhoods contained many descriptions of potentially risky outdoor play. These experiences were valued and mothers saw them as important positive influences on their own development. They recounted how they had spent most of their playtimes outside, with relatively little adult supervision, from quite young ages. As they grew older, they 'graduated' from playing in their backyards to exploring their neighbourhoods. However, these accounts were in marked contrast to the descriptions of their own children's play activities and the risks they were prepared to let their own children take:

> 'Even though I feel it's quite unlikely because I firmly believe that most abuse occurs in the home . . . it's that fear of them being alone in a situation where someone might harm them.'
>
> 'I think in this day and age we have become like that because it's in the press. It just seems to be everywhere nowadays that there is [sic] issues that you have to worry about.'[49]

This fear is not proportional to the statistical level of risk within Australia, or indeed in the UK or Europe, where children are most at risk inside the home, from people they know, or via their web-linked technologies. Thus constraining their outdoor play does not necessarily make children safer.[50] Nevertheless the anxiety over letting children outside alone endures even though parents recognize that it is not based on evidence. One explanation of why this fear persists, and contributes so strongly to the social and cultural influences on children's play, is the availability heuristic. This refers to the way in which people make quick judgements about problems, based on how easily a particular danger comes to mind or can be imagined.[51] For parents, this judgement is 'fed' by vivid media accounts of childhood dangers and harm, which are easily recalled. This creates a situation where parents are likely to overestimate the likelihood of risks for their own children and to condemn other parents who fail to guard against such well-known risks.[52] Awareness of actual levels of risk does little to allay these fears, nor does it appear to alter parents' behaviour even when they recognize and acknowledge children's opportunities to benefit from forms of positive risk-taking that nurture healthy development.[53]

This move towards a more supervised, indoor childhood has been identified in other countries as well.[54] It has been estimated that between 1981 and 2003 in the USA, children experienced a 50 per cent decrease in outdoor activities,[55] while in the UK half of adults surveyed believed that children should not be allowed out without supervision until they were 14 years of age.[56] Many adults have expressed their

concerns about these changes, as reflected in dramatic newspaper headlines that compare children's outdoor activity times
unfavourably to those of farmed chickens or prisoners.[57]
Indeed, Professor Tanya Byron, who chaired a national review
into children's online lives in the UK, concluded that the lack
of outdoor play was having harmful effects on children.

> The less children play outdoors, the less they learn to
> cope with the risks and challenges they will go on to face
> as adults . . . Nothing can replace what children gain from
> the freedom and independence of thought they have when
> trying new things out in the open.[58]

What about online play and is it a risk to children?

The play experiences of many children today differ greatly
from those of their parents. They are influenced by immediate social and family circumstances, which might include a
hurried lifestyle, diverse family structures and the availability
of childcare support. As children retreat from the outdoors,
they are likely to be spending more time in their own homes,
watching television or 'playing' online, and this shift has
caused great parental and social anxieties about the 'wrong'
sort of play and the risks children may face in the virtual
world. It is undoubtedly true that the nature of children's
interaction with media is changing. Technology has moved
from 'saturating leisure time at home to something more
significant: not so much the saturation of daily life as a complete integration into its routines and activities'.[59] Young

people in many nations are constantly 'tethered' to technology.[60] This has had a significant impact on children's experiences of play.

Children's restricted free play opportunities have coincided with increased access to new media. A significant factor within this complex situation has been the development and promotion of new play technologies for even the youngest children. Parents find themselves making difficult decisions about the age at which their children should begin using these devices, what they should use, how they can safely balance their children's technology-based play with more physically active experiences, how they can control the type of content their children see and the extent to which an activity is contributing to the development of their child. As these technologies were not necessarily something the parents grew up with, they are making choices and decisions without being able to draw on or compare to their own childhood experiences.

These days children's immersion in technologically mediated play begins early. It is now common for many 3–5 year olds to go online every day using tablet computers[61] and, in 2017, 38 per cent of 2-year-olds used a mobile device for accessing media.[62] Children's access to the internet increases with age. In the UK, their regular access rises from 33 per cent of 3–4-year-olds to 65 per cent of 5–7-year -olds, 83 per cent of 8–11-year- olds and 92 per cent of 12–15-year-olds.[63] These figures are likely to rise in line with increased ownership of mobile devices by children which have become the most popular way in which they access online games and social media.

Parents seeking to understand the impact that using digital technologies will have on their children are unlikely to be reassured by the accounts that appear across the media. For example, during 2017 media headlines indicated that technologies were:

Undermining cognitive abilities: *Just looking at your smartphone makes you less intelligent.*[64]

Creating addiction: *Tech addiction is 'digital heroin' for kids – turning children into screen junkies.*[65]

Socially isolating children: *Social media making children more isolated.*[66]

Damaging minds: *Instagram and Snapchat are damaging young people's mental health.*[67]

Impacting on family dynamics: *Parents' mobile use harms family life, say secondary pupils.*[68]

Excessive 'screen time' has been associated with obesity, sleep problems, aggressive behaviour and attention deficits in preschool children, and children's total media consumption can be a risk to their overall well-being.[69] Research which linked touchscreen technologies with poor sleep in children between 6 months and 3 years of age was widely reported in 2017.[70] Based on this study, the *Daily Telegraph* claimed that 'iPads could hinder babies' sleep and brain development, study suggests'.[71] Similarly, a widely reported conference paper in the same year stated that children under 2 years of age who played with iPads were more likely to have delayed speech skills.[72] Although this study was not published, it was reported in the media as concluding that 'Tablets and smartphones damage toddlers' speech development'.[73]

This research found that the more handheld screen time a child's parents reported, the more likely the child was to have delays in acquiring expressive speech. Such findings were used to support recommendations that children under the age of 2 should not have access to such devices.

Such headlines are worrying and many parents will welcome guidelines about when, how and which children should be using digital technologies. However, in considering the impact of these new 'play' technologies it is important to reflect on the nature of the evidence that is being presented. In particular, it is helpful to consider it within the broader context of children's development, and their family lives, rather than seeing technology as detached from the social and cultural aspects of society. So, in the previous two examples, it is reasonable to expect that infants and toddlers – in circumstances where they stay up late, playing on brightly lit and noisy devices – will spend less time sleeping at night than other children and this might impact on their development. Secondly, when toddlers spend less time talking or being talked to, this might make them slower in developing their expressive language skills. However, it is not the technology per se that is the central issue but the way it is used, plus the lack of interaction with parents and allowing technology use to impact on sleep time.

It is also worth remembering that concern that playing with new technologies is damaging children's healthy development is not a new phenomenon. An historical perspective reveals a pervasive trend in which almost every new technological development, particularly those that influence the experience of communication and information, has been a source of social anxiety. When writing was developed, Socrates (327 BCE), who was raised as a non-writer, pronounced that it would 'create forgetfulness' because people would no longer use their memories: 'They will trust to the external written characters and not remember of themselves.'[74] In the eighteenth century the popularity of books was described as 'an epidemic of reading', afflicting many young people who succumbed to an unhealthy 'reading addiction';[75] and making all children read was once viewed by medical authorities as overly demanding, unnatural and a risk to mental health.[76] Newspapers allowed the transmission of the latest information to single readers on a daily basis. Because of this, it was argued by some, they were creating socially isolated individuals, detached from the 'real-life' communication of social groups. As radio became popular in the 1920s, newspapers and magazines reported children being exposed to lurid and inappropriate stories, missing out on mealtimes, essential socialization with their families and damaging their ability to pay attention.[77] Despite the fact that people often look back with amusement on their parents' media-related anxieties, whilst being convinced that their own concerns about the internet or online games respond to real and pressing issues, it is undoubtedly the case that in twenty years' time, although the technologies will be different, the concerns will remain the same.

Research evidence of the impact of technology on children is very mixed, however, and a range of research has identified that the use of smartphones and tablets is associated with both negative and positive effects; for example, there is clear evidence that having an engaging digital device around can impact on another parallel cognitive task, although there is no experimental evidence to support claims that our attention is suffering longer term impairment. Using digital technologies as 'external memories' may mean that we recall less of our experience independently.[78] These modern examples give some support for historical concerns about the use of writing and the radio. These technologies change our abilities to interact with the world, but have come to be viewed as unproblematic because we welcome the positive things they bring to our lives.

For instance, while the study mentioned above suggested that iPads could hinder a child's sleep, the same research team emphasized that evidence for a negative impact on a toddler's cognitive development from touchscreen technology was lacking and, in a related study, they found 'no evidence to support a negative association between the age of first touchscreen usage and developmental milestones. Indeed, touchscreen use at an early age, specifically scrolling of the screen, was associated with the achievement of better motor skills.[79] Similarly, the conference paper which suggested that iPads could delay speech development referred specifically to expressive speech and found that there were no other delays, for example, in comprehension, social interactions or use of gestures.

A key issue for parents is deciding when their young child should *begin* to use play technologies. Parents commonly report worries that their children's devotion to newer screen-based play is happening at the expense of family social interactions,[80] although other researchers have pointed out that some parents use mobile technologies for exactly this purpose, implementing them as 'virtual pacifiers' or 'electronic babysitters' to reduce the amount of social interaction they have with their children (which chimes with some of the children's comments quoted earlier in the chapter that their parents told them to play when they wanted some space for themselves). This highlights an important indirect effect of play technologies on the child's social relationship with caregivers. Natalia Kucirkova and Jenny Radesky[81] evaluated the effects of new technologies, including touchscreens and electronic toys, on the development of children aged between 0 and 2 years. They found that this was not necessarily negative (although advice to parents usually recommends that the lives of children under 2 should be kept 'screen-free') and that there could be positive learning and developmental outcomes for these technologies, if they were *socially mediated*, that is, where parents played with the children and chatted about the programme or game. Although traditional books and toys may prompt more positive social play experiences than electronic gadgets, it is important to remember that it is parents and children playing together which is significant, whatever the media. Modern technologies, when used thoughtfully, can provide an engaging way for children to explore different ways of learning and communicating about their world.[82]

Other research has found that a significant factor in young (0–8yrs) children's use of televisions, computers, smartphones and tablets is their parents' own 'screen time' and attitudes to these devices.[83] The child's age, parental attitudes, and parents screen-time interact to shape how much the child plays with particular technologies. Essentially, the more parents' use, and have positive attitudes towards, a particular technology, the more their children will play with it. If parents use these technologies within social and play interactions then they can have a positive impact. A systematic review of 273 research studies that measured impact outcomes on children's development concluded that children's use of these screen technologies supported their social development when the interactions were mediated socially. When used at home, they were able to facilitate adult–child interaction and contribute positively to family relationships.[84]

As radio, cinema and new digital media have become part of children's lives, there has been a historical trend for research initially to focus on the amount of time children are spending with the new medium, and then on the consequences for children's health, morals and cognition.[85] In each case society sees parents as the gatekeepers whose role it is to keep children safe from these risks. However, digital media is not an 'add-on' that parents can eliminate from their families' lives. It is an integral part of the way families live now in many parts of the world and a part of their social interactions; research that addresses screen-time alone is too simplistic.

> [T]his long- held focus on the quantity of digital media use is now obsolete . . . parents should instead ask themselves and their children questions about screen context (where, when and how digital media are accessed), content (what is being watched or used), and connections (whether and how relationships are facilitated or impeded).[86]

Alicia Blum-Ross and Sonia Livingstone have developed research-led guidance for parents concerning 'screen-time' issues.[87] They suggest that parents (and their children) would benefit from considering the positive attributes that technologies can bring, rather than emphasizing risks alone, such as opportunities for creative play and self-expression, entertainment, access to information and a conduit to relationships. In order to do this, parents need to be able to evaluate the opportunities and risks that different media and technologies can offer, in relation to their own children and family resources. However, this 'ability' varies widely between families, and perhaps it is here that the 'risk' lies rather than with the technology itself.

How do children 'play' online?

Children's increasing access to online spaces over the last decade has enabled virtual worlds and online interactive games to become part of children's everyday lives in many parts of the world. There are hundreds of different types, designed for games consoles, mobile devices, and different operating systems, and these games are seen by children as constituting play. The scale of this phenomenon can often be underestimated by parents. A good illustration of this scale is World of Warcraft™, which was one of the first massively multiplayer online role-playing games (MMORPG). In this type of game large numbers of players interact online as game avatars. By 2008 World of Warcraft had a (paying) population about half the size of Australia, peaking at over 12 million in

2014, as other competitor games grew in popularity.[88] Games in which children control online avatars within online worlds, and take part in quests or competitions, are now ubiquitous. These games have often been thought of as a teenage phenomenon, however parents of younger children will quickly become aware of the games that have been developed for, and promoted to, them. Club Penguin™ , aimed at children from 6 years upwards, but often played by younger children, has over 200 million user accounts.[89] Children's play in these games is big business, often involving a subscription or in-game purchases to enhance their avatar or play options. Children's participation in social life is now becoming entwined with the experience of playing these games.

Another game for young children is Moshi Monsters™, played by millions of children between 5 and12 years of age. Children are attracted by the chance to 'Adopt your own pet monster! Chat with new friends! Play games and puzzles!'[90] This type of advertising explicitly draws children to the fun aspects of the game. These 'virtual worlds are societies where fun matters'[91] and having fun is the cardinal rule for designing a successful game. Surveys of players in virtual worlds reveal that fun is more important than any other feature of the game, with social networking being a secondary but intrinsic part of a 'play' experience. Children clearly see virtual worlds and online games as places for play. However, whilst parents agree that play is important for children, they may not have this type of activity in mind. This different perception can be seen in the game information provided for the parents of young children, which typically promotes the educational benefits, indicating that online play and fun are not so inherently appealing for the *parents* of children.

> Education is right at the heart of the Moshi Monsters experience . . . Successfully nurturing a Moshi Monster is no mean feat. It takes a variety of skills that your child can develop over time. Your child will need to think creatively, hypothesize, strategize, manage scarce resources, collaborate with friends, and nurture a wide variety of other skills that could extend positively into their everyday lives. (Moshi Monsters, 2009)[92]

Certainly, children can learn many useful skills from playing particular online games and engaging in virtual worlds, such as Club Penguin™, Moshi Monsters™ and World of Warcraft ™. However, promoting the 'skills' aspects to parents of younger children (where parents are stronger gatekeepers to the accessing of games) underlines a perceived difference between child and parental beliefs about play that is recognized by the game developers. Fun is not enough for parents and so play needs to be justified in relation to things adults will value.

As might be expected from children's understanding of what 'counts' as play, there is an overlap between their online game playing and their social networking activities, an overlap that brings with it the risks of accessing inappropriate content, excessive use and contact with strangers.[93] There are widespread parental concerns about children playing and exploring online virtual worlds, games and social media. These concerns are exacerbated because it can be difficult for parents to know what their children are doing. This is partly because children are increasingly using mobile devices, and also because many children do not want their online activities monitored by their parents and hide their activities from them.[94] There is also evidence from a range of countries that children may not value (or listen to) their parents' advice regarding online play. Although most parents give their children explicit advice not to talk or message people they meet online, one in ten children in a UK study said they did this.[95] A study of Indonesian children and their parents found that children saw themselves as more advanced users of new media and games than their parents.[96] Consequently, the rules which most parents set about online play were not always accepted by their children. The digital divide between generations is perhaps greater in countries such as Indonesia, but nevertheless these issues are widespread, particularly with regard to 'the latest' social media apps.[97] Parents' lack of familiarity with, or fears about, virtual environments can understandably lead many adults to limit access to online spaces, or perhaps to mistrust their children. As a consequence, parents may overly monitor their children and feel that problems exist, whereas it may be simply be the case that circumstances are different from those in their own childhood. Children should feel that they can trust their parents' judgement and responses, and a balance is needed between children being willing to share their internet activity with their parents and parents respecting their children's privacy. Parents can restrict their children's internet access, but while this reduces the risk to them, it also gives the children fewer learning opportunities and may also undermine children's willingness to share their future activities with their parents.

However, just as in the real outdoor world, it is important that parents model behaviour that supports their children's development, and help them to develop the online skills they need to transition into adult society as well as their offline skills, for example in evaluating the trustworthiness of online information.[98]

Once again, fears over children's online play are not new. Children who played Habbo Hotel ™, a virtual world which had over 270 million users, identified that the thing that 'freaks out' adults the most was that they had good friends who they had never met in real life. During 2012 investigative reporters went undercover in Habbo Hotel and reported the existence of grooming and sexual predation.[99] This and other accounts suggest that parental anxieties about this aspect of playing in online spaces are not without foundation. The current game spaces where younger children play typically have developed into well-moderated 'low risk' environments, supported by developments in monitoring technologies and dedicated specialist monitoring companies. It is in the less well-regulated space of social media, and off-game backchannels, where children report feeling less safe. A survey of over 10,000 9–16-year-old children across Europe asked open-ended questions about online experiences that the children found upsetting.[100] Younger children were most concerned about viewing upsetting content, whereas older children were concerned about risks related to contact with people online, particularly as a result of using social networking sites, sharing photos or personal information, and people pretending to be someone else.

These fears are often very real and children have reported

unintentionally accessing information which they find upsetting.

> I logged onto a game website and clicked onto action games and see Alien vs. Predator trailer. It was very blood and gory and it disturbed me. (Boy, 10, UK)
>
> One time I was looking for a game and rude pictures came on the computer, people without clothes on. (Girl, 9, Ireland)
>
> I don't like it when people speak nasty to you. (Boy, 10, Slovenia)
>
> When strangers message me on the Internet, sex sites that open without me clicking on them. (Boy, 10, Austria)
>
> Videos where older teenagers mistreat disabled children and upload the video on YouTube. (Girl, 9, Italy)[101]

These concerns are highest in countries where children make the most use of online games and social networks, and in the report quoted above about 12 per cent of children (and 8 per cent of their parents) said that they had been upset by something online in the previous year. When 10-year-old Thomas Brown carried out a child-led research project for the Open University's Children's Research Centre, 7 per cent of his sample (aged 7–11) reported viewing inappropriate online material at some point.[102] In another child-led research project, 9-year-old Rhia Auroa asked children in her school (aged 7–11) about inappropriate video games. She found that whilst some children played such games and enjoyed doing so, they were also aware of some of the negative aspects of these games. These included promoting 'bad morals', 'aggression/violence' and exposure to blood and gore.[103] Longitudinal studies also suggest that upsetting online experiences can result in long-term emotional and psychological consequences.[104] However, although these examples may be shocking, other international reviews have offered a more nuanced picture which suggests that children are *not* necessarily increasingly at risk. One reason for this is that the children who are most at risk online are also those most vulnerable offline in the real world. Factors such as family dynamics and children's risky behaviour in the real world are better predictors of their online risk than the use of particular apps or technologies.[105]

Parental concerns over children's online play are likely to change as screen-based games turn into augmented reality games. Augmented reality (AR) gives children a live view of the real world, but overlaid with additional information. This additional information can be in many forms, for example as a character from a game or a text or video label of a real-world feature. This is very different from children playing in a virtual or online environment, which 'replaces' the real world with something that can only be seen though a static screen. One of the first uses of AR was in augmented early reading books, for example using markers in books to generate 3D characters such as moving dragons[106] or interactive illustrations such as 3D models.[107] This gives children a better sense of what a complex object might look like and can also be fun. *Marvel* Comics originator Stan Lee is developing AR for children, based on his popular story characters. Children view the physical comic through their smartphone and the AR app overlays the comic with 3D character animations.[108] Real-world toys and games that require the manipulation of objects can be augmented to make them more exciting and appealing. This augmentation can be viewed through mobile phones, handheld devices or specifically designed smart 'spectacles'. These applications can allow children to play with augmented reality objects and environments socially, with their friends – they might be driving AR cars around the family kitchen, or collecting virtual icons from particular places in their home towns to gain game points. An often overlooked positive feature of AR games is the possibilities they hold for children who have a sensory impairment or learning difficulty. These games offer alternative ways in which children can explore the world around them. This might include object and picture recognition or colour-naming apps, and can make the game more interesting and accessible for a wider group of children. Because children are manipulating virtual objects within the real world, or exploring the real world in search of virtual objects, these games allow the creation of rich multi-sensory play experiences.

The summer of 2016 saw the Pokémon GO™ phenomenon, perhaps the first AR game to make a large impact on public awareness; it serves to illustrate important aspects of children's play with AR games. When the Pokémon GO trend first became news, it was accompanied by a flurry of media calls for parents to set strict guidance for their children or to stop them playing the game altogether. The game was perceived as creating specific threats to children's physical safety and well-being, so that headlines and reports proclaimed the existence of 'The Pokémon GO crime wave: Robbers, thieves and paedophiles target 300 gamers in one month'.[109] During the summer that the game launched many real-life incidents were reported in media. These reports seemed to bring together parental fears about both online and outdoor play, mentioning 'increased risk of injury, abduction, trespassing, violence, and [financial] cost'.[110] The UK's National Society for the Prevention of Cruelty to Children quickly published a parents' guide addressing the hiding of locational information and safeguarding processes.[111]

However, there are also possible significant benefits to children from playing this type of AR game. As suggested earlier, an issue for those seeking to promote children's wellbeing is that children are not playing outdoors enough. A study of Pokémon GO in the USA analysed signals from wearable sensors and data from 32, 000 users. Tim Althoff and colleagues found that playing Pokémon GO led to significant increases in physical activity and that this boost was seen regardless of a person's age or previous activity levels.[112] The game was able to reach people who had previously had very low activity levels or had been sedentary. Other research has reported similarly dramatic impacts, with 80 per cent of users playing outside for more than thirty minutes per day and being physically active for more than five hours per week.[113] A report in the *British Medical Journal* stated:

> Most health apps that promote physical activity tend to get users who want to be healthy. Pokémon GO isn't marketed as a health app, but players still end up doing a lot of walking. The possibilities for apps to make the streets an active, reclaimed playground in which to have interconnected fun are boundless. Increased physical activity is a tantalising side effect.[114]

The game became popular not because players were responding to an understanding of the benefits of physically active play but because it was fun. It is a form of play that brings increased socialization opportunities, exercise and outdoor activity, along with the previously identified risks. Because of these risks, parents' beliefs about outdoor play will have a considerable impact on young children's use of AR games and the benefits they might derive from them.

Our focus on playing with and through 'screens' reflects the use of current technology; however, this is likely to change. In particular, the development of artificially intelligent objects will have an increasing place in children's play. Young children appear keen to have 'intelligent' toys that they can play with through voice commands, touch or gestures, and parents may buy them because they see them as replacing 'screen-time'.[115] For example, the internet-connected toy Dino (a toy dinosaur) uses IBM Watson to analyse and respond to children's questions and comments.[116] This reflects the increasing use of smart software, such as Alexa and Siri, within adult life. Robotic toys that move around and navigate in the physical world have also been developed to promote the development of children with disabilities of varying kinds. Now, such technology will increasingly be seen in 'mainstream' toys and semi-autonomous play companions.[117] The impact of artificially intelligent play companions and play materials on children's development will be an important future research area.

The balance of evidence suggests that play is fun for children, is vital for their healthy development and that children need a regular broad range of play experiences, including real-world social play. However, children's experience of play is nested within a complex set of interacting influences. Cultural and economic circumstances can shape how children play as can adults' lifestyles, cultural changes and the development of exciting, new technologies. A thread running through all the research, however, is the importance of social interaction. IPads or touchscreens can be both negative and positive, depending on how they are used; as long as they are part of the parent–child relationship, rather than a substitute for it, then they need not be the bogeymen of contemporary parenting. Beliefs about play and its effects on children's development are an integral part of broader ideas about how children learn and how they should be taught. We will look at this issue in the next chapter.

What Matters in Education?

Education, and here we are principally talking about formal schooling rather than the informal types of learning that take place within homes and communities, is typically presented as a way of transmitting the knowledge and skills deemed important in any given society. Discussions on education usually build on ideas about how children learn and the most effective ways to teach them, as well as recognizing the role that education can play in helping children acquire the skills and knowledge that will help them take their place within society – particularly in the realm of attaining academic qual-ifications which lead to employment and economic security. The educational aspirations that many parents have for their children are strongly associated with these broader aspira-tions for their children's lives. Of course, not all parents globally have a choice over when and where their child can go to school and the distribution of educational opportun-ities throughout the world continues to reflect stark inequali-ties. Against this backdrop of inequality and limited opportunities, children's education represents a significant area of concern for the majority of the world's parents. In some parts of the world, this might mean anxiety over whether children will receive any education at all and whether it will be too expensive (or, even if the schooling is free, whether the books, uniforms and stationery their children need will be affordable), while in other countries parents may be concerned about the type of school their child attends and how this will influence their children's learning, social and emotional development as well as their social mobility and opportunities for the future. This chapter examines some of the concerns that parents may have regarding their child's education as well as looking at children's own views about school.

What do children want from school?

Although children are obviously and self-evidently central to schools and education systems, it is only very recently that their own views have been sought, or even deemed important. Education is often seen in terms of the parents' choices rather than the children's and a comparison of the two reveals some sharp distinctions. At a rhetorical level at least, children are increasingly positioned as having rights in relation to decisions that affect their lives (see the section in Chapter 9 on children's rights).[1] Although this idea has been formalized over the last decades in a range of policies, there are relatively few research studies that explore school from the child's point of view. Those that have done so suggest there is often a disjunction between adult and child perceptions of the same environment.[2] Children remain relatively powerless in the choice of school they attend, although some might 'vote with their feet' and one study found that 27 per cent of primary school children truanted at some time without the knowledge of their parents.[3] But learning from children about things they value about schools can at least inform the choices parents make on behalf of their children. More fundamentally, it is difficult to argue that our schools are for the benefit of children if children's own views on what is beneficial to them haven't been sought or listened to.[4]

When children are asked about their school life, and what matters most to them, one factor is consistently seen as the most important – friendship. Children are happiest at schools in which they feel that other pupils and teachers are friendly and in classrooms where they feel safe. Children place great importance on feeling safe and secure. Conversely, bullying of themselves or other children makes them feel unhappy or ill at ease,[5] and bullying is now the most significant, and consistently reported, factor raised by children when asked about how their schools could be improved.[6] Research in the UK found that between 22 and 29 per cent of secondary school pupils reported being bullied in a way that frightened or upset them within a one-year period.[7] This behaviour can take several forms, including physical violence (of those who reported being bullied, 38 per cent reported someone trying to physically hurt them), but most commonly includes verbal assault, name-calling and 'teasing'.[8] European research suggests that girls and boys bully to the same extent, but that boys are more likely to use physical methods.[9] Beyond Europe, research has found bullying to be a serious problem in many countries;[10] for example in Mongolia, the Philippines and Indonesia research has revealed children's experiences of being bullied not only by other children but also by teachers and other education professionals.[11] Young children may not mention bullying specifically, but are acutely sensitive to the fairness with which they and other pupils are treated and report feeling unhappy when other pupils are ignored by teachers, or teachers are seen as being unfair.[12]

Concerns over bullying are shared by both parents and children; parental concern about bullying also appears to be increasing internationally.[13] In a European-wide survey of thousands of parents, bullying was a cause of anxiety for many of them and was of greatest concern for parents in Spain, Italy and France, where over half of those questioned saw it as a major issue.[14] In response to such concerns, many schools have explicit policies in place to address relationships between pupils. In the UK this is often outlined in the school's behaviour policy document which may state explicitly how children's good behaviour is expected and rewarded, and how staff and parents can respond to issues such as bullying.[15] Alternatively, the school may have a whole-school approach to supporting positive social relationships. One such approach is known as Circle Time, which is popular in the UK and aims to promote pro-social behaviour and a positive school ethos through regular timetabled sessions with groups of children.[16] Children are taught the ground rules for these sessions, in which their concerns and positive experiences are discussed, and pupils commit to helping their peers.[17] Similarly, the Diana Award (DA) is a charity legacy arising out of Diana, Princess of Wales' belief that young people have the power to change the world for the better; it has pioneered a series of training programmes, such as the anti-bullying ambassador programme to address bullying in schools in the UK and to action change. The DA organizers have trained over 24,500 young people to tackle bullying in their schools and local communities.[18] Other whole-school approaches focus more directly on aggression, such as 'Behaviour Recovery' which is popular in primary schools in several countries and has an emphasis on practical approaches to common problems such as disruption in class, aggression and problems during breaktimes.[19] Other methods include a buddy system to develop a positive social network for children experiencing problems.[20] Approaches such as these can be used as explicit indicators that schools are addressing the issue of social behaviour, which has been raised as a concern by children across many countries and contexts.

Another way to understand what children want from a school is to get them to design their own. One study worked with groups of young primary school pupils in the UK to help them discuss, and draw and paint, what their ideal schools would be. The thing that they wanted most of all was that their school-time should allow them to learn in ways that were fun.

> In a fun way to do with games, not just sitting still writing things down all the time. In fun silly ways, you remember it more if you remember what you did that lesson – you remember what you learned (Child aged 9).[21]

Although they all wanted learning to be fun, children's ideas about the nature of learning reflected their current school experiences; for example, one child created 'the beach school' because it would be more fun to learn out of doors.

However, the beach was to be used for a respite from 'having to' learn things. Another child did away with the school entirely, and drew themselves sitting alone on a quiet beach with a laptop. This beach was a relaxing and peaceful place. The learning happened via the laptop, with topic quizzes for the child, the results of which were beamed immediately to the government. The children surveyed attended a school in England which placed great emphasis on performance in national tests and this emphasis on results undoubtedly affected the children's understanding of the purpose of school. Another child's new school was a 'candy workshop' whose activities were all based around chocolate. A central computer assessed children on fractions using chocolate bar imagery. In the Candy Workshop those children who learned to say the correct answers got a chocolate reward. This idea of being rewarded, in different ways, for repeating the right answer was also suggested by many other children. However, no child ever suggested that a reward was needed for any outdoor or playground activities that they devised.[22] Their imagined best schools were lovely places, but the children saw a clear division between 'fun' and 'learning' in the school activities.

Not surprisingly, the children's ideas about the nature of learning often reflected their own educational experiences. Children who appeared to have had very traditional experiences of education (where, for example, they were seen as passive and expected to simply learn or absorb information) conveyed this way of teaching into their models of the best school. Those who had had other experiences, for example as members of a centre that supported children to carry out their own research projects, were more likely to create models that reflected other, more interactive ideas about learning. Rather than seeing themselves as being passive recipients of knowledge, these children saw learning as an active process. The teacher might provide an initial question or goal, but they wanted to 'figure stuff out', through observation, exploration and experimentation.[23]

Parents too also greatly influence the epistemological beliefs of their children. Large-scale research studies with parents and children suggest that parental epistemological beliefs (i.e. their ideas about the nature of knowledge and learning) influence their parenting styles, which then translate into their children's beliefs about what knowledge is and how learning occurs. For example, parents who encourage questions and discussion to facilitate understanding of issues are likely to support the development of better reasoning skills in their children in comparison to parents who do not.[24] In contrast, children whose parents used disciplinary techniques that emphasized control and behavioural conformity were less likely to see learning and knowledge as a form of discovery.[25] Personal epistemological beliefs also interact with a range of other influences, such as beliefs about gender, social class and disability;[26] for example young children's understanding of scientific concepts can be strongly influenced by their parents through the way they respond to their children's question about how the world works. These interactions are not, however, necessarily 'equal' for boys and girls. Not only are parents more likely to expect boys to be interested in science topics[27] but, in one museum-based study, they were three times more likely to explain interactive science exhibits to sons rather than daughters.[28]

What matters to parents?

It is of course naive to think that children know 'best' when it comes to education, especially on questions of which school they should go to or how they should be taught. As suggested above, they are heavily influenced by the ways they are taught and by their parents, so it can be very hard for them (as it is for anyone whatever their age) to evaluate what makes a good school and what constitutes effective teaching. Despite the importance of listening to children, and the need for them to feel safe and supported at school, their views must be seen in conjunction with those of their parents who still make the final choices about education for their children.

Parents' thinking about what matters in education will be informed by their own understanding of many factors, including their cultural background and social aspirations for their children, their epistemological beliefs and notions of what good teaching looks like, and their ability to evaluate the choices, options and information that are available to them. The importance of each of these factors varies significantly between people and places. Nevertheless, at a general level, there is a surprising amount of agreement on what matters most to parents. A study of eleven countries found that parents care most about two things: first, the quality of the school as a safe and pleasant environment for their children, and secondly, good academic results. This study also concluded that when school quality is very important to parents, their children tend to do better at school.[29]

Parents' desire for academic success is underpinned by their expectations of the long-term consequences of this success. Parents across Europe have indicated almost unanimously that what they want from education is the promise of social and economic mobility, in order that their children can have a good life.[30] However, parents with the fewest academic qualifications, or whose children have uncertain social trajectories, including children experiencing poverty and hardship, are likely to be the most sceptical that improved social mobility is actually a possible outcome of education. There is typically a link between parental expectations of what education will 'deliver' for their children's lives and how much they become actively involved in their children's education.

When making a decision about which school their children should attend within the UK (where such a decision is possible), three school attributes consistently emerge as important for parents: 'the academic quality of the school, its socio-economic composition and the home–school distance'.[31] This means, for example, that in the UK most parents will opt for schools which appear to have higher academic standards than other schools, with fewer pupils from poorer families. So the information that they receive about the school has a strong steer on their choice. In England this information might relate to the published school performance results, and how they are presented to the public. However, several studies have found that given the choice of the same set of schools, poorer families are more likely to opt for less academic schools, with proximity to home being a significant influence on this decision.[32] This contributes to the situation in which approximately one third of all state schools in England can be identified as segregated by socio-economic status.[33]

An educational movement which has challenged this situation is that of *inclusive education*.[34] This worldwide movement supports the UN goal of 'Education for All' and has had a profound effect on educational practice and access worldwide. It developed from a belief in children's rights and a consensus that 'all children have the right to be educated together, regardless of their physical, intellectual, emotional, social, linguistic or other condition, and that inclusion makes good educational and social sense'.[35] Many countries are signatories to this and have created policies and practices designed to allow equal access to educational opportunities and to ensure that no child is excluded. Most European countries are also signatories to the Convention on the Rights of Persons with Disabilities (CRPD),[36] which in Article 24, explicitly states that 'Parties shall ensure an inclusive education system at all levels.'[37] Internationally inclusive education has been seen as a strategy to support the education of *all* children, welcoming children from all social backgrounds, classes and abilities.[38] Indonesia, for example, is the world's most diverse multi-ethnic state[39] and the government has an explicit goal to give all children at least nine years of basic education[40] and is developing inclusive schools to support this.[41]

The notion of inclusive schools highlights the broad issue of parental attitudes about who their own children should mix with at school. This issue intersects with the educational choices that are available to parents and encompasses ideas about ethnicity, poverty and religion, and their own personal beliefs and social constraints, creating a complex situation in which 'what parents want' in education is not simply a matter of how their children are taught, but also with *whom* they are taught. The outcomes of this complex interaction can be seen internationally. Within Northern Ireland an integrated education approach was instigated in the 1980s, allowing Catholic and Protestant pupils to be educated together, yet several decades later 93 per cent of pupils still predominantly attend schools of their 'own' religion.[42] In England, a quarter of primary schools and over 40 per cent of secondary schools have been described as 'ethnically segregated'.[43] Commenting on this situation, journalist and teacher Lola Okolosie concluded: 'Where there is the option to choose, there is also the choice that many [parents] aren't prepared to make: an integrated school, less segregation.'[44] In the USA the racial segregation of schools is a persistent problem, despite legalization to support schools that are open to all pupils. Research suggests that a significant factor in parental choices about a school their child might attend is the racial composition of the school and that this goes beyond race acting as a proxy indicator of important school characteristics such as exam results.[45] This means that schools may have good academic results, but if they have the 'wrong' racial composition other parents will reject them – so that, in particular, white parents will tend to select schools that have a lower proportion of African American pupils. As parents 'negotiate their local educational landscape and strive when possible to choose the highest quality and most suitable school for their children',[46] they consider many factors, such as the quality of the school premises and facilities, but also how these match with their aspirations and who they want their children to mix with.

An issue often raised by parents in relation to inclusive education is how well children learn in such schools, in particular in classes that include children with special educational needs and disabilities (SEND). This includes the question of whether some children would be better placed in segregated special schools. First, this is an issue for parents whose children may experience difficulties in learning or have sensory impairments. This group of children encompasses a vast spectrum of individual differences, ranging from children who might have some problems with literacy skills to children who, regardless of their age and life experiences, are likely to remain at an early stage of intellectual, social and communication development and require support for almost all their activities. Depending on national definitions and policies, this group can comprise roughly 15 per cent of children.[47] Secondly, special needs and disability is an issue for parents whose children have *not* been identified in this way. In many countries, children with special educational needs or disabilities are a stigmatized group, and parents do not wish their children to mix with them, or attend the same nurseries and schools.[48] Teachers and educators from across the world have reported that some parents do not want their children educated alongside those who are 'different' in any way. An early childhood centre supervisor in New Zealand commented to one researcher:

[S]ome parents are actually very prejudiced against it
[disability], and they don't want their children exposed to it.
And they can be very cruel and . . . they have pulled children
out because there are children there with a disability that
they don't want their child to be exposed to.[49]

In the UK, teachers have reported parents commenting,
'Either he goes, or I'm taking my daughter out of the school.'
[50] Parents often believe that their own children's educational
progress will be hampered if children with special educational needs or disabilities are educated within their child's
school or class.

However, research indicates that children who have peers
with special educational needs and disabilities are more
likely to have more positive attitudes towards children with
SEND and to play with them.[51] (As Chapter 8 will discuss,
however, this finding has been contested and is not always
true.) For some parents this is a positive outcome; for others
it is something to be avoided. This has created a situation
where, although there has been a significant move towards
inclusive schools, for example in the thirty-five countries who
form the Organization for Economic Cooperation and
Development (OECD), the academic and social consequences of 'schools for all' remains an important and controversial issue for parents.[52] At a general level, large-scale
studies typically find no academic advantages for children
with SEND placed in (segregated) special schools,[53] and evidence from 1,300 studies indicate marginally positive outcomes from inclusive school placements.[54] A slightly different

and more mixed picture emerges from studies that have looked at the educational outcomes for specific groups of children, defined by a special educational need, in specific curriculum areas; for example, young people with Down syndrome progressed in both in mainstream and special education settings, but their language and communications skills developed better in mainstream settings.[55] For pupils without special educational needs or disabilities, a range of research studies has indicated positive or neutral effects[56] on their academic outcomes, irrespective of their classes being attended by either more or less than 10 per cent of students with special educational needs.[57] So when parents are deciding which type of school is best for their child, the general picture from research does seem to be slightly supportive of (and certainly does not condemn) inclusive schools. Within all these studies are variations between individual children, individual schools and instructional quality, which contribute to a more nuanced situation than revealed through simple comparisons of children's school placements and their educational outcomes.[58]

What does good teaching look like?

Parental beliefs about how children learn are important in guiding how they support their children and what they expect schools and teachers to do. But some of these points of view can be contradictory in nature; for example, in the book *The Psychology of Education*, Martyn Long and his colleagues identified three competing ideas expressed by parents concerning what mattered most when teaching. They found that parents would argue variously that:

> 'Class sizes are not important; what matters most is the quality of the teaching' *or* 'Reducing class sizes would obviously result in improved learning'.

> 'Children's teachers are the most important factor in their education' *versus* 'Teachers aren't really important – the key things are a child's own knowledge and motivation'.

> 'Firm discipline and punishment are important in controlling problem behaviour' *versus* 'Positive behaviour comes from the examples of others; punishment is ineffective and simply brutalizes children'.[59]

Given the complex nature of children's educational experiences, it is difficult to resolve these issues satisfactorily. Bearing this complexity in mind, Long went on to review the international research evidence with regard to each of the above issues. He concluded that reducing class sizes – in controlled experiments – did improve pupils' learning outcomes but not by very much, but that altering the teaching approach being used was more important and could have a much greater impact. He also found that punishment was generally an ineffective long-term strategy and did not help to teach children appropriate behaviour. Finally, he showed that teachers had the greatest positive impact on younger children's academic achievements, but in comparison children's home backgrounds were associated with 'much larger' variations.[60]

As suggested previously, the epistemological beliefs of parents strongly influence the judgements they make about the education that their child receives and the type of classroom activities which they deem as educationally valuable. Similarly, teachers' beliefs about how children acquire knowledge has a significant influence on how they teach children – and this then has an impact on how both teachers and parents view 'good teaching'.[61] It is therefore important to look not only at classroom practices but at the ideas which inform these practices, particularly perspectives and ideas on how children learn.

The work of psychologists Jean Piaget and Lev Vygotsky provides two theories to explain how children learn. These theories have been debated and adapted since they first appeared in the twentieth century, but both remain highly influential today.[62] The third perspective is that of direct transmission which has also been called a traditional view of how to teach children.[63] A notable difference between these three theories is their position on the relationship between social interaction and children's cognitive development.

The first perspective is that of Jean Piaget who created a universal theory of children's cognitive development. Piagetian theory is unique in its breadth and the level of explanation it offers. It provides a model of how an infant's innate reflexes are gradually transformed over time into adult cognitive abilities. The key to this transformation is that it is driven by the internal (mental) adaptations that arise from children's active interactions with their environment. His theory is a *constructivist* one. Children construct their understanding of the world through their own direct explorations of it. This understanding is represented in psychological structures called schemas (or schemata). These begin in infants' coordinated sequences of physical actions, such as grasping an object, which are then internalized as mental representations. Piaget's theory sees children developing through a series of qualitatively different stages; the sensory-motor stage (0–2 years, pre-operational stage (2–7 years), concrete operational stage (7–11 years) and formal operational stage (11 years +).

In the sensory motor stage the young child (0–2 years) 'thinks' through developing action schemas and their intentional behaviour begins. One characteristic of this stage is the development of 'object permanence', where they come to understand that an unseen object still exists. The next preoperational stage (approximately 2–7 years) sees the child using language to represent real objects and events. A characteristic feature of this stage is that the child is egocentric, and has difficulty in seeing the world from the perspective of others. The third concrete operations stage (approximately 7–11 years) is seen when children become able to apply logical reasoning to real (rather than hypothetical) events. One feature of this stage is that the child has mastered conservation (explained below). Each stage is progressively more sophisticated and culminates in the formal operational stage, where the child is able to apply logical thought to hypothetical ideas. This final stage typically begins during the teenage years, although not all adults will achieve it.

Piaget provided detailed explanations of how children's internal schemas develop and change with the child's increasing experience of the world.[64] When a child's current level of understanding is challenged, their schema accommodates this new situation by changing to suit the environment better. For this reason, if parents or teachers want to support the development of children's thinking, then they need to create situations in which children are actively engaged in solving problems. These activities should be accessible to them, but also challenge their current mode of reasoning. Chapter 5 discussed the nature of play activities and it is easy to see why a constructivist perspective places such importance on play. Play is a self-directed and purposeful interaction with the environment. From a Piagetian perspective, it allows children to drive their own development through their active exploration and experimentation in the world. It is through these activities that children learn. Piaget's theory was informed by the results of research tasks, which he presented to children of different ages.[65] These tasks revealed ways in which children thought differently to adults and these differences underpinned his four-stage theory: for example, Piaget showed that children at the pre-operational stage had not yet developed the concept of *conservation*. This concept is an awareness that a quantity will remain the same, even if its manner of presentation changes. In a conservation of number task, children are shown two rows of eight counters, one black, one white. They are asked if the two lines have the same number. One line of counters is then spaced out, and the question is repeated. Piaget found that children of 4 or 5 years of age could usually identify that each row had the same number. However, after one row had been made longer, the children felt that there were now more in the longer row. In contrast, children who had reached the concrete operational stage understood that the number remained the same (conservation of number). Piaget argued that understanding number was not simply learning number labels. Rather than being told about numbers, children needed to explore practical number problems to develop their underpinning conceptual understanding.[66]

This means that the teachers can support children's development by creating environments for them that provide structured play activities. For very young children this might include shape-sorting tasks, block-building, balancing beams, toys or sand and water trays. The essence here is that the child is given practical first-hand experience of the 'world'. Children's understanding of conservation can be developed through activities that allow them to engage with number and volume problems that involve sorting, measuring and matching. Piaget's influence can be discerned most clearly in Western nursery education settings.

Piaget's stage theory has been useful as a framework for teachers to reflect on how children's thinking develops over time and the sort of activities that would be appropriate for their developmental stage. However, this theory has been challenged through re-creations of his classical tasks, which have been subtly altered to give them more social meaning for young children. For example, the above conservation of number task was revised to include a 'Naughty Teddy' who naughtily spread out row of counters.[67] This dramatically improved children's responses, with 72 per cent of 4 to 6-year-old children correctly identifying that the number remained the same. Other 'revised re-creations' of different tasks have produced similar improvements in the number of children being able to give correct answers to problems which had appeared beyond them in Piaget's classic tasks.[68] It has been argued that this was because the revised tasks made 'human sense' to them.[69] These studies show that socially meaningful situations can support children in applying subtle reasoning at an early age.

Lev Vygotsky's theory of development acknowledges the social environment and the way it can support the development of children's cognitive abilities. This social environment might include the way that a problem is presented (as with the 'Naughty Teddy' conservation task above) or support from peers or an adult. This external support allows the child to perform at a higher level of development than they can do alone, and this higher level subsequently becomes internalized so that the child can achieve this level without the social support. In this theory, children's advanced skills occur initially 'outside of themselves'. What they can do in supportive contexts they will later be able to do by themselves, and so it is in these supportive contexts that we can see children's potential for development, for example with their improved performance on the 'Naughty Teddy' task. This is very different from Piaget's view, in which the child is seen almost as a 'lone scientist'.[70] Vygotsky's theory is known as a *social constructivist* theory, in which the child's development of abilities can be seen in two ways: first, in interactions between people, and secondly as the actions of an individual. Development moves from the social to the individual level.[71] The social constructivist perspective emphasizes the social and cultural origins of children's cognitive development.

An important difference between Piaget's and Vygotsky's theories concerns the role of language in children's development. In essence, Piaget saw language as reflecting the cognitive development which had already taken place, following schema development. In contrast, Vygotsky saw language as leading cognitive development,[72] as children's 'external' social speech gradually becomes internalized to form their inner thoughts. There is evidence to support a Vygotskian perspective, and this includes the results of social constructivist inspired classroom activities. These approaches are based on the idea that children need to learn how to use language to collaborate with others and to make joint decisions. Children rarely receive guidance on how to do this in schools, but when it does occur it has a positive impact.[73] For example, a class-based intervention for 9–10-year-old children in the UK taught them the skills and social ground rules they needed to work collaboratively in science lessons, so that they could engage in critical questioning and negotiating decisions.[74] The children worked in groups to carry out scientific investigations, and their results were compared to a control group who had had standard lessons. The finding showed that the ' talk-focused' children performed significantly better than the control group in answering National Curriculum standardized science questions. However, they also performed significantly better on non-verbal reasoning tests. This suggested that their underpinning ability to reason (rather than just their subject-specific knowledge) had developed further using the collaborative approach. Similar improvements have been found elsewhere, for example in relation to learning mathematics, where both subject knowledge and reasoning ability in general have developed significantly.[75] These results support the Vygotskian perspective of language and social activities having the potential to lead cognitive development. The children's social interactions had a profound impact on the development of their individual thinking skills.

The third perspective on learning is that of a *direct transmission* model. A belief that children learn in this way is common worldwide. In this traditional perspective children are seen as 'passive' and learn through direct instruction by the teacher. This perspective presents 'teaching as a non-problematic [direct] transfer of knowledge and considers learning as the absorption of this process'.[76] Echoes of this belief have also been seen in teacher–pupil interactions in UK primary schools, where some studies found that approximately 90 per cent of teacher–pupil talk was a closed exchange – in which the teacher asks a question, the pupil answers, and the teacher indicates if this answer is right or wrong.[77]

Shu-Chen Wu and Nirmala Rao compared the beliefs about learning of German and Hong Kong kindergarten teachers,[78] by using a series of questions to which teachers could respond Strongly Agree, Agree, Neither Agree or Disagree, Strongly Disagree. They found some significant differences between the two groups concerning the relationship between play and learning, for example in their responses to the following statements.

· The presence of teacher at play can make children learn better.
· Children can learn better through teacher's guidance at play.
· Teachers should get involved in children's play actively.

The Chinese teachers were much stronger in their agreement with each of these statements than their German counterparts, who tended to disagree with most of them. The Chinese teachers did not see the need for, or refer to, 'free' play. They felt that as teachers they should direct children's play to give it the required educational value.[79] In Chapter 5 we discussed Chinese parents' attitudes to play and the influence of cultural beliefs; it is possible to see the same influences operating within the education system, where play can even be regarded as the 'opposite to learning'.[80] In contrast, the German kindergarten teachers' beliefs could be seen as reflecting a Piagetian perspective, and these beliefs influenced what they did within the classroom. Because they believed that children needed to explore and play in order to learn, they facilitated learning by providing 'free' time and play materials for the children to have fun with. They felt that these activities would benefit the children's development of independent thinking.

Other international research has identified huge differences in teachers' support for these different approaches. For example, teachers in Iceland and Australia were likely to strongly endorse constructivist beliefs, whereas in Malaysia and Italy teachers' views were more mixed and endorsement of both constructivist and direct transmission was common.[81] Teachers' responses to epistemological questions can also predict their classroom practices,[82] with the traditional approach generally being associated with less flexible and less effective teaching for inclusive or diverse classes.[83] However, identifying which perspective 'works best' is problematic, because of the wide variations which exist between the different contexts and cultures in which education occurs and the ways learning outcomes are assessed. International research suggests that when countries seek to improve educational achievements, a focus on teacher-training that attracts and sustains talented teachers is vital. However, the nature of the teaching approaches being used remains very varied and interacts with cultural factors;[84] for example, South Korean pupils outperform those from many other countries academically, but against a backdrop where they 'are under enormous, unrelenting pressure to perform. Talent is not a consideration – because the culture believes in hard work and diligence above all, there is no excuse for failure. Children study year-round, both in-school and with tutors.'[85]

Childhood is a time of learning, and how children learn, what they learn and why they learn it are fundamental aspects of their lives. It is not surprising that education, especially when there seem to be so many choices and contested beliefs, can seem a minefield for parents and educational decision-makers. Parents are guided in their school choices, and in their beliefs about what matters in education, by several factors including their social-cultural circumstances and ambitions, and their beliefs about how learning occurs. Consequently, parents will arrive at different decisions about where their child should go to school and whether they are happy with how their child is being taught. However, a significant voice lacking in this picture is that of the children themselves. Children's perspectives on the school that they'd like to attend and the qualities that they value remains surprisingly underrepresented in educational research and even when they are discussed they are rarely acted upon. What is clear is that both parents and children want schools to provide safety and happiness, but parents also want them to deliver academic success, social mobility and future achievements. They want schools to help socialize children in the present, but also train them for the future. It is a tricky balancing act for children, parents and their teachers.

How Can Parents and Professionals Promote Resilience and Autonomy in Children?

This chapter looks at autonomy and resilience in children, what these concepts mean and how they can be developed. Resilience has become a central concern of parents, schools and policy-makers, particularly in the Western world, in recent years and seems to offer a way to combat the mental health issues faced by so many young people today. Recent statistics have revealed that mental health problems in children are increasing (or being diagnosed) at an alarming rate. The charity YoungMinds[1] reports that one in ten children aged between 5 and 16 years of age in the UK suffer from a mental health disorder, with over 8,000 children under 10 years of age suffering from depression. A growing body of research suggests that the ability to cope – or not – with everyday challenges during childhood is a predictor for the subsequent development of stress-related illnesses such as depression and addiction in later life.[2] There are many factors which can make children vulnerable, including poor parenting, poverty, bullying or even their own responses or personalities, and yet not all children react in the same way to the same set of circumstances and some manage to overcome adversity even when they are living in very unfavourable conditions. Unfortunately there are no standard definitions of resilience and while there have been attempts to quantify and measure it, most studies look at the concept qualitatively – as one group of researchers argued: 'Rather like beauty, resilience may be said to lie in the eye of the beholder.'[3] Nevertheless, resilience is typically defined as 'positive development, or thriving, under stress'.[4] In other words, resilience looks at the ways in which children cope with, and even respond positively to, adversity.

Developing resilient behaviours, such as the ability to endure and adapt to stressful life experiences, are clearly important life skills and are associated with self-confidence, autonomy, emotional intelligence and social competence. Yet there are clear differences in how children react to stressful situations and countless parents have, over many years, questioned why it is that some children appear more able to bounce back from life's challenges and show fewer signs of anxiety than other children. Even children raised within the same family can demonstrate startling differences in how they react to and cope with stressful events. And whilst there may be agreement on the importance of supporting children's psychological and emotional development, there appears to be less agreement on what this actually means in terms of how parents raise their children and how practitioners support them in doing so.

How can parents support children's autonomy?

English paediatrician and psychiatrist Donald Winnicott's extensive research of early mother and child attachment highlights the importance of establishing responsive relationships which are attuned to the needs of the baby as well as their future needs. Winnicott is perhaps most well known for coining the term 'good enough' mother.[5] Although his work recognizes the significance and impact that early parent–child relationships can have upon children's later development, the notion of being 'good enough' is often misinterpreted.

This term is often used as a way to indicate that mothers can never be perfect (of course not – that would be impossible) and that they will always fall short of meeting all the needs of their baby – and that being 'good enough' is fine. But in fact what Winnicott was at pains to illustrate is the importance of a mother's (Winnicott also indicated that the carer of the baby needn't necessarily be the mother and can include any carer) adaptability, aligned to their baby's needs. He looked at the difference between a baby's early dependency on their carer to the increasing need for them to develop independence and to learn to manage their own emotions – and so prepare for their future lives. After the early stage of dependency, mothers who can be adaptive can instil increasing independence in their infants. By means of a gradual process in which the mother increases her time away from her baby in very short periods, the baby learns to adapt to this distance and develop a healthy sense of independence. This is quite different from the idea that babies will learn to be independent by sleeping alone in their cot in their own room as soon as is practically possible, but more about taking small steps that allow babies to learn to soothe themselves. Winnicott suggested that such a process can be helped by *holding*, *handling* and *object-presenting*; for example, mothers hold and handle their baby in different ways, from cuddling and carrying to stroking and playing, to provide comfort, security and fun. They can also provide their baby with objects, such as their breast, cuddly toys and blankets, which can also provide comfort and objects for stimulation and play. Winnicott argues that the good enough mother will do this sensitively and facilitate a sense of loosening rather than the abrupt shock of being dropped or separated from the carer. Rather than a sudden transition, this letting go comes in small and digestible steps. For Winnicott, the early years are important for teaching children self-regulation through sensitive and adaptive parenting which can also support young children in preparation for their future independence.

Perhaps one of the most powerful messages implicit within Winnicott's work is the idea that parents communicate distinct messages to infants through their parenting approaches. Interaction involves much more than what is said (as of course very young babies cannot interpret language yet) and includes how parents interact and communicate through tone, gesture and touch, and how often what parents hope not to convey to their infant is inadvertently what is communicated. A sensitive parent who feels that cuddling, holding and stroking their infant is vital for their development (or as merely an extension of their maternal or paternal love and affection) may react to their infant's cries immediately. They may also invest much of their time in cuddling, checking and carrying their infant. Despite the love and affection that is clearly important here, there are other

SCA J1G2BCb

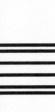

BUSINESS REPLY MAIL

FIRST-CLASS MAIL   PERMIT NO. 136   HARLAN IA

POSTAGE WILL BE PAID BY ADDRESSEE

SCIENTIFIC AMERICAN.

PO BOX 3186
HARLAN, IA 51593-2377

Subscriber Savings

VOUCHER

SEND NO MONEY NOW! MAIL TODAY!

☐ **1 Year** (12 issues) **$34.99** — SAVE 63%

☐ **2 Years** (24 issues) **$64.99** — SAVE 66%
← Best Deal!

Name _____ (please print)

Address _____

City _____ State _____ Zip _____

Email Address _____

✄ For faster service, go to **SCIAM.COM/INSIGHTS**

Savings based off annual cover price. Canadian orders include GST. Please add appropriate PST. Outside US and Canada, subscription price is $60 USD. Any applicable sales tax will be added to your order. Please allow six weeks for delivery of first issue.

COVER PRICE	$95.88
YOU SAVE	63%
YOUR COST	**$34.99**

SCIENTIFIC AMERICAN.

SCA J1G2BCb

messages that may surface. An overly protective parent may inadvertently project the message that their child needs comfort, love and affection from their parents to soothe them and help them regulate their feelings and emotions, and that they are not capable of doing this alone. What, then, are the longer term implications for this child who has to learn to manage and regulate their own emotions? In contrast, a parent who acknowledges that their own sense of 'self' as a parent is important as much as their infants' growing independence, may also provide love and affection with frequent cuddling and holding, yet balance this with periods of distance, space and separation. In this way the parent communicates to their infant that they can regulate their own emotions and do not always need Mum or Dad.

A growing body of research has linked the self-regulation and the ability of children to manage their own emotions and behaviour to positive outcomes in later childhood, adolescence and adulthood. Studies initially carried out during the 1960s and 1970s by Walter Mischel and colleagues at Stanford University demonstrated through extensive experiments that it is often the behaviour qualities and traits that infants develop and refine at a very young age that make a big difference to their later development.

Mischel[6] and his colleagues' work specifies that self-regulation develops from the child's ability to use what Mischel describes as 'cool regulation techniques', such as remaining calm and using distraction skills, in contrast to 'hot regulation techniques' which appear highly charged, emotive and often impulsive reactions, such as emotional outbursts and losing one's temper when faced with difficult situations. When relying or typically using 'hot techniques', a child may focus primarily on getting what they want and feeling satisfied immediately, and then act out, lose patience and perhaps even have a tantrum when the impulse is not satisfied. In contrast, children who have learnt 'cool techniques' display the ability to regulate and control their behaviour and so have fewer outbursts and typically use distraction skills to remain seemingly calm – or at least calmer. Mischel and his colleagues were interested in how young children resist temptation and remain calm, and so they devised a series of experiments to examine this – known as the *marshmallow test*. They presented 4-year-old pre-school children with a marshmallow and two options: first, they could ring a bell at any point to summon the experimenter and eat the marshmallow; alternatively, they could wait until the experimenter returned after around fifteen minutes and earn two marshmallows. Many of the children were simply unable to wait, called the experimenter back and ate the marshmallow straight away, whilst others were able to delay gratification (delayed gratification is the ability to resist temptation and to delay reward) and so were rewarded by two marshmallows. In follow-up experiments, Mischel and his colleagues discovered that some children were able to wait much longer if they used certain skills and techniques for distraction – such as covering their eyes or singing songs – which Mischel describes as 'cool techniques'. The children who waited longer when re-evaluated as adolescents, and then again as adults, demonstrated higher academic performance, social competence and reported higher ratings of personal self-worth and confidence. Additionally, they were rated by their parents as better able to cope with stress, apply reason and more likely to plan ahead. Statistics also reveal that as adults they were less likely to have drug problems or other addictive behaviours, get divorced or become overweight.

Psychologist Anita Sethi[7] found that 18-month- old infants who had been separated from their primary care-giver – an experience normally considered potentially anxiety-provoking and distressing for many young children – displayed less anxious behaviour if they were distracted or used distraction techniques themselves. Research carried out at the University of Montreal in 2010 discovered that infants (aged between 12 and 15 months of age) of mothers who sup-ported autonomous behaviour, such as encouraging children to go off to sleep without being cuddled, scored better in a series of tests which measured attention control in a similar way to those tested in the marshmallow experiment. Sethi proposes that parents who accommodate infant choice, autonomy and independence actually model effective self-regulatory behaviours. Similarly, Carol Dweck,[8] a psycholo-gist from Stanford University, has studied the impact of choice, belief and self-control for many years and her research argues that certain 'mindsets', or beliefs that infants acquire about themselves and others around them, provide strong indicators to how these children will develop throughout childhood and later adulthood. For those infants who learn to be more independent and autonomous, and acquire the belief that they can learn skills on their own and that they are trusted to regulate their own emotions, later develop greater problem-solving skills and social competence, which are important life-skills .

Why is it that some young children appear able to remain calm and to regulate their emotions and others don't find this quite so easy? Again, we come back to neuroscience and ideas around brain plasticity introduced earlier. For Mischel and his colleagues, whilst aspects of self-regulation reflect basic genetic make-up, ongoing research demonstrates that such behaviours can also be refined, developed and learnt at different stages throughout childhood, adolescence and even adulthood. Self-control and the regulation of emotions appear to be skills and behaviours that parents can foster and nurture in different ways. Being attuned to and sensitive to the needs of an infant is perhaps an important first step, but so is recognizing when is a good time to try and relinquish some control and provide more opportunities for children to develop greater autonomy and independence. Maggie Dent, the author of *Saving our Children from Our Chaotic World*, [9] suggests that all parents can and should strengthen their children's ability to be autonomous and resilient. She describes how many of the things which parents might feel are small and perhaps even insignificant, such as rushing to and from a raft of activities, are often the big things in so far as they are powerful and have the capacity to reduce or enhance a child's resilience to stress. Dent talks about the 'hurried child' and the 'over-scheduled' child as modern developments. She argues that over the last ten years parenting has become a type of competition and the hidden stress this places on growing children can cause many other issues that can impact emotionally, socially, mentally and cognitively. As well as highlighting the importance of parental sensitivity – in much the same way as Winnicott – Dent also talks about the importance of free play, risk-taking and child-hood independence. Children who are free to play in the natural world with limited parental/carer intervention and supervision are more likely to develop stronger 'seeking' or enquiring thinking behaviours which will serve them well as they mature into adulthood. Rather than avoid risks and sheltering children from the harsh realities that life can bring, Dent calls for parents to appreciate children's need to experience disappointment, challenge, failure and stress and to fully develop the interpersonal and personal skills that allow people to live well within society.

Why do some children appear more resilient than others?

From everyday infant separation from parents, to sibling rivalry and starting pre-school, along with making new friends and encountering different social situations, childhood is marked out by a number of potentially anxiety-provoking events. All children will have very different experiences and will interpret and react to such events in a variety of ways. Understanding why it is that some children appear better able and perhaps more equipped to endure stress has become a topic of wide debate. The term *resilience* has only recently come to the fore and other terms such as *coping*, as well as *grit*,[10] have been used to describe how children behave under stressful conditions. Psychologists, sociologists and psychiatrists all employ particular methods to try and tease out some of the influences on children's experiences and have asked (and continue to do so) a series of questions as to the origins and development of resiliency: are some children at risk by virtue of their early family experiences and the impact of their environment – or is resiliency a type of behaviour or approach to life that children are born with?

Much of the early research on resilience was longitudinal – exploring behaviour over a number of years – often from childhood through adolescence and into adulthood. The principal aim was to look at how early experiences and living conditions were in some way linked to later behaviours. Many studies tended to focus on children identified as 'at risk'; most notably, children raised within families facing adversity, such as war and natural disasters,[11] or in family circumstances of economic deprivation, separation and discord.[12]

Emmy Werner and Ruth Smith's longitudinal study of 698 Hawaiian infants, many of Asian descent, in Kauai, was published in 1982 yet was based on research which actually began in 1955. It is one of the most well-known studies of this kind.[13] All the infants who participated in the study were identified as being raised in conditions of high risk, including living in families experiencing poverty, with a parent diagnosed with a mental health disorder or where drug misuse and alcoholism were evident. The study began with an assessment of the reproductive histories and the physical and emotional condition of the mothers during each trimester of pregnancy through to delivery. Using a variety of different methods, including observation, developmental assessment and interviews, the study continued with an evaluation of the effects of stress, immediately before and after birth, and then studied the quality of the caretaking environment on the physical, intellectual and social development of the children, from infancy through to adolescence. The study revealed that whilst two thirds of the infant participants went on to develop a number of social and behavioural problems during adolescence – including aggressive and anti-social behaviour – one third developed into confident young adults at 18 years of age and 'caring and efficacious' adults by 32 years of age, who 'worked well, played well, loved well, and expected well'.[14] So the study indicates that, despite living in adverse and highly stressful family circumstances, many children have the capacity to endure hardship and to develop resilient behaviours. Werner and Smith identified both 'risk' as well as potential 'protective' factors and argued that risk factors such as poor health and poverty, for example, can be mitigated by protective factors including caring family dynamics, supportive community relationships, as well as a child's disposition, personality and outlook on life.

Psychologists Anita DeLongis and Susan Holtzman suggest that individual personality plays a central role in shaping how children react to and cope with everyday stressors.[15] Children are often described as having a pessimistic or optimistic outlook or being the type of child who sees their 'glass as half empty or half full'. Lois Barclay Murphy, a psychologist specializing in children's personality development, looked at how children deal (or not) with stressful social situations. She was one of the first psychologists to carry out research during the 1970s which systematically examined young children's coping skills and their capacity to adapt to different challenges. Through extensive observations of children, Murphy and her colleague Alice Moriarty proposed that the ability to cope owes much to children's past experiences, particularly their success and failures in adapting to and dealing with (or not) early stressful events, such as their ability to cope with everyday separations from parents and carers when starting pre-school or nursery, as well as their personality traits, particularly their openness to new experiences without causing worry or distress.[16] They argued that examining a 'child's way of getting along – with whatever equipment he has' is the only way to provide 'a full understanding of the effects of stress on children'.[17] Similarly, many contemporary psychologists now look at five basic dimensions of personality, often referred to as the big five personality traits: extraversion, agreeableness, conscientiousness, neuroticism and openness to experience when trying to understand resilience.[18] Research reveals that traits such as extraversion and conscientiousness have been linked with problem-focused coping – whereby children appear more able to demonstrate the capacity to cope with difficult situations and everyday stressors. In contrast, the personality trait of neuroticism is associated with disengagement coping, whereby children display avoidance to everyday stressors or have an intense emotional reaction to it.[19]

Studying behavioural traits and the personalities of children (as well as adults), however, is fraught with difficulties. Not only is it difficult to extract and understand personality distinct from the environments and cultures through which such traits emerge, but a number of studies exploring the links between personality and the development of resilient behaviours suggest that resilience is influenced by multiple personality components. In addition, how personality types are identified, studied and interpreted clearly differ between populations and cultural contexts.[20] It is not easy to come up with a straightforward or definitive list of risk and protective factors – they are always context-specific and different people can take on different roles in different contexts. Adults can be supportive to some children and so enhance their resilience while undermining others, while peer and sibling relationships, which play such a powerful role in children's social, emotional and cultural lives, can be ambivalent. Supportive friends can help buffer difficult experiences at home; rejection or bullying can do the opposite. Resilience therefore cannot be seen solely as a matrix in which protective and risk factors are weighed up against each other and if a child has more protective than risk factors then they will automatically be resilient. As Victoria Cooper and Andy Rixon argue, resilience is not static, and there are positive and negative factors which can enhance or undermine it: these can be described as 'adverse' and 'protective' factors.[21] For example, children may be heavily influenced in a positive way by good physical health or material wealth yet undermined by poor family relationships; similarly, while relationships may be very positive for some children, physical health can be undermined by living in conditions of poverty. There are further problems with using a resilience framework and while it is a positive way of understanding children's responses to adversity, supporting or promoting children's resilience is meaningless unless wider social circumstances are also addressed. Even the most resilient child can be overwhelmed by endemic poverty, war or natural disaster, and even the most optimistic and hopeful can be deeply affected by an acrimonious parental divorce. Resilience is no magic bullet and researchers are still trying to untangle the causes of resilience from the effects, the processes from the outcomes.

Although the idea that children are in some way predisposed to adapt to and cope with stress has remained fairly strong, the focus on exploring the links between personality and resilience has shifted more recently to include an analysis of the physiological, neurological and genetic foundations for the development of resilience in children. Studies reveal how particular regions of the brain respond to different experiences of stress and neuroscientists are attempting to understand what underlying neurobiological mechanisms contribute to the development of resilience, chiefly children's physiological vulnerability to heightened stress reactions.[22]

Children's physiological responses to stress including changes in heart rate, breathing and the release of stress hormones; the molecular pathways that control coping behaviours are now gradually being uncovered. Research carried out at Stanford University[23] has looked at glucocorticoid hormones which provide physiological feedback during acute stress and neuropeptide Y (NPY) and 5-Dehydroepiandrosterone (5-DHEA) which are thought to reduce the stress response by limiting sympathetic nervous system activation and protecting the brain from the elevated cortisol levels.[24] Dustin Albert and colleagues at Duke University in America have recently identified a specific gene variant amongst children who appear highly sensitive to their environments and are particularly vulnerable to stress. The genetic marker is part of the glucocorticoid receptor gene NR3C1 that influences the activity of a receptor which cortisol binds to which is directly involved in shaping reactions and adaptability to stress. This research indicates that a child's level of sensitivity to his or her environment is somehow related to specific differences in their genomes. Albert and his colleagues' research has looked at 'high risk' children – those identified as carrying the NR3C1 gene – and found that they are 75 per cent more likely to develop behavioural problems, including drug misuse, aggressive behaviour and anti-social personality in young adulthood without support and intervention. Whilst studies of this kind can be helpful in potentially identifying children at risk and so providing support where needed, Albert does suggest that these findings are in their early stages and so far the studies carried out have been limited to studying small groups of children and young people. More extensive research is needed before conclusions can be drawn.

Despite the emerging evidence to suggest children's reactions to stress have a neurological basis, neuroscientists are at pains to acknowledge the important part played by experiences and influences within the environment. The developmental psychologist Bruce Ellis from the University of British Columbia and the developmental paediatrician Thomas Boyce have been studying how the human genome influences children's behaviour and particularly their reactions during stressful situations. Ellis and Boyce suggest that, to a large extent, genes predispose how sensitive children are to stress during childhood. Their research identified genes linked to brain chemical receptors, which if combined with family stress can lead to later social and emotional problems. In a highly influential paper published in 2005, entitled 'Biological Sensitivity to Context', Ellis and Boyce use the Swedish metaphor of a 'dandelion child' (*amaskrosbarn*) and an 'orchid child' (*orkidebarn*) to describe children's vulnerability.[25] In order to explain this metaphor more fully, it is necessary to take a brief digression into botany and describe these two plants. The dandelion (*Taraxacum officinale*) is a tough plant species which can survive and thrive in any number of conditions, from continuously wet, cool, shady places to baking hot, dry sites. It doesn't care whether the soil is alkaline or acid, can shrug off damage to its leaves or roots and can survive and germinate, grow, flower and seed pretty much anywhere. In contrast, the orchid is quite literally a delicate flower – much more sensitive and fussy. Its seed must fall in exactly the right place and right conditions to germinate. Damage the plant and it will die. However, if these precise conditions are met, the orchid may eventually produce complex, beautiful, long-lasting and often fragrant flowers. Ellis and Boyce applied this image to children, dividing them into 'dandelion children' who appeared better able to endure and in some cases thrive in spite of adverse family and environmental conditions; and 'orchid children' who are highly sensitive to their environment and are far more likely to display anxious reactions to stressful conditions. Importantly, internal characteristics alone are not enough to determine resilience, but need to be looked at alongside the interplay between the environment and the child's personality.

Others have also looked at the relationship between environment and resilience. Psychiatrists Marilyne Essex, Marjorie Klein, Eunsuk Cho and Ned Kalin have examined how exposure to stress can result in a 'dysregulated stress response',[26] in so far as this reaction can be either too high or too low. The differences between children in terms of their levels of resiliency can be explained in relation to how they have become sensitized to react to stress. In situations where children experience insensitive parenting, they are more likely to develop a heightened physiological reaction to stress. Studies in this field suggest that early infant experiences of fear or anxiety may therefore sensitize children to react more readily to future threatening situations by heightening their stress response.[27] Whilst this heightened physiological reaction can be protective in situations of danger and threat, such a heightened response has been linked to an enhanced susceptibility to depression or anxiety in later life. This research infers that early exposure to stressful environments may influence the central nervous system in ways that may adversely affect children's later development.

Applying evolutionary principles, a number of studies, including research by Jelena Obradovic and colleagues from the Stanford Graduate School of Education, indicate that children who show heightened physiological or behavioural reactions to stress are actually more sensitive to both positive and negative environments. In a sample of pre-school children, Obradovic and colleagues found that high physiological reactivity exacerbated risk for children who were exposed to high levels of family adversity such as marital conflict, maternal depression, harsh parenting and financial stress. Conversely, in the context of low family adversity, high physiological reactivity promoted adaptive functioning such as better school competence and more pro-social behaviour. Neuroscience suggests that as the brain can be remodelled through experience and neural circuits are adaptable and dynamically regulated, it is possible to change the brain, develop coping strategies and become more resilient. Learning to adapt and cope with stress involves dynamic regulation of plasticity in brain circuits that govern stress responses (see Chapter 2 for a discussion of brain plasticity). Psychiatrist Fatih Ozbay and colleagues from the Mount Sinai School of Medicine have studied the neurobiology of human social bonding. Although the impact of neurochemical mediators to support mental health are largely unknown, preliminary studies suggest that oxytocin facilitates social bonding and may actually help reduce psychological stressors in humans. George Bonanno, a professor of clinical psychology,[28] who writes widely on this topic, suggests that, in a similar way to a child's innate *physical* immune system and capacity to endure and recover from illness, through natural selection children have developed an innate *psychological* immune system that enables them to adapt to challenging life events.

Can and should children learn to be more resilient?

If we all have the basic mechanics in place to endure stress and adapt to challenging situations, why are children's reactions so different? Individual differences in children's physiological reactions to stress are very complex and studies indicate that behaviours can be shaped by a variety of neurological processes as well as early experiences. The psychologist Suniya Luthar describes how more recent trends in research place far greater emphasis on understanding resilience as a process rather than as a particular trait or set of behaviours, and that individual adaptation results from interactive and learning processes that take place within the family and wider community.[29]

Most researchers exploring resilience would not claim that being resilient was a panacea for all problems: it is a complex idea and there are several notes of caution which must be sounded. There are some situations which are so overwhelming that children cannot cope with them and in these circumstances a resilience model may not be helpful. Resilience also varies over time and in different contexts. A baby may be resilient and very good at having his or her needs met, and an adolescent less so. Furthermore, children may be resilient in one context but not another – they may do well at school while also being depressed or anorexic, or they may be happy in their home environment and miserable elsewhere. It is also the case that what might appear to be coping or resilient behaviour may be nothing of the sort. As social workers Brigid Daniel and her colleagues note, 'Some young people who appear to be resilient may in fact be internalizing their symptoms', and while they may appear to cope in the short term, they are actually suffering greatly.[30]

It is also worth noting that not all forms of risk or adversity are necessarily harmful to children. Some degree of adversity and stress is an inevitable part of human life and learning to cope with it is an important part of growing up. Indeed, there is an argument that children who have never suffered adversity are disadvantaged when they become adults because they have not developed coping mechanisms and may react inappropriately when confronted with situations they have no resources to deal with.[31] Moreover, some psychologists argue that stress is not always harmful to children; it can be tolerable or even beneficial, and several childhood experiences, such as starting at a new nursery or having a new sibling, can become positive learning experiences as long as the child has the necessary support to deal with them. In line with Bonanno's idea of a 'psychological immune system', there is evidence that exposure to mild levels of stress that a child can cope with 'inoculates' them against the effects of stress later in the life span. Psychologist Ignacia Arruabarrena from the University of the Basque Country divides stress into three categories. First, *beneficial stress*, such as starting nursery, as mentioned above; secondly, *tolerable stress*, i.e. severe but still short-lived stress such as a death in the family, or parental divorce. Although this poses higher risks to children, with the right support from caring adults children can adapt and cope without it having a long-term negative impact or interfering with their development. Thirdly, there is *toxic stress*: 'when the adverse experiences faced by the child are chronic, repetitive, uncontrollable, and/or experienced without having access to support from caring adults.'[32]   Research into children's resilience reminds us that while the developmental consequences of living in adversity can be devastating, not all children exposed to powerful stressors sustain developmental damage. Some children develop a high degree of competence in spite of stressful environments and experiences, and the effects of adversity on children are not always as negative as supposed. In the context of war, for example, estimates of trauma in children are often lower than expected and as human ecologist James Garbarino and his colleagues argue: 'On the one hand, there is the common assumption that children exposed to danger are destined for developmental difficulties; war is not good for children and other living things. On the other hand, we have the fact that children survive danger and may even overcome its challenges in ways that enhance development.'[33] One of the early researchers on resilience, Robert Coles claimed that social crises could even stimulate moral development in some children by strengthening their empathy for human suffering, their altruistic sentiments, and by enhancing their commitment to serve other victims of violence.[34]

The pioneering work of the British psychiatrist Sir Michael Rutter[35] has been especially important for looking beyond individual personality traits that might predict how children cope under stress to look more at processes which explore how children learn and adapt within their environments. Rutter has conducted numerous studies which have looked at how young children respond to stressful life events during their early years, through childhood and into adulthood.[36] He suggests that resilient behaviours can be learnt when children are encouraged to develop positive appraisals of themselves and to recognize their own ability to cope during stressful experiences and to manage their own behaviours, for example, learning to calm or soothe themselves.[37]

Stress is a part of everyday life and whilst research focusing on 'risk' has identified the impact that stressful living circumstances can have on children's later development, research on the nature of relationships, and particularly parent–child relationships, has set out to provide a fuller explanation.

Learning to separate from parents during the very early years is recognized as an everyday stressful experience and one which has frequently been simulated through research as a way to explore young children's reactions to and adaptability to stressful episodes. Following on from her work with John Bowlby on parent–child attachment (introduced in Chapter 1), the Canadian developmental psychologist Mary Ainsworth developed the 'strange situation' procedure as a way of observing how young children – just under 2 years of age – encounter and react to anxiety-provoking situations.

The 'strange situation' consists of a series of stressful episodes (which last approximately three minutes each), all within an unfamiliar setting to the child. For each episode the child experiences a different stressful event, such as being confronted by a stranger, being left alone by their parent with the stranger, being left entirely alone and being reunited with their parent. During each of these episodes the researcher is able to observe parent/carer–child and child–stranger interaction. Based on her observations, Mary Ainsworth, along with her colleagues, identified different types of parent–child attachments, including *secure*, *insecure* and *absent*, which she suggested are important for children's early emotional development.[38] Research using the 'strange situation' scenarios suggests that a child who is securely attached will explore freely while the parent is present, using them as a 'safe base' from which to explore. The child will engage with the stranger when the parent is present, but is likely to become upset when the parent leaves and very happy when finally reunited with the parent. In contrast, a child with an insecure attachment will ignore the parent and display very little emotion when they leave or when they return. The child will not explore very much regardless of who is with them. Ainsworth argued that the seemingly detached behaviour of the avoidant child may actually mask distress and anxiety. Further, Ainsworth claimed that children with absent attachment display distress even before they became separated from their parent and are clingy and difficult to comfort when reunited. From her observations she suggested that children's secure or insecure attachment with their parent reflects the quality of their early relationships, particularly their parent's sensitivity to their needs. Although many aspects of the research around parent–child attachments and the use of the 'strange situation' to explore this have come under criticism,[39] this work still remains important today. Rather than focus primarily on parental sensitivity as an indicator for a child's ability to adapt to stressful situations, researchers now argue that both a child's temperament and a parent/carer's sensitivity are important.

The links between establishing a secure attachment in childhood and the development of subsequent behaviours has been studied by the British psychiatrist Jerry Holmes,[40] who suggests that children who have experienced consistent parental care, along with the stability which this brings, have the capacity to develop trusting relationships later in life. Yet the child who has not had the continuity of care which a secure attachment brings, and so has not experienced the mutual stability afforded by a good attachment relationship, has no 'secure base' to return to, and may therefore be weighed down by unresolved attachment issues. Such a young person has little or no inner or outer resources to help him or her deal with any threat in a socially helpful way. Peter Fonagy, American professor of psychoanalysis,[41] goes as far as to suggest that children's early attachment experiences may actually shape how they in turn become parents and form their own attachments with their children, which provides some support to the inter-generational research introduced in Chapter 2.

In their study of parenting approaches, Hamidreza Zakeria, Bahram Jowkara and Maryam Razmjoeeb[42] identify a link between parenting style and resilient behaviours in children. In their research they differentiate between *acceptance-involvement*, *psychological autonomy-granting* and *behavioural strictness supervision* parenting. Acceptance-involvement parenting refers to the responsiveness of a parent and the extent to which they respond to their children. Typically this style of parent displays warmth and sensitivity to their children's needs whilst setting clear rules and boundaries. Psychological autonomy-granting parenting styles describe a parent's tolerance to their children's opinions as well as the use of democratic reasoning for the discipline of their children. Behavioural strictness-supervision style parents set out to control and police the attitudes and behaviour of their child. Warm, sensitive and supportive parenting approaches are associated with the development of resilience and are singled out by many psychologists as protective factors that may enable children to overcome negative and stressful life events.

The potential impact of a controlling style of parenting on children's later development was examined in a longitudinal study [43] (introduced in Chapter 4) which tracked a group of children born during the 1940s through to adulthood in the 1990s. The study monitored the well-being of participants in the Medical Research Council (MRC) National Survey of Health and Development.[44] The researchers found that children who claimed that their parents had intruded on their privacy during childhood were more likely to have low scores in surveys of happiness and general well-being carried out in their teenage years and throughout their adult life. In contrast, the children who reported that their parents were more caring, warm and responsive to their needs tended to be more content well into adulthood.[45]

Yet it is not just parent–child relationships that are important. Michael Rutter describes how children learn a range of adaptability skills through their interaction with many significant people in their lives from siblings and peers to other family members. In the absence of a parent, as in the case of the orphaned children that Rutter studied in Romania, young children will form emotional bonds with others and these relationships are very important for their ongoing development. Similarly, the work of Judith Rich Harris, introduced in Chapter 4, highlights the influence of family and community, including children's relationships with siblings, peers and others, as well as parents in shaping a child's behaviour.[46]

Whilst studies indicate that aspects of resiliency have a neurological basis, how far these processes extend beyond providing a child with a predisposition or vulnerability to stress or anxiety requires far more debate. What research does reveal is that resilience – as a type of behaviour or process – shifts and changes in relation to a range of influences. Despite difficult early experiences, children can adapt and learn to manage stressful life events. In order to achieve and sustain resilient behaviour, studies indicate that early family environments are important. Children respond positively to loving, warm and caring environments which are not solely dependent on parents and can encompass a number of different supporting relationships, including siblings, peers and grandparents. Ultimately the concept of resilience has an underlying positive message: it considers what children can do rather than what they cannot and contains within it a message of hope – that recovery is possible and no matter how dire the circumstances in which children are raised, some manage to find ways to cope and grow up to be happy, autonomous, well-adjusted adults.

What Should Children Look Like?

The world, we are told, is in the middle of an obesity crisis with 41 billion children under the age of 5 overweight or obese.[1] In the USA, 20 to 25 per cent of children and adolescents are estimated to be overweight, while in the UK a third of children aged 2 to 15 were overweight or obese in 2016.[2] Italy, New Zealand, Japan and India have all identified the need to intervene to stop the rise of childhood obesity.[3] Even Sweden, often seen as the healthiest country in the world, has started to see a rise in the number of overweight or obese children.[4] Children are also becoming obese at a younger age and the prevalence of obesity of children in the USA between the ages of 2 and 5 increased from 5 per cent in the years 1976–1980 to 10.4 per cent in 2008.[5]

The health implications of these statistics are serious: according to the American Obesity Association, paediatricians are reporting increasing numbers of obesity-related diseases in children, such as type-2 diabetes, asthma and hypertension – illnesses once confined to adults. The effects of becoming obese at a young age may predispose those children to illnesses as adults such as heart disease and depression, and to premature death. Childhood obesity and being overweight also increases the risks of suffering from anxiety and depression, low self-esteem, stigma and bullying. The medical evidence clearly points to the fact that children who are larger face a higher risk of serious health problems than children with a lower BMI.[6] The economic costs are also high and it is estimated that the UK spends more on the treatment of obesity and diabetes than on the police, fire service and judicial system combined.[7]

It is unquestionable therefore that childhood obesity has become a major public health concern and there are claims that childhood obesity is a 'time bomb' and an 'epidemic' which means that today's generation of children have a lower life expectancy than their parents, reversing decades of medical progress.[8] But the problem is a contentious one and, as this chapter will go on to discuss, sociologists have questioned the anxieties that many professionals have expressed about children's bodies and concern about the ways the 'obesity crisis' has been used to control and regulate particular groups of children. While recognizing that being overweight or obese poses health risks to some children, they have examined the issue as a social problem as well as a medical one and looked at how a health issue (obesity) has been transformed into a moral one (self-indulgence and lack of self-control) and the implications here for parents. They have also queried whether the concentration on obesity and the promotion of particular ideals of attractiveness and slimness has had unintended consequences and whether it has led to increased anxiety among children, at younger ages, over how they look and what they should eat.

Why have children become so fat?

Medics and nutritionists have consistently argued that both children and adults have become larger in recent years and, on one level, the causes of this seem simple – children (and adults) are putting on weight because they are eating more calories than they are using up. Yet in reality the causes of obesity are multiple and various explanations have been offered to explain this rise in numbers, including genetic inheritance, an increasingly sedentary lifestyle, the easy availability of convenience foods, the amount of sugar in diets, the malign influence of marketing and advertising to children, larger portion sizes, children not walking to school any longer, and the rise in social media which means children spend time in their bedrooms rather than playing outside.

There is evidence that many of these influences can impact on children's weight in various ways, but no one factor can be seen in isolation. Genetic factors may well be highly significant and adults who are heavier are more likely to give birth to heavier babies, although the complex interactions of multiple genes, personal behaviour and lifestyle are still being untangled.[9] There are also environmental factors and suggestions that children's susceptibility to becoming obese may be linked to their nutritional status while in the womb. Longitudinal studies have been carried out on children who were born to women who were pregnant during the Dutch famine of 1944–5 (a famine caused by the Nazi occupation and food embargo). They found that among men whose mothers were undernourished (and who therefore also suffered from malnutrition in the womb) there was a high prevalence of obesity later on in adulthood. Researchers have suggested that this might be explained in part by understanding how, if suffering from malnutrition, the growing foetus prioritizes depositing fat while in the womb. Later on, when food is plentiful, those adults retained their tendency to store fat and therefore became obese. Similar results have been found in contemporary societies, specifically in Russia, Brazil, South Africa and China, where undernourishment in the womb, combined with rapid social changes after birth, have led to higher than expected numbers of children becoming overweight or obese.[10]

But genetic and environmental factors cannot be accepted exclusively as an explanation without also examining lifestyles and familial behaviour. Studies from the USA have identified having obese and overweight parents as the biggest risk factor in predicting whether a child will become overweight: 48 per cent of children with overweight parents became overweight compared with only 13 per cent of those with normal-weight parents. Whether this is caused by genes or is related to the parents' lifestyle, their views on food and eating behaviour is still up for debate. More recent studies have attempted to look at the interplay of multiple factors and one exploratory study, led by researchers from Stanford University, tracked 150 children and their parents from birth to the age of 5 and then used this data to predict if children would be overweight at 9.5 years old.[11] The researchers examined not only children's and parents' weight but also food behaviours and attitudes towards food, children's physical activity, their personalities and temperaments and parental views on their child's weight. While parental weight was a significant factor in how much children weighed, the study also found that parents reacted in different ways to children depending on the children's temperaments; many parents, even those of normal weight, would use food to calm and comfort a child if they thought this would end or reduce the frequency of tantrums. Sleep, too, seemed to be important, with overweight children sleeping thirty minutes a night less than normal-weight children and, although the links are not fully understood, it has been suggested that children who are overweight get less exercise during the day and therefore need less sleep at night.

The wider environment, especially in terms of the food and drink industry, has also been seen as having a significant impact on children's eating habits and weight. There are claims that food portions have got bigger, that they contain more hidden salt and sugar, and that parents are being tricked by marketers, advertisers and producers over exactly what children are eating. Breakfast cereals, for example, are often promoted as a healthy form of eating in the morning, giving energy, vitamins and roughage, and are widely given to children at home, in nurseries and in breakfast clubs. However, many contain very high levels of sugar and fat and are nutritionally quite poor. In 2016 the British government launched a plan of action to tackle childhood obesity.[12] One of the main targets was the food and drink manufacturing industry and the 'hidden' sugar in many of their products – particularly fizzy drinks. The government proposed a soft drinks levy on all manufacturers who do not lower the sugar content of fizzy drinks by 2019, challenging food and drink makers to cut sugar across a range of products, especially those popular with children, in an attempt to reduce children's sugar intake by at least 20 per cent by 2020. In doing this it is following other countries such as Mexico, Denmark, Hungary and France, although the experience in these countries has been mixed in terms of lowering rates of obesity; Denmark, which imposed a tax on sugary drinks in the 1930s, repealed it in 2014 in the face of criticism that it was ineffective. Even in Mexico where the tax has led to a noticeable fall in consumption of fizzy drinks, there are claims that people simply get calories from elsewhere and that, even if they do not, the drop in calories is not sufficient to beat obesity.[13]

Television, especially the marketing of foods high in fat, sugar and salt to children, has also been seen as a contributor to the rise of obesity. In 2007 the British media regulator Ofcom banned the advertising of such food products in and around programmes specifically targeted at, or likely to appeal to, children, arguing that this would cut the exposure of the under 9s to such adverts by 51 per cent. Although this target was not reached, there was a noticeable impact on the amount of advertising of these foods broadcast on children's TV (although not on programmes targeted at both adults and child viewers such as the family offerings on Saturday night TV where, despite high numbers of children watching, advertisers can still advertise unhealthy foods).[14] Yet this has still not yet reduced obesity in children, and studies which have looked at the relationship between television advertising and children's weight elsewhere have shown that in countries/

states where there is a ban on advertising to children, such as Sweden, Norway, Greece and Quebec, rates of childhood obesity have continued to rise despite the ban.[15] So far, most of the studies have focused on television advertising, but in the contemporary world it is unclear whether this is still children's primary exposure to advertising. Social media, the internet, bloggers and vloggers, peer to peer and viral marketing have all been enthusiastically embraced by even the youngest of children and while television advertising is relatively easy to control, these new forms of media are much harder to regulate (see Chapter 5).

What children eat is never simply about nutrition or even good health of course, but also has important social and cultural meanings tied up with ideas about good parenting. On a positive level, food is about love and intimacy – a home-cooked, nutritious meal being seen as the epitome of parental nurturance, especially good mothering, and the image of a mother in an apron cooking for her family has an enduring currency. It is also about socialization; not only should the meal be home-cooked with properly nutritious ingredients, but it should then be eaten sitting down with the family, with no distractions in the form of computers, phones or televisions – mealtimes should be a time for talking, listening and learning manners. More ambivalently, food is a marker of social status: foods become divided into high and low status foods, into adults' and children's foods, good/healthy and not good/unhealthy foods. Food is also intimately connected to body image – another issue which has become of great concern to parents in recent years as younger and younger children express dissatisfaction with the way they look and try to control their bodies through food intake – a subject which will be explored later in the chapter.

Against this backdrop, children's food consumption has become another battleground between parents and the state: another, more controversial, explanation given for the rise in childhood obesity is that it is down to poor parenting, especially poor mothering. As a headline in *The Times* newspaper put it, 'Ignorant parents are blamed for creating an obese generation'.[16] The report went on to claim that parents were wilfully ignorant of just how fat their children were, quoting the UK's Chief Medical Officer, Dame Sally Davies, as saying that parents no longer know what being overweight looks like: 'I remember in the clinic, parents thinking it was unhealthy if their children's ribs showed . . . For my generation that was normal – how have we lost this national knowledge and understanding of what is healthy?'

Is childhood obesity creating a new moral panic?

Childhood obesity is a social problem with many different, intertwining causes which are likely to play out in various ways in individual children. There is a consensus among nutritionists, the medical profession and the government that childhood obesity is a very serious problem, needing direct intervention. Yet despite the concern over children's weight, there have been a number of dissenting voices, and sociologists in particular have been critical of the language and sensationalism of the campaigns against childhood obesity. They have suggested that the perceived crisis, and reactions to it, are not entirely what they seem and mask other social anxieties and problems. The language of the debates is undoubtedly hyperbolic with references to the obesity 'time bomb' or the US Surgeon General declaring that obesity 'is a greater threat than weapons of mass destruction'. Claims that obesity is an epidemic are problematic in that obesity is not communicable so cannot, by definition, be an epidemic.[17] However, behind the terminology there are real anxieties about the nature of the claims and the idea that children are eating themselves to death has been challenged. While there is no doubt that morbid obesity can cause serious health problems to individuals, there is also concern that children's health and well-being are being reduced to measurements of size and weight without regard to the bigger picture. There are worries that the terms 'overweight' and 'obese' have been conflated, thereby making the problem seem more serious than it actually is.

Providing healthy, nutritious food has long been seen as part of the moral obligations of being a good parent, but, it is argued, childhood obesity is now being used as a way of indentifying and stigmatizing 'bad' parents. Childhood obesity is referred to as a form of child abuse, which may necessitate the intervention of the state and the punishment of the parents in some cases. As one US commentator put it, 'If you have an overweight child, that is America's most pleasurable form of child abuse.'[18] This view was echoed by the chairman of the Child Growth Foundation in the UK, who said: 'In 99 per cent of cases, obesity is so avoidable. Letting a child get fat is a form of abuse as there's a possibility they could die before their parents. It's important they are taken out of their homes and put under twenty-four-hour surveillance from doctors and nurses.'[19]

Sociologist Frank Furedi has argued that the concerns over obesity are part of the over-medicalization of people's lives and have created a situation where normal, individual anxieties, whether in relation to food, exercise or work, have been turned into medical problems which have to be 'fixed' through government policy and education.[20] Those who refuse to engage with this education or policy can be labelled ignorant or even deviant for failing to comply. Others have gone further and argued that childhood obesity is not really a concern about child health but a way of defining and then reinforcing social divisions, especially those based on class or ethnicity, and while the impact of choosing the 'wrong' foods is presented in terms of health outcomes, it is actually a way of shaming the poor and socially marginalized. Jantina De Vries from the University of Cape Town also sees concerns over obesity as a form of social control and a way of marking out children who do not conform to 'proper' or 'appropriate' body shapes (i.e. the slim, lean and fit bodies considered socially desirable) and therefore fail physically to reflect middle-class values of self-restraint and self-discipline. For her, obesity is as much of a social problem as a medical one; while it might make some children ill, it also marks out whole groups of children – usually poor ones – and stigmatizes them as different, gluttonous, lazy, feckless and lacking in self-control.[21]

Questions of ethnicity and class are raised by many sociologists who have looked at obesity, with many pointing out that the highest levels of childhood obesity are often found amongst the socially marginalized. Looking at the obesity statistics worldwide, it is clear that rates of obesity map onto structures of social and ethnic inequality. Poorer people are significantly more likely to be overweight than richer ones and those of a minority ethnic background are more likely to be overweight than members of majority white populations. In Holland, children of Moroccan or Turkish descent are more frequently obese than white Dutch children. In the USA, children of Hispanic or African American origin are thought to be at particular risk, while in the UK it is Indian and Pakistani heritage children that have the highest prevalence of diabetes and obesity. Some have tried to explain this in terms of genetics, different metabolism or other biological factors, but researchers such as De Vries see the causes of obesity in these populations as social and political as much as physiological. She argues that the political elites have seen in obesity the 'close relation between immoral behaviour and the social and economic outcasts of society; the poor and the immigrants also most readily engage in self-destructive behaviour and are thus in need of regulation that protects them from themselves. In this way, the call to take political action against childhood obesity apparently equals a call for political action against the poor and weak individuals in society.'[22]

Seen in this light, childhood obesity is less of a public health problem and more a problematic cultural, social and political concept overlaid with moral and ideological agendas which have become cloaked in the language of public health and science.[23] It can be argued that the middle classes and governments have always been concerned about the diet of the poor – and their refusal to listen to health advice – although in the past this has focused on children being underweight rather than overweight. Norwegian sociologist Vebjørg Tingstad has seen the concern over childhood obesity as part of a more generalized moral panic over 'toxic childhoods'[24] (see Chapter 9), while sociologist John Evans and his colleagues have seen the focus on reducing children's weight as part of a contemporary 'child rescue' movement which aims to regulate the behaviour of the working classes and differentiates the poor between the deserving and the undeserving, and in doing so overlooks important issues of social inequality and structural health inequalities.[25] These inequalities mean that poor children do consistently and considerably worse in terms of health than those of a higher socio-economic status. In the UK, throughout childhood, deaths from accidents, respiratory disease and, to a lesser extent, infectious diseases, show steep class gradients: for example, in the year 2000, a child in the lowest social class was twice as likely to die before the age of 15 as a child in the highest social class. The same is true in the US, with some of the worst outcomes for child health and also the greatest disparities in wealth between rich and poor.[26] As sociologist David Buckingham puts it, discussions over obesity remove 'attention from the structural causes of health inequalities, and blame the victims: people who are already second-class citizens are now seen to be responsible for their own plight, and too slothful or ignorant to do anything about it'.[27]

In terms of children, the blame for them being overweight tends to fall squarely on their parents, particularly their mothers, who are condemned as either too lazy to work and also to cook for their children or too focused on their careers and not being around to feed them. April Michelle Herndon, Professor of English and Gender Studies at Winona State University, has argued that overweight children have become yet another stick with which to beat mothers and she claims that the childhood obesity 'epidemic' has led to new forms of mother-blaming, giving mothers a new set of responsibilities and duties on top of the daily care they are already expected to provide.[28] In the US (although less so in Europe), rises in childhood obesity are seen as directly related to mothers going out to work and delegating one of their perceived primary duties of motherhood – the physical nurturance of their children – to others. Although there are no specific studies that suggest that fewer working women would lead to fewer children being overweight, it is, Herndon claims, presented as a common-sense assertion that has rarely been questioned and which fits into a socially conservative agenda that sees a woman's rightful place as being in the home.

Researchers Jeni Harden and Adele Dickson from Edinburgh and Edinburgh Napier University have conducted detailed, in-depth studies of low-income mothers' food practices and the ways that they dealt with feeding their young children.[29] They found that all the mothers had a very good knowledge about what was healthy and the sorts of food they should be feeding their children. All of them talked about the importance of home-cooked meals made with fresh produce. However, they were not able to consistently provide this and spoke of their guilt and upset that they could not. Many of them relied on benefits and in order to feed their families had to go to multiple shops in order to get the best deals and the cheapest food. Without cars, and with buggies and young children to take with them, this often became extremely difficult. If children were fussy eaters, it was hard to keep introducing new foods to them – because if one was rejected, that meant a meal wasted and there was little money for a replacement. Mothers also often lacked facilities to cook and especially to eat together as a family: many expressed a desire to do so, but in the small social housing units they lived in there was no space for a dining table so meals were often eaten in front of the TV. Despite this, however, these mothers did their best, in poor housing and with strained resources, yet felt judged and ashamed if their children became overweight.

Why do children worry about their bodies?

Being or becoming fat is not just about the potential for ill health, but is also related to social and cultural ideas about the attractive body – ideas which children pick up on and internalize at a surprisingly early age. Obese children are referred to, even by doctors, as 'freakish' and their bodies become a source of shame and visceral dislike to both themselves and others.[30] The drive to control childhood obesity has led to the imposition of intensive and sometimes invasive regulation. Children are weighed and measured in schools and nurseries, sometimes publicly, and there have been instances when those children deemed to be overweight have been shamed and forced into restrictive diets until they complied.[31] The flipside of the childhood obesity crisis, therefore, has become a 'fear of fat', an over-emphasis on body size and shape and, for some children, a sometimes overwhelming pressure to be thin and to conform to notions of the 'ideal' body.

For many years, problems around body image were seen as largely confined to girls and were thought to surface in the early teenage years. More recent research has suggested that children as young as 3 are already forming ideas about what are appropriate or inappropriate body shapes and are beginning to learn that 'thin is good and fat is bad'. Psychological tests on children between the ages of 3 and 5 have shown that they consistently rate pictures of 'chubby' children more negatively than pictures of 'thin' ones, and when asked which child was more likely to be mean are much more likely to identify the fatter child as mean than the thinner one. They also saw overweight children as angrier than non-overweight ones.[32] Studies from the USA have found that preschool children associated favourable words with a picture of an average-sized person, but associated words such as 'fights', 'cheats', 'gets teased', 'lazy', 'lies', 'mean', 'dirty' and 'stupid' with images of obese people. A 1998 study showed that both boys and girls, regardless of age, viewed an obese figure as less happy, less friendly, less popular, more likely to be teased or bullied, less attractive and lazier than an average one.[33] Studies from the UK have found that this negativity towards overweight children translates into behaviour with other children such as assigning them negative characteristics and claiming they didn't want to play with them.[34]

In popular children's culture the portrayals of fatter

children are often negative (even when hidden under a veneer of humour or fantasy) and the not very covert message of much of children's popular culture today is that slimness and beauty are not only attractive but a sign of moral virtue – in contrast to fatness which is associated with ugliness, negative characteristics and moral failings. Augustus Gloop in *Charlie and the Chocolate Factory*, Dudley in the Harry Potter series, Piggy in *Lord of the Flies* and the archetypal Billy Bunter are all portrayed as stupid, greedy, cowardly and obsessed with food. Even in animated films for children, the fatter characters are the villains; for example, Ursula the octopus in Disney's *Little Mermaid* is portrayed as both nasty and obese.

Not surprisingly, therefore, many children shun fatness in others and dislike it in themselves, so that alongside the rise in obesity has come a rise in children's insecurities about their bodies and a desire to be as thin as possible. A UK study of 300 children found that by the age of 8 girls have become very conscious of ideas about slimness, while boys too were influenced by ideas about acceptable body shapes, identifying the V shape as the most acceptable and desirable shape for them.[35] Children have internalized the message that a thin body is a good one, as well as the stereotype of 'what is beautiful is good', and try and apply that to themselves even if it is detrimental to their physical or mental health. Studies from both the UK and USA have shown that children are preoccupied with their bodies and how they look from a very young age: 45 per cent of both boys and girls aged between 8 and 11 had a desire to be thinner, while 37 per cent had tried to lose weight and 6.9 per cent were within the range for anorexia. Even younger children are not immune to these pressures and a study in 2000 in the USA found that 52 per cent of girls aged 6–8 and 48 per cent of boys would prefer to be thinner than they currently were and wanted to lose weight.[36]

Parental views on eating and their own eating and dieting practices have a significant impact on children. Girls whose mothers are dieting or who talk about losing weight are likely to imbibe the message that fat is bad, both physically and morally, and this can set up aspirations for unrealistic body shapes for the girls. Just to add to parental guilt, there are also suggestions that emphasizing healthy eating too strongly can have the exact opposite effect and that putting too much pressure on children to eat certain types of food, or placing too much importance on 'clearing your plate', can lead to anxiety about eating later on and even to eating disorders such as anorexia or bulimia.[37] This is a complicated and controversial area and it is far too simplistic to point to any one cause of anorexia, be it improbably thin-looking models on the fashion pages of *Vogue*, Barbie dolls with their unrealistic proportions or parental behaviour. What is clear, however, is that researchers have consistently found that in children aged 3–12 concerns about weight and low self-esteem are not related to a child's actual weight but to their perceptions of themselves and whether or not they believe that their parents or peers think that they are fat.[38]

Whatever parents might think about their children's weight, and whether their concerns are new or perennial, what children look like and their judgements about each other do have a significant impact on their childhood. For one group of children in particular this social pressure to conform to an ideal in terms of their appearance and anxiety about what others think of them is particularly difficult to cope with. The subject of how disabled children fit into, and think about themselves, in an increasingly body-conscious world is disquieting. The stigma of having a different physical appearance experienced by disabled children has a long and sad history. As late as 1952, the eighth edition of a textbook, *Mental Deficiency (Amentia*, by British physician Alfred Tredgold, described 'idiot or imbecile' children as 'utterly helpless, repulsive in appearance, and revolting in manners', while the 1970 *Encyclopaedia Britannica* cross-referenced Down syndrome with 'Monster'.[39] Such children were often institutionalized shortly after birth, their families were told to forget about them and start again, and they were an enduring source of shame and stigma. Even as more and more disabled children began to be integrated into mainstream schools, the labels and terminologies still focused on their impairments and located the problem in terms of what was 'wrong' with the children. Today there are many more provisions made for disabled children, and yet many are still treated as objects of pity and other children (and adults) can reinforce the feeling that not only are they different but that they are inferior.

Children who are disabled or ill tend to have a less positive body image than healthy children and feel worse about how they look; this idea is then reinforced by others' reactions to them.[40] In her study of how non-disabled children viewed those with disabilities, sociologist Angharad Beckett found that many children viewed disability negatively and saw disabled people as 'kind of not being very good' at things. Others saw disabled people as those with 'broken' bodies, who were ill, incompetent and 'not okay'.[41] Children rarely saw positive futures for those with disabilities, arguing that one of the markers of disability was that people could not work or marry or have children. Many children equated disability with ugliness, with one girl in Beckett's study claiming that disabled people just 'don't look nice'. Other researchers have found similar attitudes. Educationalist Alan Hodkinson, for example, found that non-disabled children had very negative attitudes towards disabled children, arguing that they were 'more unintelligent, ugly, boring, cowardly and poor than their non-disabled counterparts'.[42] Furthermore, although children were not always consistent in their views and attitudes, he found that it was the children who had had greater exposure and experience of interacting with their disabled peers who held the harshest opinions and were the most likely to describe them as 'ugly' and in negative terms.[43]

Children are not, of course, unique in their prejudice and their views reflect wider social attitudes towards ideas of beauty and normality. It also should be pointed out that several of the children in both studies were aware of the discrimination faced by people with disabilities and spoke of the need to love and value disabled people more highly. Moreover, the study also contradicts other research presented in Chapter 7 which suggested that one of the benefits of more inclusive education is that children mix with children who are different from them, including those with different bodies, and that this teaches tolerance and understanding. With such contrasting findings it is hard to draw definitive conclusions except to say that whatever policies are in place, and however much social attitudes have changed, there remains ambivalence about disabled children. More positively, however, other studies have suggested that disabled children themselves are much more optimistic about disability than their non-disabled peers and have very clear views of what the disability means to them and the impact it has on their daily lives.[44] While they recognized that their 'impairment' might impose physical limits on them, none of the children saw their disability as a tragedy, wished to change it or have it 'cured'. For many children their disability was not a major part of their identity and they talked about just getting on with things and coping as best they could. The children were often practical and pragmatic and did not see their disability as a major source of difference between themselves and other children. Indeed, it was parents who saw the most differences between their children and others and who were more sensitive to slights and discrimination.

Disabled children, like all other children, are heavily influenced by the views and perceptions of their parents. Even if these views are not explicitly stated, it is clear that the children pick up on well-meaning parental anxiety. Parents have a very difficult role to play – promoting their children's health and fitness, encouraging them to reach their potential, emphasizing that how they look, and the shape or size of their body, is not the most important thing about them, while also acknowledging that their children may be judged in a world that idealizes physical perfection and a very limited range of preferred body types and recognizing the risks to good health that being overweight can carry. If

3-year-olds have already internalized negative messages about difference, it is hardly surprising that disabled children are also sometimes perceived as inferior. How to acknowledge this and to ameliorate some of its impact while also promoting a child's confidence is extremely hard to achieve.

While medics and nutritionists seem consistent in their belief that children are getting fatter and that this constitutes a serious public health crisis, sociologists have, on the whole, been less sure about the accuracy of claims that there is an obesity 'epidemic'. They have tended to focus less on the medical side of the health issues and more on the way that interventions around obesity have masked other issues such as racism, social exclusion and inequality. Some have argued that claims of a health crisis among children are yet another form of mother-blaming. Certainly in order to understand childhood obesity fully, it needs to be examined as more than a health issue, and discussions about it must encompass an examination of the moral dimension which equates fatness not only with ill health but also with immorality, lack of self-control and ignorance. While aimed at tackling children's increasing weight, campaigns against obesity have, some sociologists argue, made children hyper-aware and vigilant about their bodies from a much earlier age.[45] Children are worrying more about how they look, disordered eating has become more common in children, or at least more diagnosed, and ideas that slimness and beauty are synonymous with goodness have become more overt. Not only does this exacerbate anxiety in children who are not overweight, but it also impacts on disabled children as it defines ideas of beauty increasingly narrowly. It also steps up the pressure on parents – especially mothers – who must keep their children at the correct weight while also ensuring that their children have healthy attitudes towards eating, worry just enough about their bodies not to eat too much or the 'wrong' sort of food, but not enough to make them self-conscious, unhappy or to eat less than they need to in order to conform to constrictive ideas about the socially acceptable body.

Was It Really Better in the Past?

Childhood evokes strong personal memories and emotions. It is often seen as the crucible in which characters are formed (for good or ill) and a time of life which can be remembered but never re-created. The shared culture of childhood is an endless source of fascination: in the West the memories of music listened to, TV programmes watched, games played and books read bind people to their contemporaries and form a generational as well as a national identity. Parents and grandparents are exactly the same, of course, bound to their peers by their own generational culture. Perhaps not surprisingly, each generation likes to think that things really were better in their day and that they have gone to hell in a handcart ever since – and perhaps equally unsurprising is the eye-rolling of their children as the reminiscences begin. Yet this nostalgia is undercut by sociologists and historians who tell us that a golden age is a myth: whatever we remember personally, or fervently wish to believe in, children in the past were at serious risk from death, disease and discrimination and were routinely abused, unhappy and silenced. In contrast, childhood today, in the contemporary West at least, is a time when survival is more or less guaranteed, as are good health care, education and material and social opportunities (for the majority of course; there will always be the socially marginalized and excluded for whom this is a long way from reality). This chapter will explore the currency of both these sets of ideas – that childhood today is deteriorating fast, as well as the view that today's children have never had it so good, and will use the UK as a case study for examining these ideas. In doing so it does not seek to belittle contemporary British parents' fears or to suggest that childhood today is in crisis and in terminal decline. Rather, it tries to make sense of why these ideas exist and how far they can help us evaluate the situation of contemporary children.

Is childhood in crisis today?

Ask the majority of parents throughout the world what they want for their children and how they hope they will grow up and most will answer that they want their children to be happy, healthy and successful. Yet what this means, and whether children and parents see happiness or success differently, is highly contentious. In the last twenty years there have been numerous attempts by psychologists, policy-makers, sociologists and economists to quantify childhood happiness (or, more usually, well-being) in order to draw comparisons between children in different countries.[1] The subsequent reports published by these various researchers have made for rather grim reading for parents in the UK and the USA, sparking social and media anxieties that British and American children are among the most unhappy, stressed, emotionally deprived, educationally under-achieving, friendless, obese and over-sexualized children in the world, and that childhoods are being eroded and the freedoms and fun that children had in the past are gone.[2] Despite the wealth and dynamism of both economies, the UK and the USA consistently rank at the bottom of league tables of child welfare and well-being. Today's children, claim commentators such as Sue Palmer, are 'battery reared' rather than ' free-range'. Children are perceived as being at risk as never before, as the institutions of the state, as well as their own parents, fail them. At the same time they are seen as out of control, unhappy and a risk to themselves and others.[3] In 2009 the report *A Good Childhood: Searching for values in a competitive age* was published, based on the conclusions of twelve independent experts commissioned by the Children's Society to look at the state of British childhood as part of the 'Good Childhood Inquiry'. This report found that one in five children had a mental health problem, that one in twelve children intentionally self-harmed on a regular basis, that rates of 'non-aggressive conduct problems' such as lying, stealing and disobedience have rocketed and that children no longer played outside because of their parents' fears. Such findings led the then UK Children's Commissioner, Al Aynsley-Green, to comment that: 'I believe there is a crisis at the heart of our society. We have been failing children and young people for far too long.'[4] There was also a fear that children had become estranged and alienated from adults. A survey carried out by Barnardo's in 2008 found that 49 per cent of adults felt that children were a danger to themselves and others and 43 per cent thought that adults needed to be protected from children; 45 per cent agreed with the description of children as feral and 35 per cent agreed with the statement that it feels like the streets are 'infested with children'.[5]

While some of this was dismissed by sociologists as sensationalized,[6] a report in 2007 had a much more significant impact and provided factual, statistical evidence that childhoods in both the UK and the USA really were problematic. UNICEF's *Child Poverty in Perspective: An overview of child well-being in rich countries* looked at six different aspects of children's lives: material well-being, health and safety,[7] educational well-being, family and peer relationships, behaviours and risks; and subjective well-being. Using a variety of indicators and statistics, this study compared the experiences of being a child across Europe and North America.[8] It concluded that despite being two of the richest countries in the developed world (the study included most of Europe and the USA and Canada), the well-being of children from the UK and the USA was among the lowest overall. In almost every category British and American children were near the bottom, especially in family and peer relationships (the UK was ranked 21 out of 21, the USA was 20th), children's behaviours and risks (ranked respectively 21st and 20th), and subjective well-being (the UK was ranked 20, but only because there was insufficient data from the USA). On issues such as material well-being, British children also scored lower, coming 18th and the USA 17th; on educational well-being they were ranked 17th, while the US was 12th. On health and safety, the UK was 12th, compared with 21st for the USA. A follow-up report by UNICEF in 2013 on children's well-being was more positive about the UK and showed some improvements in the UK's standing in that it rose up the table from last out of 21 to 16th out of 29 countries overall. In contrast, the USA fell to 26th place. The worst placed in the developed world appeared to be Romania, closely followed by Latvia and Lithuania. While the UK had shown an improvement, it still lagged behind Slovenia, the Czech Republic and Portugal, and there were still some areas of concern. Infant mortality rates, for example, were double those of countries such as Sweden or Finland.[9]

In contrast, the Scandinavian countries scored highly on nearly every measure, making childhood a seemingly happier and easier period of life in Northern Europe. Many reasons have been put forward for the Scandinavians' high ranking in these tables: better state-subsidized childcare, delayed entry to primary school, greater emphasis placed on pupils' social development and happiness than on their academic or school achievement, fewer league tables, flexible working for parents and low crime rates. One of the most debated reasons put forward for their high ranking, however, was that these societies were more socially equal and had a more equitable distribution of wealth and, unlike in the UK and the USA, there was less of a gap between the richest and the poorest in society.[10] Certainly the Scandinavians had very low levels of child poverty and wealth was distributed more evenly across society. This was achieved, however, through much higher levels of taxation than in the UK and the USA. The majority of Scandinavians are happy with this social contract and while the financial price may be high, they live in comfortable, peaceful societies without extremes of poverty and with largely happy children. Yet this social contract is a highly politicized and raises profound questions about the nature of the relationships between families and the state; in the UK and other countries politicians (especially, but not always, those from the right of the political spectrum) argue that parents must be responsible for children's welfare and well-being and that the best way to ensure child well-being is for children to be brought up is in a climate of low taxation, with working parents, within a stable home.[11] The Scandinavian model is rejected for encouraging people to rely too heavily on the state. Such arguments and differences of opinion about the role of government can sometimes seem rather removed from discussions of parenting but show clearly the interplay between the micro and the macro as well as the political and economic frameworks within which contemporary parenting takes place.

Is the golden age of childhood over?

The idea that childhood is in crisis has a great popular appeal and is related to the belief that, while childhood today is problematic, at some point in the past there was a golden age of childhood, now forever lost: a time when children played freely, disappearing from the house for days on end while pursuing wholesome activities in the outdoors with their friends. Communities were stronger, strangers less dangerous, junk food less prevalent, television more limited and social media yet to be invented. Not all of this vision is a myth: society was indeed less consumer-oriented, there was less to buy and fewer choices, and while teenagers were first seen as a untapped commercial market after the Second

World War, the world of younger children was less commercialized (and the concept of the 'tweenager' did not appear until the very late twentieth century).[12] Toy companies existed, making toys and dolls for children to play with and aspire to own, but the idea that children have significant purchasing power, or much influence over household spending other than a limited amount of 'pester power', is a very recent phenomenon. Prior to the invention of mobile phones, the internet and the widespread ownership of home computers, children's exposure to media was restricted and tightly controlled. In the early 1950s in the UK there was only one broadcaster of children's television and radio – the BBC – and while there are criticisms that its vision of childhood, and what was good for children, was restrictive and at times reactionary, the programmes it broadcast were still informed by a public service ethos that strove to educate and inform, as well as entertain. The BBC did not broadcast commercials and there were strict rules on ITV, when it arrived in 1955, about what should and shouldn't be marketed to children.[13] Although evidence on the impact of children's participation in the market as consumers is highly contested, it is fair to say that children's lives have become increasingly commercialized in the last forty years and many parents are concerned about the influence of the market on their children's choices and preferences and about the impact on childhood more generally. Indeed, Sue Palmer has labelled contemporary childhood as 'toxic' because of its commercialization and her belief that children have too much freedom in terms of consumer power and have come to associate happiness with having material possessions.[14]

Certainly it seems true that in the past children had greater physical freedom in terms of play and where they could do it, and much more unstructured time – as described in Chapter 5. There were fewer after-school clubs or organized activities to take part in and fewer children attended nurseries because of the social expectation that mothers would stay at home. When they were older, children also had many fewer forms of entertainment and, without this, had to devise their own; whether this involved reading, playing outside or visiting friends' homes, it was largely done without parental involvement or management. Many of those who are now adults can look back at their own childhoods in the 1950s, 60s, 70s and 80s and remember playing out of doors and visiting friends or going to the shops on their own, or going out by bicycle or bus, unaccompanied by parents from the age of around 7. In some parts of the world it is still not uncommon today to see primary school children of 4 or 5 walking two or three miles to school with their friends and siblings without any adult supervision.

By the age of 10, children in the UK during the 1930s might have had a roaming distance of around twenty miles (travelling by bus, train, bicycle or foot), but by the 1970s this distance had dropped to a mile, and today many children are not allowed out of their back gardens – indeed, it is estimated that modern children spend less than 4 per cent of their time outdoors, being driven to nursery or school by car or playing indoors.[15] Visiting friends or travelling to school has become something that is organized by parents, and while this is designed to keep children safer and better supervised, it also means that they can lose the chance of gaining independence, negotiating risk and choosing their own friends. The report, *A Good Childhood*, mentioned previously, found a sharp contrast between the age parents today were first allowed to go out unsupervised and when they allowed their own children to do so: 39 per cent of today's parents were allowed out before their tenth birthday, while only 17 per cent would allow their children the same freedom at the same age.[16] Play, as argued in Chapter 5, has gone indoors and the outdoor play enjoyed by today's parents in their childhood has largely gone. In 1971, 80 per cent of 7–8-year-olds walked to school on their own in Britain, but by 1990 this had dropped to 9 per cent, caused in part by the increase in the amount of traffic and its size and speed.[17] Today the figure is even less and those children who walk to school tend to do so with their parents. Walking in a gang or on your own is simply not conceivable and has in some cases even become criminalized: a couple in Maryland in the USA had their two children aged 6 and 10 taken into protective custody after they were found walking home from a local park alone,[18] and in Australia a mother was arrested for allowing her 6-year-old child to walk unaccompanied through the town of Miles near Brisbane. In the USA, case charges were later dropped and the law was clarified to 'allow' children to walk home unattended with their parents' permission, while in Australia the police chief reiterated that no children under 12 were to walk to school alone.[19]

This past freedom was possible partly because of what sociologist Frank Furedi in his book *Paranoid Parenting* has called a sense of 'adult solidarity'.[20] He argues that in the past there was greater trust between adults who would look out for each other's children and children, in turn, were taught to believe that they could trust adults to help them if they got into difficulties. With fewer cars on the road, children's physical safety was less of a concern and fears over malign strangers were less prevalent – children might have been told not to accept sweets from strangers, but the idea of malevolent outsiders posing an imminent risk to them seemed remote. Although, even then, the abduction and murder of children was not unknown and horrific murders of children, such as those committed by Myra Hindley and Ian Brady in the UK in the early 1960s, or the abduction and murder of the baby Lindbergh in 1932 in the USA[21]caused profound shock and anxiety for many parents.[22] Despite this, however, parents still allowed their children to roam around freely, believing that they could rely on other adults to provide help if they needed it.

As this adult solidarity has broken down, parents have become more inward-looking, more frightened of predatory paedophiles lurking in the shadows, and have kept their own children closer, protecting and looking after them while declining responsibility for others. High-profile abduction cases have played on parents' fears and also uncovered the stringent, and often vitriolic, levels of social judgement to be meted out if parents take any degree of risk, no matter how low, and something does go wrong. Overall, sociologists such as Furedi have argued, solidarity and social trust have collapsed and been swapped with suspicion and fear; the golden age of the past, when children were free and unfettered, when they could relax and trust adults, has gone and been replaced with a world in which children are both a threat to themselves and to others and where every adult must be treated with suspicion.

Or has childhood only recently come out of the dark ages?

Attitudes towards childhood in the past are inevitably con-flicting and while many look back on it as a time of happi-ness, innocence and freedom, there is also a strong contrary idea that childhood in the past was miserable, brutish and short and that the last forty years have been a period of pro-gress and greater nurturance during which society has become more child-friendly. There is plenty of evidence that childhood in the past was not characterized by innocence and freedom but by uncertainty, hard work and not much love. One does not have to look far back in history to find high infant and child mortality rates, stories of desperate family poverty, of children going out to work in hard and hazardous jobs, being sent away from over-stretched house-holds to new lives (and new exploitation) in the colonies, supporting their siblings after the death or desertion of their parents, or being subject to very harsh and potentially abu-sive discipline and punishment. Within the family, children, so the cliché went, should be 'seen and not heard', parents would 'spare the rod and spoil the child' and parenting was about demanding obedience and compliance rather than pro-viding support or nurture. King George V is supposed to have said, 'My father was afraid of his mother; I was frightened of my father, and I am damned well going to make sure that my children are afraid of me'– an attitude that was probably not confined to the aristocracy. Children and parents were dependent on each other, but often out of a painful necessity rather than out of reciprocal loving kindness and children had little protection within or outside the family.

The idea that childhood in the past was far from idyllic was articulated most forcefully in 1974 by American psycho-analyst Lloyd deMause, who published a book of essays entitled *The History of Childhood* in which he described the child's experience of childhood from the Babylonians to the present. He began his introduction to the book with a much-quoted sentence: 'The history of childhood is a nightmare from which we have only recently begun to awaken. The further back in history one goes, the lower the level of child care, and the more likely children are to be killed, abandoned, beaten, terrorized, and sexually abused.'[23] Essentially, he argued, until the recent past, childhood has been a story of universal pain and misery and throughout history children have been routinely abused by unkind and unloving parents who were unable to love or empathize with them. It was not until the mid-twentieth century that parents began to engage with children on their own terms, becoming facilitators rather than tyrants. Modern parenting, and the childhoods it has produced, are a triumph over the miseries of the past and should be supported and celebrated.

DeMause has not been well received by professional historians who have dismissed his theories as psycho-babble which have no regard for economic, social and cultural context. Historians have found plenty of evidence in diaries, in letters, in literature and even on tombstones of parents expressing great love, sympathy and kindness for their children and overwhelming grief when they died.[24] Such sentiments may not have translated directly into the ways that parents acted towards their children while alive, but even so, it is hard to believe that the fate of children before the 1970s was as relentlessly dismal as deMause has claimed. Unfortunately, too, his idea that the 1970s was a time of enlightenment when parents and adults finally began to see the light and started to concentrate on children's needs and desires rather than their own has been undermined by the revelations about the widespread sexual abuse of children and young people during that same period in the UK and by the failure of authorities and institutions to deal with, or even acknowledge, it.[25]

Yet elements of DeMause's argument remain intriguing: parents have not always treated children well, child abuse has a much longer history than many like to admit and, for many children, childhood was (and still is) a nightmare. Although contemporary levels of fears and anxieties over children's safety have risen, especially in terms of stranger-danger, one thing that has not changed is that children are at much greater risk in their own home and from their own families than they are from strangers. In 2014, according to the US National Child Abuse and Neglect Data System, 1,580 children died from abuse or neglect by their parent or primary care-giver (or 2.13 children per 100,000).[26] The younger the child, the more vulnerable they are, and children under 1 year old accounted for 44.2 per cent of fatalities, while children under the age of 3 accounted for 70.1 per cent. Similar statistics are found in the UK where between May 2007 and August 2008, there were 210 deaths of young children, or three deaths each week, attributable to violence, abuse or neglect by parents and carers.[27] The 'battered baby syndrome' was first publicly discussed in 1963 by Henry Kempe, a paediatrician concerned by the number of children appearing in his Chicago clinic with serious, non-accidental injuries, such as broken bones;,[28] and while the term is a recent one, it is obvious that child abuse in the home has existed for many centuries and state intervention has repeatedly proved ineffective.[29] There have been over seventy inquiries in the UK into child deaths by parents or carers since 1945 and while often not reported in the forensic and sometimes lurid detail that they are now, they have shown that abusive parenting is not a new phenomenon and that children have long been at risk by those meant to care for them. The report of the very first inquiry into a child's death is as horrific as the most recent one, and this and each subsequent report concluded with a plea that 'lessons must be learnt' and that such deaths must never happen again. They rarely are and inevitably do.[30]

Questions remain over definitions of harm and the extent to which the state should or could intervene to outlaw all practices it considers harmful. A prime example of this is the contentious issue of smacking. It can be argued that in the past many children were smacked and it did them no harm and was in fact beneficial for them and for society. Smacking and the physical disciplining of children supported and upheld the social order which encouraged a safer society in which children knew their place but had greater freedom. For many others smacking is a form of violence, a straightforward abuse of power, inflicted on the weak by the strong and it needs to be banned outright. Sweden banned smacking in 1979 and there is both legal sanction, and a strong social stigma, against parents who continue to smack. Some parents in the UK and the USA, however, continue to argue that smacking is an acceptable form of discipline and an effective form of training for good behaviour (see discussions of socialization in Chapter 4). As they see it, it is the only way to prevent a child from doing something that might endanger themselves or others, and banning it is an unwarranted interference by the state into their family life. Even parents who do not smack their children argue that it can be a useful tool for other parents and do not want to see it outlawed completely.[31] A 2008 study of Scottish parents found that while only a minority of parents practise smacking (16 per cent of mothers of 2-year-olds), 30 per cent agreed with the statement, 'it may not be a good thing to smack, but sometimes it is the only thing that will work'.[32] There are also questions to be asked as to whether smacking children is necessarily worse than manhandling them onto a 'naughty step' and holding them there, crying and distressed, or indeed whether a swift smack might be less stressful for children than being grounded or having a favourite toy or a mobile phone taken away. In the USA, attitudes towards smacking, or spanking as it is more usually known, appear even more entrenched and a 2005 study claimed that 94 per cent of parents report they have spanked their children.[33] There are claims that it is part of the culture of both the Christian right and African Americans and that banning it would represent an intolerable intrusion by the government into family life and the denial of parental choice about how to discipline children.

Looking cross-culturally, it is clear that world-wide children are regularly smacked or worse. In his 1989 study of violence in ninety small-scale, peasant societies, anthropologist David Levinson found only sixteen in which physical discipline was rare or non-existent.[34] When anthropologists have looked directly at why children are hit, they have received a variety of answers. Jónina Einarsdóttir of the University of Iceland, for example, asked Papel mothers in Guinea-Bissau why they smacked their children and was told that physical punishment was necessary for children to learn and that those who were not beaten would grow up lazy and discontented. One mother described the results of her dislike of physical punishment and the problems created by her refusal to beat her children: 'Children are the product of their upbringing. To have success in life children have to be prepared not to become lazy and deceitful, you understand? Because I do not have the heart to beat my children they never help me. My children never help me. Because I don't beat them, I have to do all the work myself.'[35] Parents in other places have concurred with this. According to Margery Wolf in her book on rural Taiwan in the 1950s, parents told her, 'Children ought to be hit. It does them no harm.' Indeed, it was part of a fundamental philosophy of child-rearing. As one mother said, 'Do you think that they will listen to you when you scold them? What good does that do? All you can do is grab one and really hit him hard. Then the others will be good too.'[36] Based on fieldwork conducted some years later in the 1980s, Charles Stafford concurred with this, and found that in the Taiwanese village he worked in, children were sometimes smacked for no reason other than to show them that life could be harsh and that they must learn to bear pain without complaint.[37]

Crisis, what crisis?

Given that the current state of childhood is portrayed so negatively, it is not surprising that many adults would rather believe in a time when childhood was very different. Certainly the ideal of a golden age of childhood has its attractions: who would not want today's children to have the happiness and freedom supposedly enjoyed by their parents and grandparents? But no generation can ever re-create the childhood they once had. Wider social changes make evaluating and judging the past difficult. Is the fact that children were allowed to roam freely across the neighbourhood a good thing or is it a sign of parental surrender of duty? Does giving a child a front door key and trusting them to come in from school and start a meal for themselves indicate a trusting and respectful parent encouraging their child to be independent and resilient, or a neglectful one – or one trying to earn enough to feed the family at a time when children in the West no longer contribute financially to the household? Or does such an example simply show that times have changed and what was acceptable in one generation is not considered so in another? As argued in Chapter 2, even those who had the happiest childhoods are unlikely to parent their children in exactly the same ways that they were parented.

Others would also admit that even happy childhoods in the past weren't always idyllic. On a trivial level, childhood could be at times quite boring and restrictive; endless Sunday afternoons with nothing to do and no TV to watch, visits to elderly relatives and constantly being on one's best behaviour. More seriously, child mortality rates were significantly higher and diseases such as scarlet fever could kill several children within a family in the space of a week, or polio which, even if children survived, could leave them disabled for life. It is also true that the risks to children have changed in some ways and, for example, it is much harder for children nowadays to play in the street or to cycle to the nearest park because of the increase in the amount of traffic, and the fact that the roads and cul-de-sacs where children could once play have been taken over by cars. It is also not entirely certain that children themselves value the sort of outdoors lifestyle many still associate with positive parenting and happy childhoods; one recent study has suggested that rural children are unhappier than their urban counterparts and preferred to feel protected rather than free. Alison Parkes from the University of Glasgow commented in *The Times* in June 2016: 'Research suggests that the rural idyll is a myth . . . children don't really think that the countryside is particularly safe or welcoming.'[38] Nor do urban children seem that keen on reconnecting with nature, with some seeing the city as vibrant and exciting while contact with nature was dangerous, nasty and unhygienic and might mean they were 'germed for life'.[39]

There has also been a broader social change in the role and value of children and while aspects of this (such as the push for the ban on smacking) can be controversial, Western society has certainly become more child-friendly and much more attention is now paid to children's needs. For many centuries in the West children were at the bottom of the social hierarchy, their needs and desires seen as less important than those of adults. It is only relatively recently that family relationships have become more equitable and children valued differently. Whereas once the father was the patriarchal head of the household, whose views and needs were paramount, this authority declined throughout the twentieth century so that by the 1950s it was children's needs that began to take precedence over those of adults. One example of this is the way that food was typically distributed within British families. Throughout the eighteenth and nineteenth centuries there was a strict and almost universally recognized pecking order – father ate first and ate the best, then the children, then the mother. By the 1950s, however, this had changed, and as one mother in the East End of London said: 'When I was a kid Dad always had the best of everything. Now it's the children who get the best of it. If there's one pork chop left, the kiddie gets it.'[40] It might be disputed whether this is a good thing (and whether both parents go without or just the mother), or even if the pendulum has swung too far in the other direction, but with a very few exceptions, today's children are more equal within the family and few contemporary parents base their parenting on fear and subordination and clearly prefer equality rather than hierarchy as the basis for their domestic relationships.

On a larger social scale, the value of children has altered significantly in the West and this too can be claimed as evidence of childhoods becoming progressively better. The idea that children are primarily an economic asset to be controlled by their parents has faded from modern memory. By the twentieth century in the West, labour and education reforms meant that children no longer had to work and were transformed from an economic asset into an emotional one, prized for the love and affection they brought into the family.[41] As historian Viviana Zelizer puts it: [I]n strict economic terms, children today are worthless to their parents. They are also expensive . . . In return for such expenses a child is expected to provide love, smiles, and emotional satisfaction, but no money or labor.'[42] This may place different burdens on children, but the shift in their financial worth and value, and the greater emphasis on love and mutual affection, should surely be seen as progress. Worldwide, this change has been slower to come, partly because of broader economic changes, but also because of different views of adult–child relationships and their respective roles and responsibilities within the family; children remain, in many places, important financial and social contributors to their families. Even outside the West, however, ideas about children's roles are changing. Agencies such as the United Nations have pushed for universal primary schooling for children so that work does not have to feature so strongly in their childhoods.

Most significantly of all, the 1970s saw a rethinking of the political and civic role of children and a critical re-examination of their particular needs, vulnerabilities and capacities: ideas that coalesced in the United Nations Convention on the Rights of the Child (UNCRC). The UNCRC is made up of fifty-four legally binding articles covering, among other things, children's right to healthcare, education, nationality and legal representation and, as documented in Chapter 5, the right to play. It also emphasizes the *participation* rights of children to take part in decisions made on their behalf and to have their opinion listened to. This has been contentious in some quarters because such rights represent a profound shift in relationships between adults and children, and challenge conceptualizations of children as unknowing and passive, needing adults (especially their parents) to act in their best interests. By 2018 the USA was one of only two countries (the other being South Sudan) not to have ratified the UNCRC because it remains concerned over possible infringements of state sovereignty and the perceived threat to family and parental rights it posed. The influence of the Christian Right, which sees the family in hierarchical terms that preclude equality between adults and children, has meant that the UNCRC is unlikely to be ratified soon in the USA.

The UK has ratified the UNCRC, but not without controversy, especially concerning children's participatory rights. The Children Act 1989 was the first piece of legislation brought in by the UK government in response to the UNCRC and emphasized the importance of listening to children and, for the first time in the history of the British legal system, ruled that courts should consider the wishes and feelings of the children concerned, dependent on their age and understanding. Children were allowed, by the courts and within the welfare system, to voice opinions on matters such as where they would prefer to live after a parental divorce, or whether they wished to remain at home or go into care if there were concerns about child protection.

Responses to the idea that children should have a voice and participate in decisions made about them were mixed.

Some child advocacy groups were very enthusiastic about the level of autonomy the legislation sought to offer children. Others disliked the participatory rights which they saw as having the potential to undermine parental responsibility and adult power. Some commentators called it a 'Brat's Charter' when it was first made law and warned of children divorcing their parents because they didn't have enough pocket money or demanding the right to do whatever they wanted to.[43] While this never happened, there remains a cultural battle over children's rights to participation and over children's autonomy and their role in families and in wider society. There is still much debate over whether children can truly be expected to know what is in their best interests and whether and when their parents, or other adults, must sometimes intervene, either for the good of the child, or for the family.

This debate is not limited to the West and there have been many criticisms that children's rights are applicable only to Western elites. The UNCRC is based on the notion that each child is an individual who has the right to liberty, to shelter and to freedom of expression, yet in many places children are not seen as autonomous individuals but as parents' dependants and sometimes even their property. In many countries children are viewed as being embedded in a web of relationships which come with duties, obligations and sometimes the expectation of sacrifice on behalf of the family. Anthropologist Rachel Burr has claimed that, in Vietnam and other Asian societies, 'children are most likely to be valued as part of the family collective and not as autonomous individuals holding independent positions in society',[44] while in his work on how the UNCRC was understood and introduced in Japan, another anthropologist, Roger Goodman, has argued that when the UNCRC was introduced into Japan, 'a whole new vocabulary had to be developed to explain it, as did the idea of the individual who could be endowed with such rights. Even today, individualism has strongly negative connections in Japan and is frequently associated with western concepts of selfishness.'[45] Sociologist Afua Twum-Danso Imoh, who has conducted research on views of the UNCRC in her home country of Ghana, found that many parents were vocal in their rejection of the Convention and the vision of adult–child relations it presented. They believed that children's rights would lead to division within families, cause children to become selfish and to neglect their parents and their responsibilities and reciprocal obligations. They told her 'we don't want Western children in Ghana'.[46]

In almost every cultural and geographical context, childhood today is undoubtedly very different from the past: each generation of parents raises their children differently and children's experiences of childhood are constantly changing and evolving. What is missing from many of these discussions are children's own views of their childhood and this is now emerging as a new area of research for scholars in Childhood Studies. While still relatively new, one of the central themes emerging from these studies is that children do not see their childhood in terms of crisis, misery or doom. Educationalist Kate Adams, for example, has undertaken several studies of children's own views of childhood, and when interviewing fifty-six children aged between 7 and 11 in an economically deprived town in the East Midlands found that all but one saw being a child as a positive thing.[47] When asked to give a single adjective to describe childhood, children replied with words such as 'fun', 'cool', 'exciting', 'nice', 'easy', 'good', 'interesting', 'happy', 'great', 'excellent' and 'relaxing'; the only negative word was 'annoying'. This is just one small study (albeit one of the very few done on children's views of childhood) and its findings may not hold true for all children, but it does suggest that the crisis may be in parents' and adults' views of childhood rather than in children's own perceptions. Of course, children have nothing with which to compare their own childhood – what they experience is their own reality and they don't have the rosy glow of nostalgia that their parents might have when looking back.

Looking at individual children's lives, and those of their families, in more depth also adds further weight to the argument that the crisis in childhood is not all that it seems. Sociologist Allison Pugh, in her 2009 study of low-income, African American and Latino parents who live in a dangerous US neighbourhood, gives an excellent example of how to understand the crisis differently.[48] The children and families she worked with faced multiple daily physical hazards in their neighbourhood, ranging from fast-moving traffic, drug-dealing and associated gun crime, gangs and pimps, to fly-tipping and discarded needles. They were poor, socially excluded, some of their children had put on weight and they rarely played outside, although they did have large TVs, computer games and much modern gadgetry. Their parents had been criticized and condemned as contributing to their children's obesity, low educational achievement and ill health.

These children were perceived as being in crisis and their mothers and fathers demonized as inadequate and neglectful. And yet, as Pugh argues, these parents' choices were not the result of ignorance or neglect, and the children were still given the best possible childhoods their parents could achieve. Given the context the children lived in, and the dangers they faced, providing items like a Game Boy™ or PlayStation™ that would keep children happily entertained and, most importantly, safe at home was an act of love and care and the best possible form of parenting in the circumstances. Rather being symptomatic of childhood in crisis, this form of parenting was a form of love and protection.

Despite all the difficulties and fears, the idea of childhood as a time of freedom, as well as a period of unalloyed joy, continues to beguile. One possible reason for this is that not only is it what most people want for their own children, but it also speaks to adults' needs and desires and imbues their own identities with a sense of meaning. A belief in childhood innocence and happiness can act as a way of reconnecting with some of the joy of childhood which seems increasingly hard to find in an ever-busier, more commercialized world. By celebrating and protecting children's happiness, adults can recapture some of their own childhood delight and momentarily revisit the lost Eden of childhood. This may be illusory, of course, and it may be impossible to create a happy childhood for one's own children, but the ideal remains strong and says as much about how adults think of themselves as it does about the true state of children's happiness. It has been argued, by Frank Furedi and others, that there is no crisis in childhood, but there is a crisis in adulthood, with adults feeling under threat and out of control and having lost confidence in their abilities as parents. Furedi has characterized contemporary adult –child relationships as *paranoid parenting*, arguing that the rise in the numbers of 'experts' in parenting and child-rearing has undermined parents' confidence and led to a pervasive paranoia about childhood. The fear of judgement and getting it wrong has meant that contemporary parenting is now saturated by anxiety. Parents have been constantly told that child-rearing is their responsibility and their burden and that it is up to them to keep their children healthy, happy, academically successful or the right weight, and if they do not, or they struggle, there are experts on hand at every turn to show them what they have done wrong and to judge them for failing.

One of the primary concerns is the perceived threat to child safety and the attempts to eliminate every possible risk from a child's life, even though this is not possible or indeed desirable. As sociologist Mary Jane Kehily has put it: 'An obvious manifestation of paranoid parenting can be seen in parents' approach to child safety, a matter that has escalated from a concern to a national obsession.'[49] Adults have become more frightened and anxious about their children and they project these fears onto them, in a way that has had a detrimental impact on everyone's lives and freedoms. To reiterate the point made in Chapter 5, Tim Gill, former director of the UK Children's Play Council (now Play England) has argued: 'Over the past thirty years, activities that previous generations of children have enjoyed without a second thought have been relabelled as troubling or dangerous and the adults who permit them branded as irresponsible. Childhood is being undermined by adults' increasing aversion to risk and by the intrusion of that fear into every aspect of their lives. The knock-on effect is extremely serious.'[50] While many of the problems and risks facing children may come from social inequality or poor government policy, it is also paranoid parenting, stoked by media fears, that has made childhood today seem worse than it was in the past.

The question of whether things were better in the past, or whether or not children were happier, is an impossible one to answer. There is evidence for all sorts of positions and it depends very much on what aspects of children's lives you look at. Children are undoubtedly better off materially (although many still live in relative poverty), they are less afflicted by disease and are more likely to survive childhood. Children have legal protections and a very different role in society and the family and there is a great interest and concern over their well-being. Yet there are also greater fears about their lives and experiences and greater pressures on parents to protect them. Childhood remains an emotive topic but by looking at a wide variety of evidence it becomes easier to see a middle way. Childhood has changed greatly in the last forty years, but then it also changed in the forty years before that and the forty before that. We can lament this, but most children don't, and perhaps the only certainty is that today's children will grow up and raise their own children in the ways they feel are best, but which would alarm today's parents in certain aspects.

CONCLUSION

When it comes to raising children there has been a long-term power struggle between experts and parents over who really knows children and what is best for them. It is not surprising that parents simultaneously baulk at some of the pronouncements (and the idea that parenthood is too important and difficult a job to be left to parents alone) while being desperate for advice and guidance on 'getting it right'. Similarly, those who devote their lives to caring for or researching children's lives and experiences can find it very frustrating to have their endeavours ignored or overridden by parental views claimed as 'common sense.'

This book was not written as a practical guide for parents on how to raise happy, healthy, well-behaved, confident children. Indeed, recent research has suggested that some parenting manuals may do more harm than good and the more self-help and baby books that parents (and mothers in particular) read, the lower their well-being and the higher their stress levels. There is no wish or intention to add to that pressure here.[1] Instead, the book is designed to provide some reassurance – if the experts cannot agree and everything is up for debate, then confusion and worry are understandable. Making sense of the many competing and sometimes contradictory claims is not easy, especially when raising children has become mired in anxiety and even paranoia for today's parents. This is partly because the stakes are so high. In a post-Freudian world it is taken as a universal truth that the seeds of future success or failure, happiness or unhappiness, are sown in childhood. Furthermore, we live in an information age – everything we need (or don't need) to know is available after a few clicks, and with so much research and information out there it seems counter-intuitive that those working with children, either as parents or practitioners, still don't know the answers to the fundamental question of how best to raise children. The subtitle of this book is 'What the evidence really tells us' and after reading it might be possible to conclude that the 'evidence' can tell us anything we want to hear.

Yet, as we have consistently argued throughout this book, everyday realities are not so black and white. Ideas such as success and failure, or even happiness and unhappiness, are slippery concepts. Not all parents across the world even think that these are important: the idea that a child should be happy would be met with disbelief in some cultures, and indeed in our own past it was much more important that a child was good (meaning well-behaved, meek, probably God-fearing and utterly obedient towards their parents) than happy. Being successful or confident are even more problematic – who defines success and what does it mean? Money? Sporting prowess? A loving family? And confidence, as we have seen, is not high on the list of priorities in places which emphasize obedience, filial obligations and responsibility to other family members, rather than individualism.

Today, resilience has become a buzzword in many schools, but again it can seem an unachievable goal and yet another way of setting parents or teachers up to fail. On the one hand, both parents and teachers must (ideally) protect and nurture their children, keeping them safe from harm and yet also expose them (in some degree) to risk, in order to make sure they develop resilience and know how to cope with failure as well as success. Teachers and other professionals must support parents, while also taking over some aspects of parenting such as ensuring children eat healthily and get along with their peers, as well as teaching citizenship – but at the same time they must not encroach too far on family life – another almost impossible balancing act.

Children are not simply passive subjects in all these processes and relationships and it is important to emphasize children's own strengths – their 'agency', in sociological terms. Once children were seen as blank slates, waiting to take on the imprint of their parents; later they were viewed as actively developing but incompetent beings; and it is only recently that research has started to take children's view and experiences seriously. This work, much of which has coalesced into the new field of Childhood Studies within universities, has argued that parenting is not a one-way process and that children influence their parents – and the ways they parent – as much as the other way around. This is one reason why we have placed such emphasis on children's voices in this book. Not only do they bring in another perspective, but they also show that children are active partners and that parenting is a two-way relationship rather than a unidirectional imposition. Such ideas can be challenging and difficult for adults, but ultimately they can be seen as positive and relieve some of the pressure from parents. Children can and do adapt, they can challenge and evade what their parents tell them, and while such insubordination can be infuriating on a day-to-day level, it also shows that children are aware of their own agency, and can be resilient and autonomous.

Contemporary parenting is sometimes seen as a battleground fought over by different groups – parents, children, professionals or researchers – over how to do it best and what the consequences of not doing it right might be. And yet within this struggle over what skills, beliefs behaviours etc. are needed to raise children, the less tangible aspects of parenting and caring for children are overlooked – the joy, the love and the satisfaction that children bring to their parents and other adults and vice versa. It is an area which is very rarely mentioned in parenting research or books on parenting manuals and yet it is central to parents' (and children's) lives. So often happy families and communities are presented as impossibilities, or as part of a sentimentalized vision of the past, and yet many people still gain the greatest pleasure, contentment and happiness within their family and in raising their children or working with them in other contexts. Parenting (whoever does it) can be hard work: frustrating, boring and repetitive at times and one's best efforts can be met with ingratitude and defiance. Yet it can also bring moments of transcendental happiness and insight. Parenting can sometimes seem like an impossible juggling act, but ultimately the overwhelming majority of parents do their very best, make mistakes sometimes, but raise children who, as discussed in the chapter on resilience, 'work well, play well, love well, and expect well'.

Notes

INTRODUCTION

1. Drawing upon interviews with parents of children with differences including dwarfism, autism, schizophrenia and struggles with gender identity, Solomon discusses the many challenges that parents face and also reflects on his own experience as a gay parent. Solomon, A. (2012) *Far From the Tree. Parents, children and the search for identity*. London: Chatto and Windus, p. 8.

2. Cunningham, H. (1991) *Children of the Poor. Representations of childhood since the seventeenth century*. Oxford: Blackwell.

3. Plomin, R., DeFries, J. C., McClearn, G. E. and Rutter, M. (1997) *Behavioral Genetics*, 3rd edn. New York: W. H. Freeman.

4. For an excellent, contemporary account of different parenting cultures, see the contributors to Lee, E., Bristow, J., Faircloth, C., and Macvarish, J. (eds) (2014) *Parenting Culture Studies*. Basingstoke: Palgrave Macmillan.

5. Caroline Gatrell writes that her 'book is about the sociology of parenthood, but the focus is on mothers because when writers and governments talk with authority about "parenting" they are by implication (especially in relation to very young children) talking about mothers'. Gatrell, C. (2005). *Hard Labour: the sociology of parenting*. Maidenhead: Open University Press, p. 3.

6. Churchill, H. (2011) *Parental Rights and Responsibilities*. Bristol University: Policy Press.

7. Alanen, L. and Mayall, B. (2001) *Conceptualizing Child–Adult Relationships*. London: Routledge.

CHAPTER 1: HOW SHOULD BABIES BE LOOKED AFTER?

1. Meyer-Rochow, V. B. (2009) 'Food taboos: their origins and purposes'. *Journal of Ethnobiology and Ethnomedicine*, 5: 18. Available at <https://ethnobiomed.biomedcentral.com/articles/10.1186/1746-4269-5-18>.

2. *Newsweek* (2015) 'How stress can affect you and your unborn baby', 22 March 2015. Available at <http://europe.newsweek.com/how-calm-your-anxiety-during-pregnancy-315242?rm=eu> (accessed 31 July 2017)

3. Lee, E. (2014) 'Policing pregnancy: the pregnant woman who drinks', in E. Lee, J. Bristow, C. Faircloth and J. Macvarish (eds) *Parenting Culture Studies*. Basingstoke: Palgrave Macmillan.

4. Jones, K. L, Smith, D. W. (1973) 'Recognition of the fetal alcohol syndrome in early infancy'. *The Lancet*, 302: 7836, 999–1001.

5. For a critical analysis of the 'discovery' of FAS and the methods used to detect it, see Armstrong, E. M. (1998) 'Diagnosing moral disorder: The discovery and evolution of Fetal Alcohol Syndrome'. *Social Science and Medicine*, 47: 12, 2025–42.

6. See Armstrong, 1998; Lee, 2014.

7. Sayal, K., Draper, E., Fraser, R., Barrow, M., Davey Smith, G. and Gray, R. (2013) 'Light drinking in pregnancy and mid-childhood mental health and learning outcomes'. *Archives of Diseases in Childhood*, 98: 2, 2 107–11.

8. Mamluk, L. et al. (2017) 'Low alcohol consumption and pregnancy and childhood outcomes: time to change guidelines indicating apparently "safe" levels of alcohol during pregnancy? A systematic review and meta-analyses'. BMJOpen. Available at <http://bmjopen.bmj.com/content/7/7/e015410> (accessed 25 September 2017).

9. Niclasen, J., Andersen, A-M. N., Teasdale, T. W. and Strandberg-Larsen, K. (2014) 'Prenatal exposure to alcohol, and gender differences on child mental health at age seven years'. *Journal of Epidemiology and Community Health*, 68: 3, 224–32.

10. It is notoriously difficult to research the impact of drinking during pregnancy. The stigma attached to it means that many women are reluctant to admit to health professionals or researchers that they drank anything at all during pregnancy, or else they are asked to remember a year or two later how much they drunk when pregnant, which they may not remember accurately. One 2017 study from the Norwegian Institute of Public Health suggested that British women were the most likely to drink, with 28.5 per cent drinking during pregnancy, compared with only 4.1 per cent of Norwegians. However, 'drinking' covers a multitude of behaviours and the researchers claimed that one unit of alcohol a month while pregnant

constituted drinking – an amount which is still within UK government guidelines. Perhaps more cynically one might ask whether Norwegian women were less likely to tell the truth than British women or, given the price of alcohol in Norway, less able to afford it. See Mårdby, A-C., Lupattelli, A. and Hensing, G. (2017) 'Consumption of alcohol during pregnancy –A multinational European study'. *Women and Birth: Journal of the Australian College of Midwives*, 30: 4, 207–13.

11. Sayal, K., Heron, J., Golding, J. and Emond, A. (2007) 'Prenatal alcohol exposure and gender differences in childhood mental health problems: A longitudinal population-based study'. *Pediatrics*, 119: 2, 426–34.

12. Meehan, C. L. and Crittenham, A. N. (eds) (2016) *Childhood: Origins, evolution and implications*. Albuquerque: University of New Mexico Press.

13. Fildes, V., Marks, L. and Marland, H. (2013) *Women and Children First: International maternal and infant welfare, 1870 –1945*. London: Routledge.

14. Aitkins, K. (2006) *A Pharmacy of Her Own: Victorian women and the figure of the opiate*. PhD Dissertation, Tufts University, Medford, MA.

15. Behrmann, B. (2003) 'A reclamation of childbirth'. *The Journal of Perinatal Education*, 12:3, vi–x.

16. Behrmann, 2003, p. 4.

17. McKenzie-Mohr, S. and Lafrance, M. (2014) *Women Voicing Resistance: Discursive and narrative explorations*. London: Routledge.

18. In August 2017, the president of the UK's College of Midwives, Professor Cathy Warwick, announced the end of the College's 'campaign for normal birth', claiming it led many women to feel like failures if they did not have a vaginal birth without intervention. Furthermore, only four out of ten women in the UK have a delivery without Caesarean, induction, instruments or epidural, making it more normal to do so than not. 'Midwives back down on natural childbirth', *The Times*, 12 August 2017, p. 1.

19. See, for instance, Bowlby, J. (1982) *Attachment*. New York: Basic Books; Mercer, J. (2011) 'Attachment theory and its vicissitudes: toward an updated theory'. *Theory and Psychology*, 21: 1, 25–45; Rutter, M. (1995) 'Clinical implications of attachment concepts: retrospect and prospect'. *Journal of Child Psychiatry and Psychology*, 36: 4, 549–71; Waters, E. and Cummings, E. M. (2000) 'A secure case from which to explore close relationships'. *Child Development*, 71: 1, 164–72.

20. Birns, B. (1999) 'Attachment theory revisited: challenging conceptual and methodological sacred cows'. *Feminism and Psychology*, 9: 1, 10–21.

21. NHS England (2014) *2014–15 National Health Visiting Core Service Specification*. Available at < https://www.england.nhs.uk/wp-content/uploads/2014/03/hv-serv-spec.pdf > (accessed 31 January 2018), p. 9.

22. Milford, R. and Oates, J. (2009). 'Universal screening and early intervention for maternal mental health and attachment difficulties'. *Community Practitioner*, 82: 8, 30–33.

23. Bowlby did acknowledge that 'mother' could mean more than the woman who gave birth and might be any maternal figure to whom the child became attached.

24. Tizard, B., and Rees, J. (1975) 'The effect of early institutional rearing on the behavior problems and affectional relationships of four-year-old children'. *Journal of Child Psychology and Psychiatry*, 16: 1, 61–73.

25. LeVine, R. and LeVine, S. (2016) *Do Parents Matter? Why Japanese babies sleep soundly, Mexican siblings don't fight, and American families should just relax*. New York: Public Affairs, Perseus Books.

26. Hollway, W. (2015) *Knowing Mother: Researching maternal identity change*. Basingstoke: Palgrave Macmillan.

27. Birns, 1999.

28. Birns, 1999.

29. Lamb, M. E. (2010) *The Role of the Father in Child Development*. Chichester: John Wiley.

30. Hewlett, B. (1991) *Intimate Fathers: The nature and context of Aka pygmy paternal infant care*. Ann Arbor: University of Michigan Press.

31. Working Families/Brighter Horizons (2017) *The Modern Families Index*. London: Working Families/Brighter Horizons. Available at <https://www.workingfamilies.org.uk/wp-content/uploads/2017/01/Modern-Families-Index_Full-Report.pdf> (accessed 31 July 2017).

32. LeVine and LeVine, 2016.

33. Heather Montgomery's grandmother was told this after the birth of her son (Heather's father) in 1937.

34. Brown, A. (2016). *Breastfeeding Uncovered: Who really decides how we feed our babies?* London: Pinter and Martin Ltd.

35. Brown, 2016.

36. Levenstein, H. (1983) '"Best for Babies" or "Preventable Infanticide"? The controversy over artificial feeding of infants in America, 1880–1920'. *Journal of American History*, 70: 1, 75–94.

37. Hardyment, C. (2007) *Dream Babies: Childcare advice from John Locke to Gina Ford*. London: Francis Lincoln.

38. Quoted in Hardyment, 2007, p. 247.

39. These concerns led, in 1977, to a boycott being launched against Nestlé in protest at its supposedly aggressive marketing of infant formula in parts of Africa and Asia.

40. Editorial (2016) 'Breastfeeding: achieving the new normal'. *The Lancet*, 387: 10017, 404.

41. Wolf, J. H. (2003) 'Low breastfeeding rates and public health in the United States'. *American Journal of Public Health*, 93: 12, 2000–10; Leung A. K., Sauve, R. S. (2005) 'Breast is best for babies'. *Journal of the National Medical Association*, 97: 7, 1010–19.

42. Hendrick, H. (2016) *Narcissistic Parenting in an Insecure World*. Bristol University: Policy Press.

43. Hendrick, 2016.

44. Rainbow Day Nursery, in Cambridge, UK, for example, encourages nursery staff to wear slings and baby carriers for those children whose parents practise attachment parenting. See *The Times*, 9 October, 2017.

CHAPTER 2: WHAT ARE THE INFLUENCES ON BECOMING A PARENT?

1. A growing body of research continues to examine emotional responses, mood changes and rates of depression amongst pregnant women and following birth. See Borthwick, R., Macleod, A., Stanley, N. (2004). *Antenatal Depression: developing an effective and co-ordinated service response*. Available at <www.positivelypregnant.org> (accessed August 2017); Crawley R., A, Dennison, K., Carter, C. (2003) 'Cognition in pregnancy and the first year post-partum', *Psychology and Psychotherapy: Theory, research and practice*. 76: 1, 69–84; Buckwalter, J. G., Stanczyk, F. Z., McCleary, C. A., et al. (1999) 'Pregnancy, the post-partum, and steroid hormones: effects on cognition and mood'. *Psychoneuroendocrinology* 24: 1, 69–84.

2. Many women report memory fog and forgetfulness during pregnancy and in the early stages following birth. A proportion of women during pregnancy and following birth also describe changes in mood. Many of these symptoms are a focus of research. For a more detailed discussion see Crawley, R. A., Dennison, K. and Carter, C. (2003) 'Cognition in pregnancy and the first year post-partum'. *Psychology and Psychotherapy: Theory, research and practice*, 76: 1, 69–84; Crawley, R., Grant, S. and Hinshaw, K. (2008) 'Cognitive changes in pregnancy: mild decline or societal stereotype?' *Applied Cognitive Psychology*, 22: 8, 1142–62 ; Oatridge, A., Holdcroft, A., Saeed, N., et al. (2002) 'Change in brain size during and after pregnancy: study in healthy women and women with pre-eclampsia',

American Journal of Neuroradiology, 23: 1, 19–26; Pilyoung, K., Leckman, J. F., Mayes, L.C., et al. (2010) 'The plasticity of human maternal brain: longitudinal changes in brain anatomy during the early postpartum period'. *Behavioral Neuroscience* 124: 5, 695–700.

3. Oatridge, Holdcroft, Saeed, et al., 2002.

4. Recent research indicates that pregnancy involves hormone surges and biological adaptations. However, the effects of pregnancy on the human brain are still unknown. One prospective ('pre' and 'post' pregnancy) study involved first-time mothers and fathers and control groups, and indicated that pregnancy renders substantial changes in brain structure, primarily reductions in grey matter (GM) volume in regions of the brain identified as being for social cognition. The GM volume changes in pregnancy predicted measures of maternal attachment following birth, suggestive of an adaptive process serving the transition into motherhood. Another follow-up session showed that the GM reductions endured for at least two years post-pregnancy. Hoekzema, E., Barber-Miller, E., Pozzobon, C., Picado, M., Lucco, F., García-García, D., Soliva, J. C., Tobeña, A., Desco, M., Crone, E. A., Ballesteros, A., Carmona, S. and Vilarroya, O. (2017) 'Pregnancy leads to long-lasting changes in human brain structure'. *Nature Neuroscience*, 20: 2, 287–96.

5. Hoekzema et al., 2017.

6. Bartels, A. and Zeki, S. (2004) 'The neural correlates of maternal and romantic love'. *Neuroimage*, 21: 3, 1155–66.

7. LaFrance, A. (2015) 'What happens to a woman's brain when she becomes a mother?' Available at <http://www.theatlantic.com/health/archive/2015/01/what-happens-to-a-womans-brain-when-she-becomes-a-mother/384179/> (accessed 2 July 2017).

8. Feldman, R., Monakhov, M., Pratt, M. and Ebstein, R. P. (2016) 'Oxytocin pathway genes; Evolutionary ancient system impacting on human affiliation, sociality, and psychopathology'. *Biological Psychiatry*, 79: 3, 174–84.

9. Kim, P. (2016) 'Human maternal brain plasticity: adaptation to parenting'. *New Directions for Child and Adolescent Development*, 153, 47–58.

10. Abraham, E., Hendler, T., Shapira-Lichter, I., Kanat-Maymon, Y., Zagoory-Sharon, O., Feldman, R. (2014) 'Father's brain is sensitive to childcare experiences'. *Proceedings of the National Academy of Sciences of the United States of America*, 111: 27, 9792–7.

11. Swain, J. (2008) 'Baby stimuli and the parent brain: functional neuroimaging of the neural substrates of parent-infant attachment'. *Psychiatry*, 5: 8, 28–36.

12. Abraham, Hendler, Shapira-Lichter, Kanat-Maymon, Zagoory-Sharon and Feldman, 2014.

13. A number of researchers debate the extent to which neuro-biology can provide an explanation as to the significance of the first five years in a child's brain development and its links to intellectual development. See Bruer, J. T., (1999) *The Myth of the First Three Years, a new understanding of early brain development and lifelong learning.* New York: Free Press; Kagan, J. (1998) 'The allure of infant determinism', in J. Kagan (ed.) *Three Seductive Ideas.* Harvard, MA: Harvard University Press, pp. 83–151; Macvarish, J., Lee, E. and Lowe, P. (2014) 'The "first three years" movement and the infant brain: A review of critiques'. *Sociology Compass*, 8:6, 792–804.

14. LeVine, R., Dixon, S., LeVine, S., Richman, A., Leiderman, P. H., Keefer, C. and Brazelton, Y. B. (2005) *Childcare and Culture: Lessons from Africa.* Cambridge. Cambridge University Press.

15. Scheper-Hughes, N. (1992) *Death Without Weeping: The violence of everyday life in Brazil.* Berkeley: University of California Press.

16. LeVine et al., 2005.

17. Furedi, F. (2001) *Paranoid Parenting.* London: Allen Lane.

18. Hollway, W. (2015) *Knowing Mother: Researching maternal identity change.* Basingstoke: Palgrave Macmillan.

19. Belsky, J., Conger, R. and Capaldi, D. M. (2009) 'The intergenerational transmission of parenting: introduction to the special section'. *Developmental Psychology*, 45:5, 1201–04.

20. Roskam, I. (2013) 'The transmission of parenting behaviour within the family: An empirical study across three generations'. *Psychologica Belgica*, 53: 3, 49–64.

21. Solomon, A. (2013). *Far From the Tree. Parents, children and the search for identity.* London: Chatto and Windus.

22. James, O. (2001) *They F*** You Up: How to Survive Family Life.* London: Random House.

23. James, O. (2010) *How Not To F*** Them Up.* London: Random House.

24. Michael Rutter talking about his professional career on the Life Scientific for BBC Radio 4. http://www.bbc.co.uk/programmes/b04581j9

25. Pinker, S. (2002) *The Blank Slate. The modern denial of human nature.* London: Penguin Books, p. 399.

26. Murphy, L and Moriarty, A. (1976) *Vulnerability, coping and growth.* New Haven, CT: Yale University Press.

27. Freud, S. (2002) *The Psychopathology of Everyday Life*, translated by Anthea Bell. London: Penguin Books (first published in German in 1901 and in *Gesammelte Werke* in 1941).

28. Gerhardt, S. (2004) *Why Love Matters: how affection shapes a baby's brain*, Abingdon: Routledge.

29. Brain plasticity is a term used by neuroscientists and researchers to refer to the human brain's ability to change. Brain plasticity science is the study of these physical changes. Grey matter (GM) within the brain, for instance, can shrink or thicken. Neural connections can be established and weakened or severed. Changes in the brain manifest as changes in human cognitive processes (including memory, language and thought) and behaviour.

30. Feldman, R. (2015) 'The adaptive human parental brain: implications for children's social development'. *Trends in Neurosciences*, 38: 6, 387–99.

31. Having a child is increasingly financially demanding. Ongoing studies conducted by the UK's Centre for Economics and Business Research indicate that the cost of raising a child to the age of 21 has risen from £222,458 in 2016 to £227,266 in 2017 which is more than the cost of an average semi-detached house in the UK. On average parents will spend more than £70,000 for babysitting and childcare and incur £74,000 education-related expenses for things including school uniforms, school lunches, textbooks and trips. These figures are tallied for a child attending a state school. Parents who opt to send their child to a private school can expect to spend approximately £373,000. Available at <https://cebr.com/?s=cost+of+raising+a+child> (accessed August 2017).

32. See <http://www.ons.gov.uk/peoplepopulationandcommunity/births deathsandmarriages/families/bulletins/familiesandhouseholds/2015-01-28#lone-parents> (accessed June 2017).

33. See <http://www.oneplusone.org.uk/content_topic/day-to-day-life/working-mothers/ (accessed May 2017).

34. A number of media straplines refer to recent research exploring the impact of working parents, for example from the *Daily Mail*, 'Working mothers risk damaging their child's prospects'. Available at <http://www.dailymail.co.uk/news/article-30342/Working-mothers-risk-damaging-childs-prospects.html> (accessed June 2017); or from the *Daily Telegraph*, 'Working mums listen up! We're in danger of getting our kids kicked out of class'. Available at <http://www.telegraph.co.uk/women/mother-tongue/11340513/Working-mums-Were-in-danger-of-getting-our-kids-excluded.html> (accessed July 2017).

35. Ermisch, J. and Francesconi, M. (2001) 'The effect of parents' employment on outcomes for children'. York: Joseph Rowntree Foundation. Available at <https://www.jrf.org.uk/report/effect-parents-employment-outcomes-children > (accessed 21 September 2017).

36. The BHPS began in 1991 and followed the same representative sample of individuals until 2011. The study included interviews with every adult member of the sampled households. The first panel consisted of 5,500 households and 10,300 individuals drawn from 250 areas of Great Britain. Additional samples of 1,500 households each in Scotland and Wales were added to the main sample in 1999, and in 2001 a sample of 2,000 households was added from Northern Ireland. Ermisch and Francesconi drew upon the BHPS to compare differences in parental employment patterns and outcomes between 516 pairs of siblings born in the UK during the 1970s.

37. Brooks-Gunn, J., Han, W., Waldfogel, J. (2010) 'First-year maternal employment and child development in the first 7 years'. *Child Development*, 75: 2, 7–9.

38. Using data from the Australian Bureau of Statistics Time Use Survey (1997), Lyn Craig conducted an in-depth study (over 4,000 randomly selected households) to compare the time allocation of employed fathers, employed mothers and mothers who are not in the labour force. The research shows how parents maintained their time commitments to both work and childcare. The strategies identified were (1) reducing the time devoted to other activities (principally sleep, leisure, bathing, dressing, grooming, eating); (2) rescheduling activities (from weekends to weekdays or changing the time of day at which particular activities are undertaken). Available at <https://www.sprc.unsw.edu.au/media/SPRCFile/DP136.pdf > (accessed June 2017).

39. Craig, L. (2007) *Contemporary Motherhood. The impact of children on adult time*. Abingdon: Ashgate.

40. Cummings, E. M. and Davies, P. T. (1994) 'Maternal depression and child development'. *Journal of Child Psychology and Psychiatry*, 35: 1, 73–112; Winsler, A. and Wallace G. L. (2002) 'Behavior problems and social skills in preschool children: parent–teacher agreement and relations with classroom observations'. *Early Education and Development*, 13: 1, 41–58.

41. For a more detailed discussion of research exploring the links between parental well-being and children's social-emotional development, see Crnic, K.A. and Low, C. (2002) 'Everyday stresses and parenting', in M.H. Bornstein (ed.), *Handbook in parenting. Practical issues in parenting*, Vol. 5, Hove, UK: Psychology Press; Dix, T. and Meunier, L. N. (2009) 'Depressive symptoms and parenting competence: an analysis of 13 regulatory processes'. *Developmental Review*, 29: 1, 45–68; Goodman, J. H. (2004) 'Paternal postpartum depression, its relationship to maternal postpartum

depression: and implications for family health'. *Journal of Advanced Nursing*, 45: 1, 26–35; Gross, H. E., Shaw, D. S., Moilanen, K. L., Dishion, T. J., and Wilson M. N. (2008) 'Reciprocal models of child behavior and depressive symptoms in mothers and fathers in a sample of children at risk for early conduct problems'. *Journal of Family Psychology*, 22: 5, 742–75; Jarvis P. A., Creasey, G. L. (1991) 'Parental stress, coping, and attachment in families with an 18-month-old infant'. *Infant Behavior and Development*, 14: 4, 383–95.

42. Talge, N. M., Neal, C. and Glover, V. (2007) 'Antenatal maternal stress and long-term effects on child neurodevelopment: how and why?' *Journal of Child Psychology and Psychiatry*, 48: 3–4, 245–61.

43. O'Donnell, K., O'Connor, T. G. and Glover, V. (2009) 'Prenatal development and neurodevelopment of the child: Focus on the HPA axis and the role of the placenta'. *Developmental Neuroscience*, 31, 285–92.

CHAPTER 3: WHAT IS 'FAMILY' AND ARE SOME FAMILIES BETTER THAN OTHERS?

1. Giddens, A. (1998) *Sociology*. Cambridge: Polity Press, p. 140.

2. Piaget, J. (1928) *Judgment and Reasoning in the Child*. London: Kegan Paul.

3. Roe, A., Bridges, L., Dunn, J. and O'Connor, T. G. (2006) 'Young children's representations of their families: A longitudinal follow-up study of family drawings by children living in different family settings'. *International Journal of Behavioural Development*, 30: 6, 529–36.

4. Mason, J. and Tipper, B. (2008) 'Being related: how children define and create kinship'. *Childhood*, 15: 4, 441–60.

5. Smart, C., Neale, B. and Wade, A. (2001) *The Changing Experience of Childhood. Families and divorce*. Cambridge: Polity Press, p. 42.

6. In 2016 the Human Fertilisation and Embryology Authority (HFEA) announced that the number of single women seeking IVF treatment has doubled since 2007. Available at <http://www.hfea.gov.uk/ > (accessed August 2017).

7. Golombok, S. (2015) *Modern Families*. Cambridge: Cambridge University Press.

8. Blake. L., Casey, P., Jadva, V. and Golombok, S. (2013) '"I was quite amazed": Donor conception and parent–child relationships from the child's perspective'. *Children and Society*, 28:6, 425–37, p. 433.

9. Blake et al., 2013, p. 426.

10. Morrow, V. (1998) *Understanding Families. Children's perspectives*. London: National Children's Bureau.

11. Morrow, 1998, pp. 24–5.

12. Morrow, 1998, p. 27.

13. Sutton, C. (2017) *What Counts as Happiness for Young People*, unpublished PhD dissertation, Open University, Milton Keynes, p. 108.

14. Punch, S. (2008) '"You can do nasty things to your brothers and sisters without a reason": siblings' backstage behaviour'. *Children and Society*, 22: 5, 333–44; see also Edwards, R., Hadfield, L., Lucey, H., Mauthner, M. (2006) *Sibling Identity and Relationships: Sisters and Brothers*. Abingdon: Routledge; McIntosh, I. and Punch, S. (2009) '"Barter", "deals", "bribes" and "threats": exploring sibling interactions'. *Childhood*, 16: 1, 49–65.

15. Weisner, T. and Gallimore, R. (1977) 'My brother's keeper: child and sibling caretaking'. *Current Anthropology*, 18: 2, 169–90.

16. Howe, N. and Recchia, H. (2014) 'Sibling relations and their impact on children's development', in *Encyclopaedia of Early Childhood Development*. Available at <http://www.child-encyclopedia.com/peer-relations/according-experts/sibling-relations-and-their-impact-childrens-development >.

17. Morrow, 1998, p. 31.

18. Punch, 2008, p. 338.

19. Morrow, V. (2009) 'Children, young people and their families in the UK', in H. Montgomery and M. Kellett (eds) *Children and Young People's Worlds: Developing Frameworks for Integrated Practice*. Bristol University: Policy Press.

20. Hylton, C. (1995) *Coping with Change. Family transitions in multi-cultural communities*. London: National Stepfamily Association.

21. Kramer L., Baron, L. A. (1995) 'Parental perceptions of children's sibling relationships'. *Family Relations: Journal of Applied Family and Child Studies*, 44: 1, 95–103.

22. Ross, H. S. (2014) 'Parent mediation of sibling conflict: addressing issues of fairness and morality', in C. Wainryb and H. Recchia (eds) *Talking about Right and Wrong: Parent–child conversations as contexts for moral development*. Cambridge: Cambridge University Press.

23. Brooks, F., Klemera, E., Offredy, M., Hill, C., Cook, L. and Clark, R. (2009) *Do Grandparents Matter? The impact of grandparenting on the well-being of children*. University of Hertfordshire: Family Matters Institute. Available at <http://www.familymatters.org.uk/researchpublications/Do_Grandparents_Matter.pdf > (accessed 10 September 2017).

24. Ross, N., Hill, M., Sweeting, H. and Cunningham-Burley, S. (2005) *Relationships Between Grandparents and Teenage Grandchildren*. Edinburgh: Centre for Research on Families and Relationships.

25. Solomon, J. C. and Marx, J. (1995) '"To grandmother's house we go": health and school adjustment of children raised solely by grandparents'. *The Gerontologist*. 35: 3, 386–94.

26. The Pew Research Centre, which maps demographic trends in America, notes that the percentage of children raised by a single parent has risen sharply from 9 per cent during the 1960s to over 25 per cent in the 2000s. The Office for National Statistics indicates that in 2014 in the UK there were 2.0 million lone parents with dependent children, rising from 1.9 million in 2004, and that 11 per cent of same-sex cohabiting couple families have dependent children. Despite these figures a stigma remains against non-traditional families. Seven out of ten Americans, for example, comment that the trend towards more single women having children can be potentially damaging for society, suggesting that children raised by single parents face more challenges than other children and children of gay and lesbian couples face many more challenges, such as social stigma and social exclusion. Available at <http://www.pewsocialtrends.org/2010/11/18/the-decline-of-marriage-and-rise-of-new-families/2/#ii-overview > (accessed May 2017).

27. For a summary and discussions of such findings, see Dunn, J., Deater-Deckard, K., Pickering, K. and O'Connor, T. G. (1998) 'Children's adjustment and prosocial behaviour in step-, single-parent, and non-stepfamily settings: Findings from a community study'. *Journal of Child Psychology and Psychiatry*, 39: 8, 1083–95; O'Connor, T. G., Dunn, J., Jenkins, J. M., Pickering, K. and Rabash, J. (2001) 'Family settings and children's adjustment: differential adjustment within and across families'. *British Journal of Psychiatry*, 179: 2, 110–15.

28. Wallerstein, J. and Blakeslee, S. (1989) *Second Chances: Men, women and children a decade after divorce*. New York: Houghton Mifflin; Wallerstein, J. and Blakeslee, S. (2002) *The Unexpected Legacy of Divorce: a 25-year landmark study*. London: Fusion.

29. Wallerstein and Blakeslee, 1989, p. 299.

30. Grady, D. (2012) 'Judith S. Wallerstein, Psychologist Who Analyzed Divorce, Dies at 90', *New York Times*, 20 June. Available at <http://www.nytimes.com/2012/06/21/health/research/judith-s-wallerstein-psychologist-who-analyzed-divorce-dies-at-90.html >.

31. Grady, 2012.

32. Smart, C. (2003) 'New perspectives on childhood and divorce'. *Childhood*, 10:2, 123–9.

33. Dunn, J. and Layard, R. (2009) *A Good Childhood. Searching for values in a competitive age.* London: Penguin.

34. Dunn, J. (2004) 'Children's relationships with their non-resident fathers'. *Journal of Child Psychology and Psychiatry*, 45:4, 659–71.

35. Maes, S., De Mol, J. and Buysse, A. (2011) 'Children's experiences and meaning construction on parental divorce: A focus group study'. *Childhood*, 19: 2, 266–79.

36. Mishcon De Reya and Place2Be (eds) (2016) *Splitting Up – A child's guide to a grown up problem.* London: Mishcon De Reya, p. 10.

37. Smart et al., 2001.

38. Jaffee, S., Moffitt, T. E., Caspi, A. and Taylor, A. (2003) 'Life with (or without) father: the benefits of living with two biological parents depend on the father's antisocial behavior'. *Child Development*, 74: 1, 109–26.

39. McLanahan, S. and Sandefur, G. (1994) *Growing Up with a Single Parent: What hurts, what helps.* Cambridge, MA: Harvard University Press.

40. Amato, P. R., and Gilbreth, J. G. (1999) 'Nonresident fathers and children's well-being: A meta-analysis'. *Journal of Marriage and the Family*, 61, 557–73.

41. Research from the Thomas Coram Research Unit at University College London has found that 87 per cent of men retain some contact with their children after a separation, although only 49 per cent claim to see them regularly at weekends or school holidays. Even so, 81 per cent of fathers reported a close relationship with their non-resident children. TCRU (2017) *Who are Fathers?* Available at <http://www.modernfatherhood.org/themes/who-are-fathers/?view=key-facts-and-figures > (accessed 31 July 2017).

42. O' Brien, M., Alldred, P. and Jones, D. (1996) 'Children's constructions of family and kinship', in J. Brannen and M. O' Brien (eds) *Children in Families: research and policy.* London: Falmer Press.

43. Jaffee et al., 2003.

44. Europa.eu (2016) *Parental Responsibility.* Available at http://europa.eu/youreurope/citizens/family/children/parental-responsibility/index_en.htm

45. Kruk, E. (2013). '"Bird's Nest" co-parenting arrangements: when parents rotate in and out of the family home', *Psychology Today*, 16 July 2013, Available at <https://www.psychologytoday.com/blog/co-parenting-after-divorce/201307/birds-nest-co-parenting-arrangements >.

46. Jaffee et al., 2003, p. 110.

47. Quoted in Faircloth, C. (2014) 'Intensive fatherhood? The (un)involved dad', in E. Lee, J. Bristow, C. Faircloth and J. Macvarish (eds) *Parenting Culture Studies*. Basingstoke: Palgrave Macmillan, p. 184.

48. Moynihan, D. (1965) *The Negro Family: The case for national action*. Washington, DC: Office of Policy Planning and Research, US Department of Labor.

49. Stack, C. (1974) *All Our Kin*. New York: Basic Books.

50. Biblarz, T. and Stacey, J. (2010) 'How does the gender of parents matter?' *Journal of Marriage and Family*. 72: 1, 3–22.

CHAPTER 4: HOW SHOULD CHILDREN BE SOCIALIZED?

1. Thornton, J., D. (2011) *Brain Culture: Neuroscience and Popular Media*. New Brunswick, NJ: Rutgers University Press.

2. Macvarish, J., Lee, E. and Lowe, P. (2014) 'The "first three years" movement and the infant brain: A review of critiques'. *Sociology Compass*, 8; 6, 792–804.

3. Available at <https://neuroethics.upenn.edu/about-us/ > (accessed June 2017).

4. Huttenlocher, P. R. and Dabholkar, A. S. (1997) 'Regional differences in synaptogenesis in human cerebral cortex'. *Journal of Comparative Neurology*, 387: 2, 167–78.

5. Goldman-Rakic, P., Bourgeois, J. and Rakic, P. (1997) 'Synaptic substrate of cognitive development: synaptogenesis in the prefrontal cortex of the nonhuman primate', in N. A. Krasnegor, G. R. Lyon, and Patricia S. Goldman-Rakic (eds) *Development of the Prefrontal Cortex: Evolution, Neurobiology, and Behaviour*. Baltimore, MD: Paul H. Brookes Publishing Co.

6. Bruer, J. (1999) 'Neural connections: some you use, some you lose'. *Phi Delta Kappan*, 81: 4, 264–77. Available at < https://www.jsmf.org/about/j/neural_connections.htm > (accessed August 2017).

7. Jha, A. (2012) 'Childhood stimulation key to brain development, study finds'. *The Guardian*, 14 October 2012. Available at <https://www.theguardian.com/science/2012/oct/14/childhood-stimulation-key-brain-development > (accessed July 2017).

8. Hackman, D. A., Betancourt, L. M., Gallop, R., Brodsky, A., Giannetta, J. M., Hurt, H. and Farah, M. J. (2014) 'Mapping the trajectory of socioeconomic disparity in working memory: Parental and neighborhood factors'. *Child Development*, 85: 4, 1433–45.

9. Chatterjee, A. and Farah, M. J. (2013) *Neuroethics in Practice: Medicine, Mind and Society*. New York: Oxford University Press.

10. Macvarish, Lee and Lowe, 2014.

11. Macvarish, Lee and Lowe, 2014.

12. Rutter, M. (2002) 'Nature, nurture, and development: from evangelism through science toward policy and practice', in *Child Development*, 73: 1, 1–21.

13. McCabe, D. P. and Castel, A. D. (2008) 'Seeing is believing: The effect of brain images on judgments of scientific reasoning'. *Cognition*, 107: 1, 343–52.

14. McCabe and Castel, 2008.

15. Weisberg, D. S., Keil, F. S., Goodstein, J., Rawson, A. and Gray, J. (2009) 'The seductive allure of neuroscience explanations'. *Journal of Cognitive Neuroscience*, 20: 3, 470–77.

16. Stokes, M. (2013) 'There's a lot more to neuroscience than media "neuromania"'. *The Guardian*, 25 June 2013. Available at <https://www.theguardian.com/science/blog/2013/jun/25/neuroscience-media-neuromania > (accessed 21September 2017).

17. 'Thrive to five' represents a branch of Kate Cairns Associates (KCA) which was established in 2011 to bring together the work of Kate Cairns and a group of experienced practitioners and trainers across the UK to provide training and resources to support practitioners working with vulnerable people.

18. See <http://www.fivetothrive.org.uk/ >.

19. The Urban Child institute, see <http://www.urbanchildinstitute.org/why-0-3/baby-and-brain > (accessed June 2017).

20. See Hendrick, H., '"It's me or the dog": me, myself and child training in an uncertain world', a revised and extended version of a seminar paper originally delivered at the Department of Social Policy, University of Edinburgh on 27 April 2012.

21. Inevitably it has been heavily criticized. Suggesting that while it might provide initial compliance, it also risks damaging the bond between parent and child, and that withdrawing love as a means of exerting control can leave children anxious and insecure in the long term.

22. Baumrind, D. (1967) 'Child care practices anteceding three patterns of preschool behaviour'. *Genetic Psychology Monographs*, 75: 1, 43–88.

23. Steinberg, L., Lamborn, S. D., Dornbusch, S. M. and Darling, N. (1992) 'Impact of parenting practices on adolescent achievement: authoritative parenting, school involvement, and encouragement to succeed'. *Child Development*, 63, 1266–81; Stassen Berger, K. (2011) *The Developing Person Through the Life Span*, 8th edn. Basingstoke: Palgrave Macmillan; Hoskins,

D. (2014) 'Consequences of parenting on adolescent outcomes', *Societies* 4, 506–31; Uji, M., Sakamoto, A., Adachi, K. and Kitamura, T. (2014) 'The impact of authoritative, authoritarian, and permissive parenting styles on children's later mental health in Japan: focusing on parent and child gender'. *Journal of Child and Family Studies*, 23, 293–302.

24. Stafford, M., Kuh, D. L., Gale, C. R., Mishra, G. and Richards, M. (2015). ' Parent–child relationships and offspring's positive mental wellbeing from adolescence to early older age'. *Journal of Positive Psychology*, 11: 3, 326–37.

25. Wintre, M. G., and Gates, S. K. E. (2006) 'Relationships with parents, spousal reciprocity, and psychological distress in middle-age adults'. *Journal of Adult Development*, 13: 2, 84–94;

26. Rodgers B. (1996) 'Reported parental behaviour and adult affective symptoms. 2. Mediating factors', *Psychological Medicine*, 26: 1, 63–77; Charles, S. T. and Carstensen, L. L.(2010) 'Social and emotional aging'. *Annual Review of Psychology*, 61, 383–409; Richards, M. and Hatch, S. L. (2011) 'A life course approach to the development of mental skills'. *The Journals of Gerontology Series B: Psychological Sciences and Social Sciences*, 66 (Supll 1): i26–i35.

27. Maccoby, E. E. and Martin, J. (1983) 'Socialization in the context of the family: parent–child interaction', in P. H. Mussen and E. M. Hetherington (eds) *Socialization, Personality, and Social Development*. New York: Wiley, pp. 1–101.

28. Steinberg, L., Lamborn, S. D., Darling, N., Mounts, N. S. and Dornbusch, S. N. (1994) 'Over-time changes in adjustment and competence among adolescents from authoritative, authoritarian, indulgent, and neglectful families'. *Child Development*, 65: 3, 754–70; Knutson, N. F., DeGarmo, D. S. and Reid, J. B. (2004) 'Social disadvantage and neglectful parenting as precursors to the development of antisocial and aggressive child behavior: Testing a theoretical model'. *Aggressive Behavior*, 30: 3, 187–205.

29. McCrae R. R., Costa Jr., P. T. (1988) 'Recalled parent–child relations and adult personality'. *Journal of Personality*, 56: 2, 417–34; Mackinnon A. J., Henderson A. S. and Andrews, G. (1991) 'The parental bonding instrument: a measure of perceived or actual parental behavior?' *Acta Psychiatrica Scandinavica*, 83: 2, 153–9.

30. Baumrind, 1967.

31. Overbeek, G. and Håkan, Stattin, N. (2007) 'Parent–child relationships, partner relationships, and emotional adjustment: a birth-to-maturity prospective study'. *Developmental Psychology*, 43:2, 429–37.

32. Harris, J. R. (1998) *The Nurture Assumption: Why children turn out the way they do*. New York: Free Press, pp. 357–8.

33. Proto-conversation is an interaction between an adult and baby that includes sounds, gestures and words that aim to convey meaning before a child learns language.

34. LeVine, R., Dixon, S., LeVine, S. (1994) *Child Care and Culture: Lessons from Africa*. Cambridge: Cambridge University Press.

35. Lancy, D. (2007) 'Accounting for variability in mother-child play'. *American Anthropologist*, 109: 2, 273–84.

36. A cradleboard is a baby carrier traditionally used by Native Americans. The baby is swaddled (wrapped tightly in a small blanket) and strapped to a flat board, usually made of wood plank which can be carried in the mother's arms, worn on her back or propped up on the ground like a baby chair.

37. Small, M. (1998) *Our Babies, Ourselves: How biology and culture shape the way we parent*. New York: Anchor Books.

38. Lythcott-Haims, J. (2015) *How to Raise an Adult: Break free of the overparenting trap and prepare your kid for success*. London: Bluebird.

39. Mogel, W. (2010) *The Blessing of a B Minus: Using Jewish teachings to raise resilient teenagers*. New York: Scribner.

40. Mogel, 2010, p. 104.

41. Chua, A. (2011) *Battle Hymn of the Tiger Mother*. London: Bloomsbury Publishing.

42. Furedi, F. (2001) *Paranoid Parenting*. London: Allen Lane.

43. UNICEF (2001) *A League Table of Child Deaths by Injury in Rich Nations*, Innocenti Report Card No. 2. Florence: UNICEF Innocenti Research Centre. Available at <https://www.unicef-irc.org/publications/pdf/repcard2e.pdf> (accessed July 2017).

44. Ginott, H. G. (1967) *Between Parent and Teenager*. New York: Macmillan.

45. Segrin, C., Woszidlo, A., Givertz, M. and Montgomery, N. (2013) 'Parent and child traits associated with overparenting'. *Journal of Social and Clinical Psychology*, 32: 6, 569–95.

CHAPTER 5: HOW SHOULD CHILDREN PLAY?

1. There will be a discussion of children's rights and the United Nations Convention on the Rights of the Child in Chapter 9. Article 31 of the Convention states that: '1. States Parties recognize the right of the child to rest and leisure, to engage in play and recreational activities appropriate to the age of the child and to participate freely in cultural life and the arts. 2. States Parties shall respect and promote the right of the child to participate

fully in cultural and artistic life and shall encourage the provision of appropriate and equal opportunities for cultural, artistic, recreational and leisure activity.' Available at <www.un.org/documents/ga/res/44/ a44r025. htm> (accessed 31 January 2018).

2. Roopnarine, J. L. (2012) 'Cultural variations in beliefs about play, parent–child play, and children's play: meaning for childhood development', in P. Nathan and A. D. Pellegrini (eds) *The Oxford Handbook of the Development of Play*. Oxford: Oxford University Press, pp. 19–40.

3. Haight, W. L., Wang, X. L., Fung, H. H., Williams, K. and Mintz, J. (2015) 'Universal, developmental, and variable aspects of young children's play: a cross-cultural comparison of pretending at home'. *Child Development*, 70: 6, 1477–88.

4. Lancy, D. F. (2007) 'Accounting for variability in mother/child play', *American Anthropologist*, 109: 2, 273–84.

5. Jiang, S., Han, M. (2015) 'Parental beliefs on children's play: comparison among mainland Chinese, Chinese immigrants in the USA, and European-Americans'. *Early Child Development and Care,* 186: 3, 341–52.

6. Naftali, O. (2016) *Children in China*. Chichester: John Wiley.

7. Chen, L. Y. (2015) 'Latest craze for Chinese parents: preschool coding classes'. Bloomberg online, 17 November 2015. Available at <http://www. bloomberg.com/news/features/2015-11-17/latest-craze-for-chinese-parents-preschool-coding-classes > (accessed 1 July 2016)

8. Jiang and Han, 2015.

9. Singh A. and Gupta, D. (2012) 'Contexts of childhood and play: Exploring parental perceptions'. *Childhood*.19: 2, 235–50.

10. LaForett, D. R., Mendez, J. L. (2016) 'Play beliefs and responsive parenting among low-income mothers of preschoolers in the United States'. *Early Childhood Development and Care*, 187: 3, 1359–71.

11. Roopnarine, 2012, p. 8.

12. Parten, M. (1933) 'Social play among preschool children'. *Journal of Abnormal and Social Psychology*, 28: 2, 430–40.

13. Brooker, L., Woodhead, M. (2013) *Early Childhood In Focus 9. The Right to Play*. Milton Keynes: Open University.

14. Whitebread, D. D. (2012) 'The Importance of Play'. Cambridge: Toy Institute of Europe. Available at <http://www.importanceofplay.eu/IMG/pdf/dr_david_whitebread_-_the_importance_of_play.pdf > (accessed 21 September 2017).

15. Lowe, R. J. (2012) 'Children deconstructing childhood'. *Children and Society*, 24: 6, 269–79.

16. Glenn, N. M., Knight, C. J., Holt, N. L. (2012) 'Meanings of play among children'. *Childhood*, 20: 2, 185–99, p. 191.

17. Gleave, J. (2009) *Children's Time to Play: A literature review*. London: Play England for National Children's Bureau (NCB). Available at <http://www.playday.org.uk/wp-content/uploads/2015/11/children%E2%80%99s_time_to_play___a_literature_review.pdf > (accessed 21 September 2017), p. 2.

18. IKEA (2015) *The Play Report*. Available at <http://www.ikea.com/ms/en_US/pdf/reports-downloads/IKEA_Play_Report_2015.pdf > (accessed 21September 2017).

19. IKEA, 2015, p. 14.

20. Glenn et al., 2012, p. 12.

21. Lester, S. and Russell, W. (2008) *Play for a Change: Play, Policy, and Practice: A review of contemporary perspectives*. London: National Children's Bureau.

22. IKEA, 2015.

23. Edwards, C. P. (2005) 'Children's play in cross-cultural perspective: a new look at the Six Cultures study'. *Cross-Cultural Research*, 34: 4, 318–38.

24. Vygotsky, L. S. (1967) 'Play and its role in the mental development of the child'. *Psychology*, 5: 3, 6–18, p. 16.

25. Brooker and Woodhead, 2013.

26. Singer, D. G., Singer, J. L., Agostino, H. D., Delong, R. (2009) 'Children's pastimes and play in sixteen nations. Is free-play declining?' *American Journal of Play*, 1: 3, 283–312.

27. Roopnarine, 2012.

28. Kennedy-Moore, E. (2015) 'Do boys need rough and tumble play?' *Psychology Today*, 30 June 2015. Available at <https://www.psychologytoday.com/blog/growing-friendships/201506/do-boys-need-rough-and-tumble-play> (accessed 5 September 2017).

29. Kennedy-Moore, 2015.

30. Whitebread, 2012.

31. Jarvis, P., Newman, S., Swiniarski, L. (2014) 'On "becoming social": the importance of collaborative free play in childhood'. *International Journal of Play*, 3:1, 1–16.

32. Colwell, M. J. and Lindsey, E. W. (2005) 'Preschool children's pretend and physical play and sex of play partner: connections to peer competence'. *Sex Roles*, 52: 7–8, 497–509.

33. Tannock, M. (2011) 'Observing young children's rough-and-tumble play'. *Australasian Journal of Early Childhood*, 36: 2, 13–20.

34. Edwards, C. P., Knoche, L. and Kumru, A. (2001) 'Play patterns and gender', in J. Worell (ed.) *Encyclopedia of Women and Gender: Sex*

similarities and differences and the impact of society on gender. San Diego, CA: Academic Press.

35. Berk, L. E., Meyers, A. B. (2013) 'The role of make-believe play in the development of executive function status of research and future directions'. *Amercian Journal of Play*, 6: 1, 98–110.

36. Eggum-Wilkens, N., Fabes, R., Castle, S., Zhang, L., Hanish, L. and Martin, C. (2014) 'Playing with others: head start children's peer play and relations with kindergarten school competence', *Early Childhood Research Quarterly*, 1: 29, 345–56.

37. Lin, Y-C.,Yawkey, T. (2014) 'Parents' play beliefs and the relationship to children's social competence'. *Education*, 1, 107–14.

38. Brooker and Woodhead, 2013.

39. Lansdown, G. (2013) 'Challenges to realising children's right to play', in L. Brooker and M. Woodhead (eds) *Early Childhood in Focus: The Right to Play*. Milton Keynes: Open University, p. 34.

40. Brooker and Woodhead, 2013.

41. IKEA, 2015.

42. Little, H., Wyver, S., Gibson, F. (2011) 'The influence of play context and adult attitudes on young children's physical risk-taking during outdoor play'. *European Early Childhood Education Research Journal*, 19: 1, 113–31.

43. Wilson, C. (2015) 'Improve your children's vision'. *New Scientist*, 23 May, 226: 3022, 37.

44. Lansdown, 2013, p. 34.

45. Little, H. (2013) 'Mothers' beliefs about risk and risk-taking in children's outdoor play'. *Journal of Adventure Education and Outdoor Learning*, 15: 1, 24–39.

46. Little, 2013, p. 29.

47. Little, H., Sandsetter, E. B. H. andWyver, S. (2012) 'Early childhood teachers' beliefs about children's risky play in Australia and Norway'. *Contemporary Issues in Early Childhood*, 1 January, 13: 4, 300–316.

48. Little et al., 2012, p. 305.

49. Little, 2013, p. 34.

50. Moss, S. (2012) *Natural Childhood*. London: National Trust.

51. Buchanan, K., Anand, P. and Joffe, H. (2002) 'Perceiving and understanding the social world', in D. Miell, A. Phoenix and K. Thomas (eds) *Mapping Psychology*. Milton Keynes: Open University Press, pp. 57–109.

52. Pimentel, D. (2012) 'Criminal child neglect and the "free range kid": Is overprotective parenting the new standard of care?'*Utah Law Review*, 947:2, 1–53.

53. Little, 2013.

54. Pimentel, 2012.

55. Gleave, 2009.

56. Moss, 2012.

57. Carrington, D. (2016) 'Three-quarters of UK children spend less time outdoors than prison inmates – survey'. *The Guardian*, 25 March. Available at <https://www.theguardian.com/environment/2016/mar/25/three-quarters-of-uk-children-spend-less-time-outdoors-than-prison-inmates-survey> (accessed 21September 2017).

58. Stevens, C. (2013) *The Growing Child: Laying the foundations of active learning and physical health*. Abingdon: Routedge, p. 82.

59. Chatfield, T. (2012) *How to Thrive in the Digital Age*. London: Pan Macmillan, p. 29.

60. Savin-Baden, M. (2015) *Rethinking Learning in an Age of Digital Fluency: Is being digitally tethered a new learning nexus?* Abingdon: Routledge.

61. Marsh, J., Plowman, L., Yamada-Rice, D., Bishop, J.C., Lahmar, J., Scott, F., Davenport, A., Davis, S., French, K., Piras, M., Thornhill, S., Robinson, P. and Winter, P. (2015) *Exploring Play and Creativity in Pre-Schoolers' Use of Apps: Final Project Report*. Available at <http://www.techandplay.org/reports/TAP_Final_Report.pdf> (accessed 21 September 2017).

62. Haughton, C., Aiken, M. and Cheevers, C. (2015) 'Cyber babies: the impact of emerging technology on the developing infant'. *Psychology Research*, September, 5: 9, 504–18.

63. Ofcom (2014) *Children and Parents: Media use and attitudes report 2014*. London: Ofcom. Available at <https://www.ofcom.org.uk/__data/assets/pdf_file/0027/76266/childrens_2014_report.pdf?lang=default> (accessed 15 October 2017).

64. McGoogan, C. and Titcomb, J. (2017) 'Just looking at your smartphone makes you less intelligent, study finds'. *Daily Telegraph*, 27 June 2017.

65. Nagash, A. (2017) 'Tech addiction is "digital heroin" for kids – turning children into screen junkies'. *Metro*, 5 January 2017.

66. Noah, S. (2017) 'Social media making children more isolated warns author Michael Morpurgo'. *Irish News*, 29 April 2017.

67. Britton, A. (2013) 'Instagram and Snapchat are damaging young people's mental health'. *Daily Mirror*, 19 May 2017.

68. Burns, J. (2017) 'Parents' mobile use harms family life, say secondary pupils'. BBC News online, 23 April 2017. Available at <http://www.bbc.co.uk/news/education-39666863>(accessed 22 September 2017).

69. Rosen, L. D., Lim, A. F., Felt, J., Carrier, L. M., Cheever, N. A., Lara-Ruiz, J. M. et al. (2014) 'Media and technology use predicts ill-being among children, preteens and teenagers independent of the negative health

impacts of exercise and eating habits'. *Computers in Human Behavior*, 35, 364–75.

70. Cheung, C., Bedford, R., Saez De Urabain, I. R., Karmiloff-Smith, A. and Smith, T. J. (2017) 'Daily touchscreen use in infants and toddlers is associated with reduced sleep and delayed sleep onset'. *Nature Scientific Reports*, 7, 46104. Available at <https://www.nature.com/articles/srep46104> (accessed 1 September 2017).

71. Donnelly, L. (2017) 'iPads could hinder babies' sleep and brain development, study suggests'. *Daily Telegraph*, 13 April 2017.

72. AAP News (2017) 'Handheld screen time linked with speech delays in young children', 4 May 2017. Illinois: American Academy of Pediatrics. Available at <http://www.aappublications.org/news/2017/05/04/PASScreenTime050417> (accessed 1 September 2017).

73. Knapton, S. (2017) 'Tablets and smartphones damage toddlers; speech development'. *Daily Telegraph*, 4 May 2017.

74. Malki, D. (ed.) (2011) *Wondermark*. Quoting Socrates on writing, from Plato, *Phaedrus*, translated by B. Jowett. Available at <http://wondermark.com/socrates-vs-writing/> (accessed 12 February 2016).

75. Furedi, F. (2015) 'The media's first moral panic'. *History Today*, 65: 11, 46–8.

76. Bell, V. (2010). 'Don't touch that dial. A history of media technology scares, from the printing press to Facebook'. *Slate*, 15 February. Available at <http://www.slate.com/articles/health_and_science/science/2010/02/dont_touch_that_dial.html>(accessed 12 February 2016).

77. Wartella, E. A. and Jennings, N. (2000) 'Children and computers: New technology – old concerns'. *Future of Children*, 10:2, 31–43.

78. Wilmer, H. H., Sherman, L. E. and Chein, J. M. (2017) 'Smartphones and cognition : a review of research exploring the links between mobile technology habits and cognitive functioning'. *Frontiers in Psychology*, April: 8, 1–16.

79. Bedford, R., Saez de Urabain, I. R., Cheung, C. H., Karmiloff-Smith, A. and Smith, T. J. (2016) 'Toddlers' fine motor milestone achievement is associated with early touchscreen scrolling'. *Frontiers in Psychology*, August: 7, 1–8.

80. Livingstone, S., Haddon, L. Görzig, A. and Ólafsson, K. (2014) EU *Kids Online*. London: LSE. Available at <http://www.lse.ac.uk/media%40lse/research/EUKidsOnline/EU%20Kids%20II%20(2009-11)/EUKidsOnlineIIReports/Final%20report.pdf> (accessed 21 September 2017).

81. Anand, P. and Roope, L. (2016) 'The development and happiness of very young children'. *Social Choice and Welfare*, 47: 4, 825–51.

82. Plowman, L. and McPake, J. (2013) 'Seven myths about young children and technology'. *Childhood Education*, 89: 1, 27–33.

83. Lauricella, A. R., Wartella, E. and Rideout, V. J. (2015) 'Young children's screen time: The complex role of parent and child factors'. *Journal of Applied Developmental Psychology*, 36, 11–17.

84. Hsin, C.-T., Li, M.-C. and Tsai, C.-C. (2014) 'The influence of young children's use of technology on their learning: a review'. *Journal of Educational Technology & Society*, 17: 4, 85–99.

85. Wartella and Jennings, 2000.

86. Blum-Ross, A. and S. Livingstone (2016) *Families and Screen Time: Current advice and emerging research*. Media Policy Brief 17. London: Media Policy Project, London School of Economics and Political Science, p. 4.

87. Blum-Ross and Livingstone, 2016.

88. Ransom-Wiley, J. (2008) WoW surpasses 10 million subscribers, now half the size of Australia. Available at <https://www.engadget.com/2008/01/22/world-of-warcraft-surpasses-10-million-subscribers-now-half-the/>(accessed 21 September 2017)

89. Grimes, S. M. (2013) 'Playing by the market rules: Promotional priorities and commercialization in children's virtual worlds'. *Journal of Consumer Culture*, 15: 1, 110–34.

90. Sheehy, K., Ferguson, R., and Clough, G. (eds) (2010) *Virtual Worlds: Controversies at the Frontier of Education*. Hauppauge, New York: Nova Science Publishers.

91. Castronova, E. (2007) *Exodus to the Virtual World*. Basingstoke: Palgrave Macmillan.

92. Quoted in Ferguson, R., Sheehy, K. and Clough, G. (2010) 'Introduction: challenging education in virtual worlds', in Sheehy, Ferguson and Clough (eds), 2010.

93. Byron, T. (2008) *Safer Children in a Digital World. The Report of the Byron Review*. Nottingham: DCSF Publications. Available at <https://www.iwf.org.uk/sites/default/files/inlinefiles/Safer%20Children%20in%20a%20Digital%20World%20report.pdf>.

94. Internet Matters (2015) *Pace of Change Report* .Available at <http://www.internetmatters.org/wp-content/uploads/2015/12/Internet_Matters_Pace_of_Change_report-vs2.pdf> (accessed 21 September 2017).

95. Internet Matters, 2015.

96. Hendriyani, Hollander, E., d'Haenens, L. and Beentjes, J. (2014) 'Views on children's media use in Indonesia: Parents, children, and teachers'. *International Communications Gazette*, 76: 4–5, 322–39.

97. Internet Matters, 2015.

98. Boyd, D. (2008) *Taken Out of Context: American teen sociality in networked publics*. PhD Dissertation, University of California, Berkeley, CA.

99. Pearson, D. (2015) 'Sulake: 15 years of Habbo Hotel'. Online article, 16 April 2015, gamesindustry.bz. Available at <http://www.gamesindustry.biz/articles/2015-04-16-sulake-15-years-of-habbo-hotel> (accessed 5 January 2016).

100. Livingstone et al., 2014, pp. 9–12.

101. Livingstone, S., Kirwil, L., Ponte, C. and Staksrud, E. (2014) 'In their own words: What bothers children online?' *European Journal of Communication*, 29: 3, 271–88, p. 271.

102. Brown, T. (2015) 'Use of visual media by primary aged children in my school'. Report available at < http://www.open.ac.uk/researchprojects/childrens-research-centre/children-and-young-peoples-voices/research-children-young-people> (accessed 31 January 2018).

103. Arora, R. (2014) 'Do children in my KS2 class play age inappropriate video games?' Milton Keynes: Open University Children's Research Centre. Available at <http://www.open.ac.uk/researchprojects/childrens-research-centre/research-children-young-people/aged-9-10> (accessed 22 February 2016).

104. Livingstone and Smith, 2014.

105. Livingstone and Smith, 2014.

106. Drake, E. and Steer, D. A. (2009) *Drake's Comprehensive Compendium of Dragonology*. Somerville, MA: Candlewick, p. 192.

107. Ha, T., Lee, Y., Woo, W. (2011) 'Digilog book for temple bell tolling experience based on interactive augmented reality'. *Virtual Reality*, 15: 4, 295–309.

108. Knapp, A. (2016) 'Stan Lee introduces augmented reality for his kids universe'. *Forbes Magazine*, 2 November 2016. Available at <http://www.forbes.com/sites/alexknapp/2016/11/02/stan-lee-introduces-augmented-reality-for-his-kids-universe/#13f5a73d184d> (accessed 15 November 2016).

109. Greenwood, C. (2016) 'The Pokemon Go crimewave: Robbers, thieves and paedophiles target 300 gamers in one month'. *Daily Mail*, 30 August 2016. Available at <http://www.dailymail.co.uk/news/article-3764307/The-Pokemon-crimewave-Robbers-thieves-paedophiles-target-300-gamers-one-month> (accessed 21 September 2017)

110. Althoff, T., White, R. W. and Horvitz, E. (2016) 'Influence of Pokémon Go on physical activity: study and implications'. *Journal of Medical Internet Reserach*, 18: 2, e315 (published online).

111. National Society for the Prevention of Cruelty to Children (2016) *Pokémon Go: a parent's guide*. Available at <https://www.nspcc.org.uk/preventing-abuse/keeping-children-safe/online-safety/pokemon-go-parents-guide/> (accessed 1 November 2016).

112. Althoff et al., 2016.

113. North American financial company Manulife comissioned a survey to look at physical activity and Pokemon in July 2016. The results can be found at <http://www.manulife.com/Master-Article-Detail?content_id=a0Q5000000KEyHeEAL>.

114. McCartney, M. (2016) 'Game on for Pokémon Go'. *British Medical Journal*, 354: i4306. Available at < http://www.bmj.com/content/354/bmj.i4306>.

115. McReynolds, E., Hubbard, S., Lau, T. and Saraf, A. (2017). 'Toys that listen: a study of parents, children, and internet-connected toys'. *Proceedings of the 2017 CHI Conference on Human Factors in Computing Systems*, 5197–5207. Available at < http://chi2017.acm.org/>

116. Hill, S. (2016) 'CogniToys Dino Toy review'. *Digital Trends*, 27 July 2016. Available at <https://www.digitaltrends.com/smart-toy-reviews/cognitoys-dino-review/>.

117. Sheehy, K., Ferguson, R. and Clough, G. (2014) *Augmented Education: Bringing real and virtual learning together*. New York: Palgrave Macmillan.

CHAPTER 6: WHAT MATTERS IN EDUCATION?

1. Sheehy, K. and Bucknall, S. (2008) 'How is technology seen in young people's visions of future education systems?', *Learning, Media and Technology*, 33: 2, 101–14.

2. Morgan, M., Gibbs, S., Maxwell, K., Britten, N. (2002) 'Hearing children's voices: Methodological issues in conducting focus groups with children aged 7–11 years'. *Qualatative Research*, 2: 1, 5–20.

3. Reid, K. (2005) 'The causes, views and traits of school absenteeism and truancy'. *Research in Education*, 74: 1, 59–82.

4. Jordan, A. (2013) 'Fostering the transition to effective teaching practices in inclusive classrooms', in S. E. Elliott-Johns and D. H. Jarvis (eds) *Perspectives on Transitions in Schooling and Instructional Practice*. Toronto: University of Toronto Press, pp. 1689–99; Jordan, A., Schwartz, E. and McGhie-Richmond, D. (2009) 'Preparing teachers for inclusive classrooms'. *Teaching and Teacher Education*, 25: 4, 535–42.

5. Nind, M., Rix, J., Sheehy, K., Simmons, K. (2013) *Curriculum and Pedagogy in Inclusive Education: Values into practice*. Abingdon: Routledge.

6. No Bullying.com. (2015) 'Bullying in Indonesia'. *Bullying Facts*, 22 December 2015. Available at<http://nobullying.com/bullying-in-indonesia/>.

7. Department for Education (2012) *Pupil behaviour in schools in England: an evaluation*, report. Available at <https://www.gov.uk/government/uploads/system/uploads/attachment_data/file/184078/DFE-RR218.pdf>

8. Department for Education, 2012.

9. McGuckin. C. and Corcoran, L. (2018) 'Cyberbullying', in K. Sheehy and A. J. Holliman (eds) *Education and New Technologies: Perils and promises for learners*. Abingdon: Routledge.

10. Patton, D. U., Hong, J. S., Patel, S. and Kral, M. J. (2017) 'Systematic review of research strategies used in qualitative studies on school bullying and victimization'. *Trauma, Violence, & Abuse*, 18: 1, 3–16.

11. United Nations Children's Fund (2012) *Child Protection in Educational Settings: Findings from six countries in East Asia and the Pacific*. Strengthening Child Protection Systems Series No. 2. Bangkok: UNICEF EAPRO. Available at <http://www.unicef.org/eapro/CP-ED_Setting.pdf>.

12. Brown, C. S. and Bigler R. S. (2005) 'Children's perceptions of discrimination: a developmental model'. *Child Development*, 76:3, 533–53.

13. IKEA (2015) *The Play Report*. Available at <http://www.ikea.com/ms/en_US/pdf/reports-downloads/IKEA_Play_Report_2015.pdf > (accessed 21September 2017).

14. United Nations Children's Fund, 2012.

15. Department for Education, 2012.

16. Rix, J. and Sheehy, K.(2014) 'Nothing special: The everyday pedagogy of teaching', in L. Florian (ed.) *The Sage Handbook of Special Education*, Vol. 2. London: Sage, pp. 459–74.

17. Long, M., Wood, C., Littleton, K., Passenger, T. and Sheehy, K. (2010) *The Psychology of Education*. Abingdon: Routledge, p. 2.

18. See <http://www.antibullyingpro.com/researchhome>.

19. Rogers, B. (2004) *Behaviour Recovery*. London: Sage.

20. Cooper, P. and Jacobs, B. (2011) *Evidence of Best Practice Models and Outcomes in the Education of Children with Emotional Disturbance/Behavioural Difficulties: An international review*. Trim, County Meath: National Council for Special Education.

21. Sheehy and Bucknall, 2008, p. 104.

22. Sheehy and Bucknall, 2008.

23. Sheehy and Bucknall, 2008.

24. Shiao En Chng, G. (2012). *Children's Informal Reasoning Skills and Epistemological Beliefs within the Family: The role of parenting practices, parental epistemological beliefs and family communication patterns*. PhD dissertation, Bielefeld University, Germany. Available at <http://pub. uni-bielefeld.de/publication/2519185> (accessed 15 October 2017).

25. Shiao En Chng, 2012.

26. Jordan, A., Glenn, C., McGhie-Richmond, D. (2010) 'The Supporting Effective Teaching (SET) project: the relationship of inclusive teaching practices to teachers' beliefs about disability and ability, and about their roles as teachers'. *Teaching and Teacher Education*, 26:2, 259–66.

27. Saucerman, J. and Vasquez, K. (2014) 'Psychological barriers to STEM participation for women over the course of development'. *Adultspan Journal*, 13: 1, 46–64.

28. Crowley, K., Callanan, M. A., Tenenbaum, H. R. and Allen, E. (2001) 'Parents explain more often to boys than to girls during shared scientific thinking'. *Psychological Science*, 12: 3, 258–61; Saucerman et al., 2014.

29. PISA (2015) *What do parents look for in their child's school?* (Vol. 44). Available at <http://www.oecd.org/pisa/pisaproducts/pisainfocus/ PIF-51(eng)-FINAL.pdf> (accessed 15 October 2017).

30. Ule, M., Živoder, A., du Bois-Reymond, M. (2105) '"Simply the best for my children": patterns of parental involvement in education'. *International Journal of Qualatative Studies in Education*, 28: 3, 329–48.

31. Burgess, S., Greaves, E., Vignoles, A., Wilson, D. (2014) 'What parents want: school preferences and school choice'. *The Economic Journal*, 125: 587, 1262–89, p. 1262.

32. Burgess et al., 2014.

33. Institute of Community Cohesion (the iCoCo foundation) (2016) *Understanding Segregation in England: 2011–2016*. London: TheChallenge/ SchoolDash/iCoCo foundation/ Available at <http://tedcantle.co.uk/ wp-content/uploads/2013/03/Understanding-School-Segregation-in-England-2011-2016-Final.pdf >(accessed 15 October 2017).

34. Lindsay, G. (2007) 'Educational psychology and the effectiveness of inclusive education/mainstreaming'. *British Journal of Educational Psychology*, 77: 1, 1–24.

35. UNESCO (1999) *Salamanca: Five years on. A Review of* UNESCO *activities in the light of the Salamanca statement and framework for action*. Paris: UNESCO, p. 9.

36. Stein, M., Stein, P., Weiss, D., Lang, R. (2007) 'Health care and the UN Disability Rights Convention', *The Lancet*, 374: 9704, 1796–8.

37. United Nations Department of Economic and Social Affairs (2011) *Disabilities Conventions Gets 100th Ratification*. New York: United Nations. Available at <http://www.un.org/en/development/desa/news/social/disability-ratification.html>.

38. Budiyanto (2011) *Best Practices of Inclusive Education in Japan, Australia, India and Thailand: Implications for Indonesia*. Tsukuba, Japan: Centre for Research on International Cooperation in Educational Development (CRICED).

39. Direktorat Pembinaan Sekolah Dasar (2008) *Profil Pendidikan Inklusif di Indonesia* 1('Inclusive Education Profile in Indonesia 1'). Jakarta: Kementerian Pendidikan Nasional.

40. Ramos-Mattoussi, F. and Milligan, J. A. (2013) *Building Research and Teaching Capacity in Indonesia Through International Cooperation*. New York: Institute of International Relations, p. 15.

41. Budiyanto, 2011.

42. Hughes, J. and Loader, R. (2015). '"Plugging the gap": Shared education and the promotion of community relations through schools in Northern Ireland'. *British Educational Research Journal*, 41: 6, 1142–55.

43. iCoCo foundation, 2016.

44. Okolosie, L. (2017) 'Segregated schools persist because parents maintain the divide'. *The Guardian*, 24 March 2017. Available at <https://www.theguardian.com/commentisfree/2017/mar/24/schools-segregated-parents-children-integration>.

45. Billingham, C. M. and Hunt, M. O. (2016) 'School racial composition and parental choice: new evidence on the preferences of White parents in the United States'. *Sociology of Education*, 89: 2, 99–117.

46. Billingham and Hunt, 2016.

47. Department for Education (2016) *Special Educational Needs in England January 2016*. Available at <https://www.gov.uk/government/uploads/system/uploads/attachment_data/file/539158/SFR29_2016_Main_Text.pdf> (accessed 15 October 2017).

48. UNICEF (2012) *The Right of Children with Disabilities to Education: A rights-based approach to inclusive education*. Geneva: UNICEF Regional Office for CEECIS.Available at <http://www.inclusive-education.org/publications/right-children-disabilities-education-rights-based-approach-inclusive-education> (accessed 15 October 2017); Werner, S., Corrigan, P., Ditchman, N. and Sokol, K. (2012). 'Stigma and intellectual disability: A review of related measures and future directions'. *Research in Developmental Disabilities*, 33: 2, 748–65.

49. Stark, R., Gordon-Burns, D., Purdue, K., Rarere-Briggs, B. and Turnock, R. (2011). 'Other parents' perceptions of disability and inclusion in early

childhood education: Implications for the teachers' role in creating inclusive communities'. *He Kupu*, 2: 4, 4–18.

50. 'Secret Teacher' (2015) 'Secret teacher: I am all for inclusion in principle, but it doesn't always work'. *The Guardian*, 23 May 2015. Available at <https://www.theguardian.com/teacher-network/2015/may/23/secret-teacher-support-inclusion-but-not-at-any-cost>

51. Ruijs, N. M., Van der Veen, I. and Peetsma, T. T. D. (2010) 'Inclusive education and students without special educational needs'. *Educational Research*, 52: 4, 351–90.

52. Canadian Council on Learning. (2009) 'Does placement matter? Comparing the academic performance of students with special needs in inclusive and separate settings'. Ottawa: University of Ottawa. Available at <www.ccl- cca.ca/pdfs/LessonsInLearning/03_18_09E. p . 2> (accessed 15 October 2017).

53. Rix and Sheehy, 2014.

54. Lindsay, 2007.

55. Buckley, S., Bird, G., Sacks, B. and Archer T. (2006) 'A comparison of mainstream and special education for teenagers with Down syndrome: Implications for parents and teachers'. *Down Syndrome Research and Practice*, 9: 3, 54–67.

56. Kalambouka, A., Farrell, P., Dyson, A. and Kaplan, I. (2007). 'The impact of placing pupils with special educational needs in mainstream schools on the achievement of their peers'. *Educational Research*, 49: 4, 365–82.

57. Ruijs et al., 2010.

58. Rix, Jonathan (2015) *Must Inclusion be Special? Rethinking educational support within a community of provision.* London: Routledge.

59. Long et al., 2010, p. 2.

60. Long et al., 2010.

61. Stanovich, P. and Jordan, A. (1998) 'Canadian teachers' and principals' beliefs about inclusive education as predictors of effective teaching in heterogeneous classrooms'. *Elementary School Journal*, 98: 3, 221–38; Brownlee, J., Schraw, G. and Berthelsen, D. (2012) *Personal Epistemology and Teacher Education.* London: Routledge; Tumkaya, S. (2012) 'The investigation of the epistemological beliefs of university students according to gender, grade, fields of study, academic success and their learning styles'. *Educational Sciences: Theory and Practice*, 12: 1, 88–95.

62. Lourenço, O. (2012) 'Piaget and Vygotsky: many resemblances, and a crucial difference'. *New Ideas in Psychology*, 30: 3, 281–95.

63. Lee, J., Zhang, Z., Song, H. and Huang, X. (2013) 'Effects of epistemological and pedagogical beliefs on the instructional practices of teachers: a Chinese perspective'. *Australian Journal of Teacher Education*, 38: 12, 119–46.

64. Müller, U., Burman, J. T., Hutchison, S. M. (2013) 'The developmental psychology of Jean Piaget: a quinquagenary retrospective'. *Journal of Applied Developmental Psychology*, 34: 1, 52–5.

65. Opper, S. (1977) 'Piaget's clinical method'. *Journal of Children's Mathmetical Behavior*, 1: 4, 90–107.

66. Piaget, J. and Szeminska, A. (1952) *The Child's Conception of Number*. London: Routledge and Kegan Paul.

67. Donaldson, M. (1982) 'Conservation: What is the question?' *British Journal of Psychology*,73: 2, 199–207.

68. Donaldson, M. (1993) *Human Minds: An exploration*. London: Allen Lane.

69. Hughes, M. and Donaldson, M. (1979) 'The use of hiding games for studying the coordination of viewpoints', *Educational Review*, 31:2, 133–40.

70. Wu, S.-C. and Rao, N. (2011) 'Chinese and German teachers' conceptions of play and learning and children's play behaviour'. *European Early Childhood Educational Research Journal*, 19: 4, 469–81.

71. Daniels, H. (2014) 'Vygotsky and Dialogic Pedagogy'. *Cultural Historical Psychology*, 10: 3, 19–29; Vygotsky, L. S. (1931/1978) *Mind in Society: The development of higher psychological processes*. Cambridge, MA: Harvard University Press, p. 57.

72. Lourenço, 2012.

73. Mercer, N., Dawes, L., Wegerif, R. and Sams, C. (2004) 'Reasoning as a scientist: ways of helping children to use language to learn science'. *British Educational Research Journal*, 30: 3, 359–77.

74. Mercer et al., 2004.

75. Mercer, N. and Sams, C. (2006) 'Teaching children how to use language to solve maths problems'. *Language and Education*, 20: 6, 507–28; Littleton, K. and Mercer, N. (2010) 'The significance of educational dialogues between primary school children', in C. Howe and K. Littleton (eds) *Educational Dialogues*. Abingdon: Routledge.

76. Elliott, B. and Chan, K. W. (1998) 'Epistemological beliefs in learning to teach: resolving conceptual and empirical issues'. Paper presented at the European Conference on Educational Research Ljubljana, Slovenia, 17–20 September 1998, p. 821.

77. Mercer and Sams, 2006.

78. Wu and Roa, 2011.

79. Wu and Roa, 2011, p. 478.

80. Wu and Roa, 2011, p. 471.

81. OECD (2009) *Creating Effective Teaching and Learning Environments: First results from TALIS*. Paris: OECD, p. 95. Available at <https://www.oecd.org/edu/school/43023606.pdf>(accessed 15 October 2015).

82. Lee et al., 2013; Jordan, A. and Stanovich, P. (2003) 'Teachers' personal epistemological beliefs about students with disabilities as indicators of effective teaching practices'. *Journal of Research into Special Educational Needs*, 3:1, 1–14.

83. Shirvani, H. (2005) 'Does your elementary mathematics methodology class correspond to constructivist epistemology?' *Journal of Instructional Psychology*, 36: 3, 245–58; Jordan, 2013; Jordan et al., 2009.

84. Ganimian, A. J., Murnane, R. J. (2014) 'Improving educational outcomes in developing countries', NBER Working Paper No. 20284. Cambridge, MA: National Bureau of Economic Research.

85. Choi, Amy (2014) 'What the best education systems are doing right'. Ideas. Ted.Com, 4 September 2014. Available at <http://ideas.ted.com/what-the-best-education-systems-are-doing-right/> (accessed 31 January 2018).

CHAPTER 7: HOW CAN PARENTS AND PROFESSIONALS PROMOTE RESILIENCE AND AUTONOMY IN CHILDREN?

1. See website <https://youngminds.org.uk/> (accessed August 2017).

2. Stress and early life adversity, including physical, sexual, emotional or verbal abuse, neglect and social deprivation, has been linked to ongoing developmental issues during childhood and adolescence (Guarjardo, N. R., Snyder, G. and Peterson, R. (2008) 'Relationships among parenting practices, parental stress, child behaviour, and children's social-cognitive development', *Infant child development*, 18: 1, 37–60; Lupien, S. J., McEwen, B. S., Gunnar, M. R. and Heim, C. (2009) 'Effects of stress throughout the lifespan on the brain, behaviour and cognition', *Nature Reviews: Neuroscience*, 10, 434–45.

3. Gilligan, R., De Castro, E., Vanistendael, S. and Warburton, J. (2014). *Learning from Children Exposed to Sexual Abuse and Sexual Exploitation: Synthesis report of the Bamboo Project study on child resilience*, Geneva: Oak Foundation, p. 1.

4. Liebenberg, L. and Ungar, M. (2009) 'Introduction: The challenges in researching resilience', in L. Liebenberg and M. Ungar (eds) *Researching Resilience*. Toronto: University of Toronto Press, pp. 3–25, p. 5.

5. Winnicott, D. (1964) *The Child, the Family and the Outside World*, London: Pelican Books.

6. Mischel, W. (2014) *The Marshmallow Test. Understanding self-control and how to master it.* London: Penguin.

7. Cited in Mischel, 2014.

8. Dweck, C. S. (2006) *Mindset: The New Psychology of Success*. New York: Ballantine Books.

9. Dent, M. (2003) *Saving our Children from Our Chaotic World. Teaching children the magic of silence and stillness*. Australia: Pennington Publications.

10. Angela Duckworth has written extensively on the notion of 'grit' and it is the basis of her TED talk, April 2013. Available at <https://www.ted.com/talks/angela_lee_duckworth_grit_the_power_of_passion_and_perseverance> (accessed August 2017).

11. Garmezy, N. and Rutter, M. (1985) 'Acute reactions to stress', in M. Rutter and L. Hersov (eds) *Child and Adolescent Psychiatry: Modern approaches*, 2nd edn. Oxford: Blackwell Scientific Publications.

12. Sameroff, A., J, Seifer, R., Barocas, R., Zax, M. and Greenspan, S. (1987) 'Intelligence quotient scores of 4-year-old children: social-environmental risk factors'. *Pediatrics*, 79: 3, 343–50.

13. Werner, E. E. and Smith, R. S. (1982) *Vulnerable But Invincible: A longitudinal study of resilient children and youth*. New York: McGraw Hill.

14. Werner and Smith, 1982, p. 92.

15. DeLongis, A. and Holtzman, S. (2005) 'Coping in context: The role of stress, social support and personality in coping'. *Journal of Personality*, 73: 6,1633–56.

16. Murphy, L. B. and Moriarty, A. E. (1976) *Vulnerability, Coping and Growth from Infancy to Adolescence*. New Haven: Yale University Press.

17. Murphy and Moriarty, 1976, p. 71. Murphy and Moriarty describe how a group of children, observed at the Menninger Foundation in America from birth through adolescence, attempted to deal with internal and external stresses, and how the stress often promoted growth. Murphy and her fellow researchers examined the different ways in which children behave, adapt and cope with everyday life stressors and look at the range of factors which potentially influence a child's capacity to cope and demonstrate resilience. These factors include the child's temperament, as well as that of their chief care-giver and other carers within their family and immediate environment, and the quality of family relationships.

18. John, O. P and Srivastava, S. (1999) 'The Big-Five trait taxonomy: history, measurement, and theoretical perspectives', in L. A. Pervin and O. P. John (eds), *Handbook of Personality: Theory and research*. New York: Guilford Press, pp. 102–38. Available at <http://moityca.com.br/pdfs/bigfive_John.pdf > (accessed 26 August 2017).

19. Carver, C.S. and Connor-Smith, J.K. (2010) 'Personality and coping'. *The Annual Review of Psychology*, 61, 679–704.

20. Eley, D. S., Cloninger, C. R., Walters, L., Laurence, C., Synnott, R. and Wilkinson, D. (2013) 'The relationship between resilience and personality traits in doctors: implications for enhancing well being'. *PeerJ*, 19 November 2013, 1:e216. Available at <https://peerj.com/articles/216/> (accessed 30 June 2017).

21. Cooper, V. L. and Rixon, A. (2017) 'Wellbeing', in V. L. Cooper and A. Rixon (eds) *Making a Difference: Working with children and young people*. Milton Keynes: Open University Press. Available at < https://learn2.open.ac.uk/pluginfile.php/2225911/mod_resource/content/3/ke206_bk1_c1.pdf>.

22. See Boyce, W. T. and Ellis, B. J. (2005) 'Biological sensitivity to context: an evolutionary-developmental theory of the origins and functions of stress reactivity'. *Developmental Psychopathology*. 17: 2, 271–301; Obradovi, J. (2013) 'Physiological responsivity and executive functioning: implications for adaptation and resilience in early childhood'. *Child Development Perspectives*, 10: 1, 65–70; Charney, D. S. (2004) 'Psychobiological mechanisms of resilience and vulnerability: implications for successful adaptation to extreme stress'. *American Journal of Psychiatry*, 161: 2, 195–216.

23. Obradovi, 2013.

24. Charney, 2004.

25. Boyce and Ellis, 2005.

26. Essex, M., Klein, M., Cho, E. and Kalin, N. (2002) 'Maternal stress beginning in infancy may sensitize children to later stress exposure: effects on cortisol and behaviour'. *Biological Psychiatry*. 52: 8, 776–84.

27. Heim, C. and Nemeroff, C. B. (2001) 'The role of childhood trauma in the neurobiology of mood and anxiety disorders: Preclinical and clinical studies'. *Biological Psychiatry*, 49: 12, 1023–39.

28. Bonanno, G. A. (2004) 'Loss, trauma, and human resilience: Have we underestimated the human capacity to thrive after extremely aversive events?' *American Psychologist*, 59: 1, 20–28.

29. Luthar, S. and Zigler, E. (1991) 'Vulnerability and competence: A review of research on resilience in childhood'. *American Journal of Orthopsychiatry*, 61: 1, 6–22.

30. Daniel, B., Wassell, S. and Gilligan, R. (2010) *Child Development for Child Care and Protection Workers*, 2nd edn. London: Jessica Kingsley Publishers, p. 70.

31. Luthar, S. S. and Barkin, S. H. (2012) 'Are affluent youth truly "at risk"? Vulnerability and resilience across three diverse samples'. *Development and Psychopathology*, 24: 2, 429–49.

32. Arruabarrena, I. (2014) 'Maltreated children', in A. Ben-Arieh, F. Casas, I. Frønes and J. E. Korbin (eds) *Handbook of Child Well-Being. Theories, methods and policies in global perspectives*. Dordrecht: Springer, pp. 2669–96.

33. Garbarino, J., Kostelny, K. and Dubrow, N. (1991) 'What children can tell us about living in danger'. *American Psychologist*, 461: 4, 376–83, p. 378.

34. Coles, R. (1967) *Children of Crisis: A study in courage and fear*, vol. 1, Boston, MA: Atlantic-Little and Brown.

35. Rutter, M. (1987) 'Psychosocial resilience and protective mechanisms'. *American Journal of Orthopsychiatry*, 57: 3, 316–31.

36. Rutter, 1987.

37. Rutter, M. (1985) 'Resilience in the face of adversity: protective factors and resistance to psychiatric disorder'. *British Journal of Psychiatry* 147: 6, 598–611.

38. Ainsworth, M., Blehar, M., Waters, E. and Wall, S. (1978) *Patterns of Attachment: A psychological study of the strange situation*. Hillsdale, NJ: Erlbaum.

39. A number of theorists have critiqued the use of the 'strange situation' and particularly the focus on parental sensitivity as a key indicator of a child's resilience. Jerome Kagan suggests that the temperament of the child must also be taken into consideration, indicating that children with different temperaments will have different attachment types (Kagan, J. (1998) 'The allure of infant determinism', in J. Kagan (ed.) *Three Seductive Ideas*. Harvard, MA: Harvard University Press, pp. 83–151). Nathan Fox (1989) found that babies with an 'Easy' temperament (those who eat and sleep regularly and adapt to new experiences) are likely to develop secure attachments. Infants with a 'slow to warm up' temperament (those who took a while to get used to new experiences) are likely to have insecure-avoidant attachments. Babies with a 'Difficult' temperament (those who eat and sleep irregularly and who reject new experiences) characteristically have insecure-ambivalent attachments (Fox, N. A. (1989) 'Infant temperament and security of attachment: a new look'. Paper presented at International Society for Behavioral Development, Jyväskyla, Finland). Jay Belsky and Michael Rovine propose an interactionist theory to explain the different attachment types. They suggest that a child's attachment type is a result of both the child's temperament and how the parent/carer responds to them, i.e. the parent's sensitivity level (Belsky, J. and Rovine, M. (1987) 'Temperament and attachment security in the strange situation: an empirical rapprochement'. *Child Development*, 58: 3, 787–95. Mario Marrone argues that, although the Strange Situation has been criticized for being stressful, and so is potentially an unethical study, it is simulating everyday experiences, as parents/carers do leave their babies for brief periods of

time (Marrone, M. (1998) *Attachment and Interaction*. London: Jessica Kingsley Publishers). Furthermore, Ainsworth's original study sample is somewhat biased – consisting of 100 middle-class American families. Therefore it is difficult to generalize the findings outside of America and to working-class families.

40. Holmes, J. (2001) *The Search for the Secure Base: Attachment theory and psychotherapy*. Hove, Sussex: Routledge.

41. Fonagy, P. (2001) *Attachment Theory and Psychoanalysis*. New York: Other Press.

42. Zakeria, H., Jowkara, B. and Razmjoeeb, M. (2010) 'Parenting styles and resilience'. *Procedia Social and Behavioral Sciences*, 5, 1067–70.

43. Cooper, C. (2015) 'Overly-controlling parents cause their children lifelong psychological damage, says study', *The Independent*, 3 September 2015, Available at <http://www.independent.co.uk/life-style/health-and-families/overly-controlling-parents-cause-their-children-lifelong-psychological-damage-says-study-10485172.html> (accessed June 2017).

44. Stafford, M., Kuh, D. L., Gale, C. R., Mishra, G. and Richards, M. (2015). ' Parent–child relationships and offspring's positive mental wellbeing from adolescence to early older age'. *Journal of Positive Psychology*, 11: 3, 26–37.

45. The research findings come from a study which has followed more than 5,000 children since their birth in 1946. Examples of controlling behaviour described in the study include invasions of children's privacy and a reluctance to let children make their own decisions. Despite many critiques of this type of study, which relies on recollections of childhood experiences and self-reporting, the researchers argue that these findings align with previous studies which have shown that children who are able to form secure emotional bonds with parents are more likely to display emotional security in later life.

46. Harris, J. (1998) *The Nurture Assumption. Why children turn out the way that they do*. New York: Touchstone.

CHAPTER 8: WHAT SHOULD CHILDREN LOOK LIKE?

1. WHO (2016) *Obesity and Overweight*, factsheet. Geneva: World Health Organization. Available at <http://www.who.int/mediacentre/factsheets/fs311/en/> (accessed 30 November 2016).

2. HM Government (2016) *Childhood obesity: a plan for action*, paper. London: Department of Health and Social Care. Available at <https://www.gov.uk/

government/publications/childhood-obesity-a-plan-for-action/childhood-obesity-a-plan-for-action> (accessed 30 November 2016).

3. Children are defined as overweight when their body mass index (BMI) is between the 85th and 95th percentile for children and teens of the same age and sex, while obesity is defined as being at or above the 95 per cent percentile. BMI is a figure based on a calculation which divides a person's weight in kilograms by the square of height in metres. Unlike BMIs for adults, BMIs for children and are age- and sex-specific, reflecting the fact that children's body compositions vary between boys and girls and change as they age. BMI levels in children are therefore relative to other children of the same age and weight. The Centers for Disease Control and Prevention (2016) *Defining Childhood Obesity* factsheet. Atlanta, GA: CDC. Available at <https://www.cdc.gov/obesity/childhood/defining.html> (accessed 31 July 2017).

4. Hewitt-Taylor, J., Alexander, J. and McBride, J. (2004) *Overweight and obesity in children: A review of the literature.* Poole, Dorset: Bournemouth University. Available at <http://eprints.bournemouth.ac.uk/11685/> (accessed 1 December 2016)

5. Burgess, J. N. and Broome, M. E. (2012) 'Perceptions of weight and body image among preschool children: A pilot study'. *Pediatric Nursing*, 38: 3, 147–76.

6. The Centers for Disease Control and Prevention (2017) *Childhood Obesity: Causes and consequences*, factsheet. Atlanta, GA: CDC. Available at <https://www.cdc.gov/obesity/childhood/causes.html> (accessed 31 July 2017).

7. HM Government, 2016. *Childhood Plan for Obesity*. Available at <https://www.gov.uk/government/publications/childhood-obesity-a-plan-for-action/childhood-obesity-a-plan-for-action> (accessed 31January 2018).

8. In 2003 the then chairman of the UK's Food Standards Agency claimed that life expectancy was likely to fall for the first time in over a century because of obesity. Ahmed, K., Revill, J. and Hinsliff, G. (2003) 'Official: fat epidemic will cut life expectancy'. *The Observer*, 9 November 2003.

9. Yang, W., Kelly, T., He, J. (2007) 'Genetic epidemiology of obesity'. *Epidemiologic Review*, 29: 1, 49–61.

10. Panter-Brick, C. (2013) 'Achieving health for children', in H. Montgomery (ed.) *Local Childhoods, Global Issues*. Bristol University: Policy Press.

11. Agras, W. S., Hammer, L. D., McNicholas, F. and Kraemer, H. C. (2004) 'Risk factors for childhood overweight: a prospective study from birth to 9.5 years'. *Journal of Pediatrics*, 145: 3, 424.

12. HM Government, 2016. *Childhood Plan for Obesity*. Available at <https://www.gov.uk/government/publications/childhood-obesity-a-plan-

for-action/childhood-obesity-a-plan-for-action> (accessed 31 January 2018).

13. See Rosenberg, T. (2015) 'How one of the most obese countries on earth took on the soda giants'. *The Guardian*, 3 November 2015. Available at <https://www.theguardian.com/news/2015/nov/03/ obese-soda-sugar-tax-mexico>.

14. Buckingham, D. (2011) *The Material Child. Growing up in consumer culture*. Cambridge: Polity Press.

15. Buckingham, 2011; Tingstad, V. (2009) 'Discourses on child obesity and TV advertising in the context of the Norwegian welfare state', in A. James, A. T. Kjørholt and V. Tingstad (eds) *Children, Food and Identity in Everyday Life*. Basingstoke: Palgrave Macmillan.

16. Gibbons, K. (2016) 'Ignorant parents are blamed for creating an obese generation'. *The Times*, 4 November 2016.

17. Buckingham, 2011, p. 105.

18. MeMe Roth, National Action Against Obesity (NAAO), quoted in Herndon, A. M. (2010) 'Mommy made me do it. Mothering fat children in the midst of the obesity epidemic'. *Food, Culture and Society*, 13: 3, 332–49, p. 332.

19. Evans, J., Davies, B. and Rich, E. (2008) 'The class and cultural functions of obesity discourse: our latter day child saving movement'. *International Studies in Sociology of Education*, 18:2, 117–32, p. 126.

20. Furedi, F. (2001) *Paranoid Parenting*. London: Allen Lane.

21. De Vries, J. (2007) 'The obesity epidemic: medical and ethical considerations'. *Science and Engineering Ethics*, 13: 3, 55–67.

22. De Vries, 2007, p. 64

23. Gard, M. and Wright, J. (2005) *The Obesity Epidemic: Science, morality and ideology*. New York: Routledge.

24. Tingstad, 2009.

25. Evans et al., p. 2008.

26. Montgomery, H. (2013) 'Children, poverty and social inequality', in H. Montgomery (ed.) *Local Childhoods, Global Issues*. Bristol University: Policy Press.

27. Buckingham, 2011, p. 122.

28. Herndon, 2010.

29. Harden, J. and Dickson, A. (2015) 'Low-income mothers' food practices with young children: A qualitative longitudinal study'. *Health Education Journal*, 74: 4, 381–91.

30. De Vries, 2007, p. 56.

31. Evans et al., 2008.

32. Su, W. and Di Santo, A. (2012) 'Preschool children's perception of overweight peers'. *Journal of Early Childhood Research*, 10: 1, 19–31.

33. Tiggemann, M. and Wilson-Barrett, E. (1998) 'Children's figure rating to self-esteem and negative stereotyping'. *International Journal of Eating Disorders*, 23:1, 83–8.

34. Grogan, S. (2008) *Body Image: Understanding body dissatisfaction in men, women and children*. London: Routledge.

35. Grogan, 2008.

36. Herbozo, S., Tantleff-Dunn, S., Gokee-Larose, J. and Thompson, J. K. (2004) '*Beauty and thinness messages in children's media*: A content analysis'. *Eating Disorders*, 12: 1, 21–34.

37. Buckingham, 2011.

38. Rees, R., Oliver, K., Woodman, J. and Thomas, J. (2009) *Children's Views About Obesity, Body Size, Shape and Weight. A systematic review*. London: Institute of Education, University of London. Available at <http://eppi.ioe.ac.uk/cms/Portals/0/Obesity%20Views%20Children%20R2009Rees.pdf?ver=2010-12-22-121209-040> (accessed 31 January 2018).

39. Sheehy, K. (2010) 'Stigmatising and removing defective children from society: the influence of eugenic thinking', in L. Brockliss and H. Montgomery (eds) *Childhood and Violence in the Western Tradition*. Oxford: Oxbow Books.

40. Pinquart, M. (2013) 'Body image of children and adolescents with chronic illness: a meta-analytic comparison with healthy peers'. *Body Image*, 10: 2, 141–8.

41. Beckett, A. (2013) 'Non-disabled children's ideas about disability and disabled people'. *British Journal of Sociology of Education*, 35: 6, 856–75.

42. Hodkinson, A. (2007) 'Inclusive education and the cultural representation of disability and disabled people: recipe for disaster or catalyst of change? An examination of non-disabled primary school children's attitudes to children with disabilities'. *Research in Education*, 77: 1, 56–76, p. 70.

43. Beckett, 2013.

44. Shakespeare, T., Preistly, M. and Barnes, C. (1999) *Life as a Disabled Child: A qualitative study of young people's experiences and perspectives*, final report. University of Leeds: Centre for Disability Studies. Available at <http://disabilitystudies.leeds.ac.uk/files/2011/10/life-as-a-disabled-child-report.pdf> (accessed 7 December 2015).

45. De Vries, 2007; Tingsted, 2009; Buckingham, 2011.

CHAPTER 9: WAS IT REALLY BETTER IN THE PAST?

1. The term 'well-being' was developed to explore children's quality of life, moving from a focus on basic needs and what children lacked to a more positive emphasis on the strengths of their present lives. Most importantly, it was designed so that children's own perceptions of their life were taken into account alongside a calculation of their material standards of living. It is a term that is now used regularly by policy-makers, practitioners and academics, but has been controversial and rejected as conceptually vague. For an overview of the arguments for and against its use, see Punch, S. (2013) 'Resilience and well-being', in H. Montgomery (ed.) *Global Childhood: Local Issues*. Bristol University: Policy Press.

2. Morrow, V. and Mayall, B. (2009) 'What is wrong with children's well-being in the UK? Questions of meaning and measurement'. *Journal of Social Welfare and Family Law*, 31: 3, 217–29.

3. Kehily, M. J. (2010) 'Childhood in crisis? Tracing the contours of "crisis" and its impact upon contemporary parenting practices'. *Media, Culture and Society*, 32: 2, 171–85.

4. Quoted in *The Guardian*, 16 May 2007. Available at <https://www.theguardian.com/society/2007/may/16/childrensservices.uknews>.

5. Barnardo's (2008) 'The shame of Britain's intolerance of children', press release. 17 November 2008. Available at <http://www.barnardos.org.uk/news_and_events/media_centre/press_releases.htm?ref=42088>.

6. Kehily, M. J. (2013) 'Childhood in crisis? An introduction to contemporary Western childhood', in M. J. Kehily (ed.) *Understanding Childhood: A cross disciplinary approach*. Bristol University: Policy Press.

7. One specific aspect of children's health – their weight and the current obesity crisis – is explored in more detail in the previous chapter, Chapter 8.

8. UNICEF (2007) *Child Poverty in Perspective: An overview of child well-being in rich countries*. Florence: UNICEF Innocenti Research Centre.

9. UNICEF (2013) *Child Well-Being in Rich Countries. A comparative overview*. Florence: UNICEF Innocenti Research Centre.

10. Wilkinson, R. and Pickett, K. (2010) *The Spirit Level. Why equality is better for everyone*. London: Penguin.

11. For a fuller discussion of the relationships between the state, social welfare and children's well-being, see Parton, N. (2012) 'Reflections on "Governing the Family": the close relationship between child protection and social work in advanced Western societies – the example of England'. *Families, Relationships and Societies*, 1: 1, 87–101.

12. Cross, G. (2004) *The Cute and the Cool: Wondrous innocence and modern American children's culture*. New York: Oxford University Press.

13. Buckingham, D. (2011) *The Material Child. Growing up in consumer culture*. Cambridge: Polity Press.

14. Palmer, S. (2006) *Toxic Childhood. How the modern world is damaging our children and what we can do about it*. London: Orion.

15. Barkham, P. (2013) 'No freedom to play or explore outside for children', *The Guardian*, 13 July 2013. Available at <https://www.theguardian.com/lifeandstyle/2013/jul/13/no-freedom-play-outside-children>.

16. Dunn, J. and Layard, R. (2009) *A Good Childhood. Searching for values in a competitive age*. London: Penguin.

17. Hillman, M., Adams, J. and Whitelegg, J. (1990) *One False Move: A study of children's independent mobility*. London: Policy Studies Institute.

18. Holpuch, A. (2015) '"Free-range" kids taken into custody again – parents had to sign "safety plan"', *The Guardian*, 13 April 2015. Available at <https://www.theguardian.com/society/2015/apr/13/free-range-children-taken-into-custody-again-maryland>.

19. *Courier Mail* (Australia) (2016) 'Do your kids walk or ride to school by themselves? You could be breaking the law', 5 August 2016, Available at <http://www.couriermail.com.au/news/queensland/do-your-kids-walk-or-ride-to-school-by-themselves-you-could-be-breaking-the-law/news-story/d45f1daefac034cb0a7aef961285c88b> (accessed 31 January 2018).

20. Furedi, F. (2001) *Paranoid Parenting*, London: Allen Lane, p. 10.

21. Fass, P. (1997) *Kidnapped. Child Abduction in America*. Oxford: Oxford University Press.

22. The number of children abducted and murdered by strangers has remained constant for many decades, at around eleven a year, and the threat to children, especially under the age of 10, posed by those outside the family, is very small. While each case is a terrible familial tragedy, what is interesting is not only that the rates have remained so stable but that the fears surrounding this risk have sky-rocketed, so that the fear of 'stranger danger' eclipses all other parental anxieties. It has been claimed, for example, that parents are more worried about their children being murdered than they are about them getting obese, despite the risk of the latter being very much greater than the former. BBC News online (2010) 'Parents "more worried about murder than obesity" threat'. 18 May 2010. Available at <http://www.bbc.co.uk/news/10120160> (accessed 22 October 2018).

23. DeMause, L. (1976) *The History of Childhood*. London: Souvenir Press, p. 1.

24. Pollock, L. A. (1983) *Forgotten Children: parent–child relations from 1500 to 1900*. Cambridge: Cambridge University Press.

25. Rocked by scandals about the widespread sexual abuse of children by entertainers at the BBC, within the Catholic and Protestant churches and elsewhere, the then British Home Secretary Theresa May launched the Independent Inquiry into Child Sexual Abuse on 7 July 2014. It was established to examine how the country's institutions handled their duty of care to protect children from sexual abuse.

26. Child Welfare Information Gateway (2014) *Child Abuse and Neglect Fatalities 2014: Statistics and interventions*. Washington, DC: US Department of Health and Human Services. Available at <https://www.childwelfare.gov/pubPDFs/fatality.pdf> (accessed 22 October 2017).

27. NSPCC (2010) *Child Protection Register Statistics*. Available at <http://www.nspcc.org.uk/Inform/research/statistics/child_protection_register_statistics_wda48723.html> (accessed 17 September 2017).

28. Kempe, C. H., Silverman, F. N., Steele, B. F., Droegemuller, W. and Silver, H. K. (1962) 'The battered child syndrome'. *Journal of the American Medical Association*, 181, 17–24.

29. Brockliss, L. and Montgomery, H. (eds) (2010) *Childhood and Violence in the Western Tradition*. Oxford: Oxbow Press.

30. The highest profile ones in the UK have been into the deaths of Dennis O'Neill (1945), Maria Colwell (1973), Tyra Henry (1984), Jasmine Beckford (1984), Kimberley Carlile (1987), Martin Nicoll (1991), Victoria Climbié (2000), Lauren Wright (2000), Ainlee Labonte (2002), John Gray (2003) and Peter Connelly (2007). Hopkins, G. (2007). 'What have we learned? Child death scandals since 1944'. Community Care website, 10 January 2007. Available at <www.communitycare.co.uk/2007/01/10/what-have-we-learned-child-death-scandals-since-1944> (accessed 22nd October 2017)

31. There is a similar set of beliefs among teachers. While some of the practices that went on in schools before the Second World War, such as the flogging and beating of boys and girls in the name of both education and discipline, would now seem abhorrent, corporal punishment was widespread in British schools and viewed as an important disciplinary tool for teachers until the late 1970s. It is now banned (as of 1987 in state schools and 1999 in private schools) and if it occurred it would be classified as assault. However, a poll of 6,162 UK teachers carried out in 2008 found that 22 per cent of secondary school teachers would still back caning in extreme cases. Bloom, A. (2008) 'Survey whips up debate on caning'. *Times Educational Supplement*, 10 October 2008.

32. Centre for Research on Families and Relationships (2008) 'Parenting practices and support in Scotland'. Briefing Paper no. 40, October 2008. Edinburgh: University of Edinburgh.

33. Donnelly, M. and Straus, M. A. (2005) *Corporal Punishment of Children in Theoretical Perspective*. New Haven: Yale University Press.

34. Levinson, D. (1989) *Family Violence in Cross-Cultural Perspective*. London: Sage.

35. Einarsdóttir, J. (2000) *"Tired of Weeping". Child Death and Mourning among Papel Mothers in Guinea-Bissau*. Stockholm Studies in Social Anthropology. Stockholm: Almquist & Wiksell Intl.

36. Wolf, M. (1972) *Women and the Family in Rural Taiwan*. Stanford: Stanford University Press, p. 69.

37. Stafford, C. (1995) *The Roads of Chinese Childhood: Learning and identification in Angang*. Cambridge: Cambridge University Press.

38. Alison Parkes, University of Glasgow, quoted in Horne, M. (2016) 'Rural idylls make for discontented children', *The Times*, 30 June 2016, p. 23.

39. Wells, K. (2002) 'Reconfiguring the radical other: urban children's consumption practices and the nature/culture divide'. *Journal of Consumer Culture*, 2: 3, 261–77.

40. Quoted in Cunningham, H. (2006) *The Invention of Childhood*. London: BBC Books, p. 214.

41. This statement is only partially true, however, and many children still work in the home, providing care for their parents, looking after siblings or working in part-time work where they are paid considerably less than adults. Despite this, childhood is still conceptualized as a separate space from adulthood where children are not expected to work, to remain at home or at school and where they are, to a greater or lesser extent, cocooned from the concerns of the adult world. See Morrow, V. (1996) 'Rethinking childhood dependency: children's contributions to the domestic economy'. *Sociological Review*, 44: 1, 58–77.

42. Zelizer, V. (1985) *Pricing the Priceless Child*. Princeton: Princeton University Press, p. 3.

43. Lansdown, G. (1994) 'Children's rights', in B. Mayall (ed.) *Children's Childhoods: observed and experienced*. London: Falmer Press.

44. Burr, R. (2004) 'Children's rights: international policy and lived practice', in M. J. Kehily (ed.) *An Introduction to Childhood Studies*. Maidenhead: Open University Press, p. 152.

45. Goodman, R. 1996. 'On introducing the UN Convention on the Rights of the Child into Japan', in R. Goodman and I. Neary (eds), *Case Studies on Human Rights in Japan*. Richmond, Surrey: Japan Library, Curzon Press, p. 131.

46. Twum-Danso, A. (2009) 'Reciprocity, respect and responsibility: the 3Rs underlying parent–child relationships in Ghana and the implications for children's rights'. *International Journal of Children's Rights*, 17: 3, 415–32.

47. Adams, K. (2013) 'Childhood in crisis? Perceptions of 7–11-year-olds on being a child and the implications for education's well-being agenda'. *International Journal of Primary, Elementary and Early Years Education*, 41: 5, 523–37

48. Pugh, A. J. (2009) *Longing and Belonging: Parents, children, and consumer culture*. Berkeley: University of California Press.

49. Kehily, 2013, p. 8.

50. Hill, A., Davies, C. and Hinsliff, G. (2009) 'Are our children really in crisis, or the victims of parents' anxiety'. *The Observer*, 1 February 2009. Available at <http://www.guardian.co.uk/society/2009/feb/01/child-welfare-inquiry> (accessed 7 July 2016).

CONCLUSION

1. Harries, V. and Brown, A. (forthcoming) 'The association between use of infant parenting books that promote strict routines, and maternal depression, self-efficacy, and parenting confidence'. *Early Child Development and Care*, 1–12. See also Swansea University press release. Available at <http://www.swansea.ac.uk/media-centre/latest-research/newresearch findslinkbetweensomebabybooksandpostnataldepression.php>.

Further Reading

CHAPTER 1: HOW SHOULD BABIES BE LOOKED AFTER?

DELOACHE, JUDY and GOTTLIEB, ALMA (2000) *A World of Babies: Imagined childcare guides for seven societies.* Cambridge: Cambridge University Press.

A fascinating and beautifully written series of essays composed by anthropologists as if they were indigenous people writing childcare manuals. The authors give accounts of parenting among the Puritans of seventeenth-century Massachusetts as well as contemporary practices in the Ivory Coast, Bali, Turkey, West Africa, Micronesia and Aboriginal Australia. The book conveys with great warmth the love and concern people everywhere have for their children, as well as their different customs in looking after them.

LEVINE, ROBERT and LEVINE, SARAH (2016) *Do Parents Matter? Why Japanese babies sleep soundly, Mexican siblings don't fight, and American families should just relax.* New York: Public Affairs, Perseus Books.

A highly accessible summary of anthropological research on how people in other cultures parent their children and look after their infants. The book challenges the idea that parents are as important as they think they are in socializing children and uses anthropological examples to caution against universal theories. For every parent who has ever felt overwhelmed by conflicting advice, it is reassuring to read this book and to know that there are many ways to raise happy and healthy children.

LEE, ELLIE, BRISTOW, JENNY, FAIRCLOTH, CHARLOTTE and MACVARISH, Jan (2014) *Parenting Culture Studies*. London: Palgrave Macmillan.

Written by academics who have pioneered the field of Parenting Studies in the UK, this is an edited collection of essays which critically analyses many of the modern 'sacred cows' of parenting. The four authors explore many aspects of contemporary parenting, including the rise of the experts, how pregnancy is policed, and whether attachment is as important as we have been led to believe. A challenging and sometimes uncomfortable read, it nevertheless brilliantly critiques some of the ideas that modern parents hold most dear.

FREEMAN, HADLEY (2016) 'Attachment parenting: the best way to raise a child – or maternal masochism?' *The Guardian*, 13 July. Available at <https://www.theguardian.com/lifeandstyle/2016/jul/30/attachment-parenting-best-way-raise-child-or-maternal-masochism>

An article written by a journalist and new mother which explores the world of attachment parenting. While concluding it is not for her, she gives a balanced account of the realities, the pros and cons of the approach, and talks to mothers who practise it. Well worth reading for an account of the ideas behind attachment parenting and why it has proved so popular.

SMALL, MEREDITH (1998) *Our Babies, Ourselves: How biology and culture shape the way we parent*. New York: Anchor Books.

An excellent summary and commentary on cross-cultural and evolutionary studies of infant care which looks at how much of what we do in children's earliest days is biological and how much is cultural. The book explores in detail how people in different cultures parent, how long they breastfeed for, how long they let their children cry and where they encourage them to sleep.

CHAPTER 2: WHAT ARE THE INFLUENCES ON BECOMING A PARENT?

HOLLWAY, WENDY (2015) *Knowing Mothers: Researching maternal identity change.* Basingstoke: Palgrave Macmillan.

This book provides an in-depth exploration of mothers' experiences of parenthood and the identity changes involved in becoming a parent for the first time. This book refers to an extensive body of research in the field of psycho-social studies.

GERHARDT, SUE (2015) *Why Love Matters: How affection shapes a baby's brain.* New York: Routledge.

Drawing upon contemporary research exploring neurobiological findings and psychological studies, this book examines why early relationships with young children are important for brain development and are linked to future psychological health and well-being.

CHAPTER 3: WHAT IS 'FAMILY' AND ARE SOME FAMILIES BETTER THAN OTHERS?

GOLOMBOK, SUSAN (2015) *Modern Families.* Cambridge: Cambridge University Press.

An authoritative account of changing family structures in the UK, written by the director of the Centre for Family Research at Cambridge University. This book looks at the social and personal impact of new reproductive technologies such as IVF, surrogacy and egg and sperm donation. Its central argument is that it is the quality of family relationships, and the wider social context, that matter most to children and have the greatest impact on their development rather than how they were conceived, their biological relatedness to their parents, the number of parents they have or their sexual orientation.

Layard, Richard and Dunn, Judy (2009) *A Good Childhood: Searching for values in a competitive age.* London: Penguin Books.

Written for a general readership, this book came out of the Good Childhood Inquiry, commissioned by the Children's Society in 2006 to look at the state of British childhood and at ways of improving children's well-being. Chapter 2 on the family gives an excellent summary of the different research carried out on parental conflict, separation and divorce.

SMART, CAROL, NEALE, BREN and WADE, AMANDA (2001) *The Changing Experience of Childhood. Families and Divorce.* Cambridge: Polity Press.

Written by a team from Leeds University, this is a sociological examination of children's views about divorce and parenting. Children are interviewed and quoted extensively and the result is a sensitive and nuanced account of the impact of divorce on children as well on how this impact has changed over the years and how best to support children negotiating this transition in their family.

CHAPTER 4: HOW SHOULD CHILDREN BE SOCIALIZED?

LYTHCOTT-HAIMS, JULIE (2015) *How to Raise an Adult: Break free of the overparenting trap and prepare your kid for success.* London: Bluebird.

In this book Lythcott-Haims draws on research as well as her own reflections as a mother and as a student dean to examine the ways in which over-parenting may harm children and actually induce anxiety amongst parents. This is a very engaging and humorous book which manages to combine research evidence with insightful reflections.

FUREDI, FRANK (2002) *Paranoid Parenting: Why ignoring the experts may be best for your child.* London: Allen Lane.

In this seminal and very accessible book, Frank Furedi challenges many of the assumptions about what makes a good parent and how easy it is for parents to become over-sensitive to the wealth of claims made by so-called experts in the field.

CHAPTER 5: HOW SHOULD CHILDREN PLAY?

IKEA (2015) *The Play Report*. Available at <http://www. kidsandyouth.com/wp-content/uploads/2015/12/>

This is a readable, and well-illustrated, report of the largest research study of children's play. Interviews were carried with 30,000 parents and children across twelve countries. The report presents many interesting insights into children's experiences of play at different times and in different countries.

BROOKER, LIZ, and WOODHEAD, MARTIN (eds) (2013) *The Right to Play, Early Childhood in Focus 9*. Milton Keynes: Open University. Available at <https://bernardvanleer.org/publications-reports/the-right-to-play/>

This illustrated booklet offers short summaries of theory, research and policy issues. It examines several of the issues raised within Chapter 5, such as the cultural influences on children's play, children's own views on play and the benefits of play.

CHAPTER 6: WHAT MATTERS IN EDUCATION?

BURKE, CATHERINE and GROSVENOR, IAN (2015) *The School I'd Like: Revisited: Children and young people's reflections on an education for the 21st century*. London: Routledge.

This book offers engaging and informative insights into children's views and visions about schools and schooling. It includes children's pictures and poems, and shows the importance of listening to 'children's voices' in designing better educational experiences.

LONG, MARTYN, WOOD, CLARE, LITTLETON, KAREN, PASSENGER, TERRI, and SHEEHY, KIERON (2010) *The Psychology of Education*, 2nd edn. London: Routledge.

This is a large and comprehensive text. It adopts an evidence-based approach to examine many educational issues. It offers practical solutions to improving students' outcomes using real-world examples and is also a useful resource for looking up reliable information about specific educational theories, interventions and debates.

PISA in Focus (2015). *What do parents look for in their child's school?* (Issue no. 51). Paris: OECD Publishing. Available at <http://www.oecd.org/pisa/pisaproducts/pisainfocus/PIF-51(eng)-FINAL.pdf>

This is an illustrated summary report of an eleven-country research study that examined what parents care about when selecting a school for their children. It includes a consideration of the 'recipe for an ideal school' and parental influences on their children's progress.

CHAPTER 7: HOW CAN PARENTS AND PROFESSIONALS PROMOTE RESILIENCE AND AUTONOMY IN CHILDREN?

GINSBURG, KENNETH (2014) *Building Resilience in Children and Teens: Giving kids roots and wings*. Illinois: American Academy of Pediatrics.

This book explores the challenges and everyday stresses that children face today and sets out a series of strategies for children dealing with peer and social difficulties, family tension and the pressure to succeed and perform academically. An easy read, this book is targeted to existing and new parents.

SELIGMAN, MARTIN (1995) *The Optimistic Child*. New York: Houghton Mifflin (pbk edn, 2007: New York: HarperCollins).

Seligman questions why it is that despite a decade of research around self-esteem and resilience, rates of depression amongst children and young people have risen and mental health issues continue to be an issue. Drawing upon a range of research findings, Seligman provides a guide to help children and young people cope with life's everyday challenges.

CHAPTER 8: WHAT SHOULD CHILDREN LOOK LIKE?

BUCKINGHAM, DAVID (2011) *The Material Child: Growing up in consumer culture*. Cambridge: Polity Press.

Written by a sociologist who has spent decades writing about children and the media, this book, especially chapter 6, 'The Fear of Fat', examines some of the claims around the 'obesity epidemic'. Challenging and sometimes controversial, this is an easy-to-read account of alternative perspectives.

JAMES, ALLISON, KJØRHOLT, ANNE-TRINE and TINGSTAD, VEBJØRG (eds) (2009) *Children, Food and Identity in Everyday Life*. London: Palgrave Macmillan.

An edited collection of academic chapters on children's relationships to food, not just in relationship to obesity. It examines the role of food in children's lives and the battles for control that can occur between parents, children and advertisers. It looks at how far children can and do exercise control and choices over what they eat.

National Center for Education in Maternal and Child Health (2012) 'Overweight and Obesity in Children and Adolescents'. Available at <https://www.ncemch.org/knowledge/overweight.php>. Washington DC: Georgetown University.

Although the causes and impacts of childhood obesity are much debated, the medical/biological aspects are important too and have generated many academic and medical papers and suggested interventions. This webpage acts as a clearinghouse (and is regularly updated) of contemporary and authoritative resources for the prevention, identification, management and treatment of overweight and obesity in children. There are sections for parents, schools and health professionals.

WATSON, NICK, SHAKESPEARE, TOM, CUNNINGHAM-BURLEY, SARAH and BARNES, COLIN (2005) *Life as a Disabled Child: A qualitative study of young people's experiences and perspectives*. ESRC Research Programme. Available at <http://disability-studies.leeds.ac.uk/files/2011/10/life-as-a-disabled-child-report.pdf>

This research report looks at the everyday experiences of disabled children across all aspects of their lives. The section on identity examines how children view their disability within a culture that prizes the perfect body.

CHAPTER 9: WAS IT REALLY BETTER IN THE PAST?

FUREDI, FRANK (2002) *Paranoid Parenting: Why ignoring the experts may be best for your child*. London: Allen Lane.

In an incisive and much-quoted and referenced book, Furedi examines the idea of risk and considers why people are now so paranoid about their children's safety and well-being, even in an age when they have never been safer. Challenging but highly readable, this puts a lot of contemporary parental fears into perspective.

CUNNINGHAM, HUGH (2006) *The Invention of Childhood*. London: BBC Books.

Based on a BBC Radio 4 series, Cunningham looks at how ideas about childhood have changed over the centuries, from the Anglo-Saxon period onwards. Although he sees unique and distinctive changes occurring in adult–child relationships after the Second World War, the book also shows that childhood has always been associated with moral panics and the notion that things are getting worse.

KEHILY, MARY JANE (2010) 'Childhood in crisis? Tracing the contours of "crisis" and its impact upon contemporary parenting practices'. *Media, Culture and Society*, 32: 2, 171–85.

One of the most recent and widely read commentators on the 'Childhood in Crisis' debate has been Mary-Jane Kehily, who argues, like Cunningham, that the idea of childhood being in crisis is part of a cyclical series of moral panics which have often focused on the young. She examines how the debate has been shaped by the media and by international reports that have painted a bleak picture of today's children – especially those in the UK – and the impact this has had on parenting.

Index

[Text to come]

INDEX